The five Love Languages of Teenagers

The **five** Love Languages *of* Teenagers

Gary Chapman

NORTHFIELD PUBLISHING
CHICAGO

All Scripture quotations, unless indicated, are taken from the *Holy Bible: New International Version®*. NIV®. Copyright © 1973, 1978, 1984 by International Bible Society. Used by permission of Zondervan Publishing House. All rights reserved.

The "NIV" and "New International Version" trademarks are registered in the United States Patent and Trademark Office by International Bible Society. Use of either trademark requires permission of International Bible Society.

Scripture quotations marked NKJV are taken from the New King James Version. Copyright © 1979, 1980, 1982 by Thomas Nelson, Inc. Used by permission. All rights reserved.

ISBN: 1-881273-83-0

1 3 5 7 9 10 8 6 4 2

Printed in the United States of America

to
Shelley and Derek,
without whom I would never have written this book

CONTENTS

ACKNOWLEDGMENTS

Through the years, people have asked, "When are you going to write a book on parenting teenagers?" My stock answer has been, "When I finish with my own." Now that our youngest is thirty-one, I think I am far enough removed from the process that I can write objectively, both from my successes and my failures. Karolyn and I were not perfect parents. Our years with teenagers were not without trauma, but through it all we sought to love, and love has made all the difference. Today we enjoy relating to our former teens as mature, caring young adults. They bring us much joy and encouragement. I write this volume with confidence that if parents are successful in loving teenagers, they will be successful parents.

Much of what you will read in this book, I learned from Shelley and Derek. Without my experience of walking with them through the teen years, I would not have been able to empathize with other parents or write with passion. Thus, I have dedicated this book to them. I take this occasion to publicly acknowledge my indebtedness to each of them for letting me "practice" on them. Because of what they taught me, I hope to do even better with my grandchildren.

I am also deeply grateful to Dr. Davis McGuirt, who rendered invaluable help as my research assistant on this project. His expertise in exploring both current and historical studies on parenting teens, and his exceptional organizational skills in digesting this material made my task much easier. "Thanks, Davis. I hope that all your research will help you and Mary Kay as you raise your own teenagers."

As always, I am deeply appreciative of those parents who have shared with me their successes and struggles in raising teens. Both in the counseling office and "on the road," hundreds of parents have been my teachers. Your pain has made me more sensitive. Your success has given me encouragement.

A special tribute is due Tricia Kube, my administrative assistant for the past sixteen years, who computerized this material and gave technical advice. She and her husband, R. A., have raised their own teenager, Joe, who is now a successful young adult, and who with his wife Angela have made Tricia and R. A. grandparents. "I can see it now, Tricia. In a few more years, you will be reading this manuscript again, as your granddaughter becomes a teenager."

INTRODUCTION

I think it is safe to say that in no generation has the task of parenting teenagers been more perplexing than at the present time. The plethora of teenage violence is no longer limited to the fictional world of the movies but is a regular part of the evening news. Reports of teens killing teens, parents, and sometimes themselves have become commonplace. The fact that such behavior is no longer limited to the impoverished areas of our major cities but has come to permeate middle-class suburbia has raised deep concern in the hearts of parents of all social classes.

As I lead nationwide marriage seminars, many of the parents I meet are in a panic mode. This is especially true of parents who have discovered that their own teenager has a sexually transmitted disease, is pregnant, or has had an abortion. Some parents have discovered that their teenager is not only using drugs but is a drug pusher in the local high school. Others are distraught when they get a call from the local police department saying that their teenager has been arrested and charged with possession of a firearm. For those parents, their overriding question comes not from a philosophical, detached, intellectual interest in today's social problems but rather flows from deep pools of personal pain: "What did we do wrong?"

"We tried to be good parents; we've given them everything they wanted. How could they do this to themselves and to us? We just don't understand," they say. Having been a marriage and family counselor for the past thirty years, I am deeply sympathetic with these parents. I also feel great empathy for the thousands of parents whose teenagers are not involved in the destructive behavior noted above, but who live with the reality that if it happened to those teenagers, it could also happen to their teenagers.

There is no simple answer to the unrest in the soul of the contemporary teenager. The reality is that today's teenager lives in a world unknown to his predecessors. It's a global world with satellite TV, the Internet, and much more. Modern technology is exposing our teens to the best and worst of all human cultures. No longer does the homogenous environment of the deep South or the expansive Northwest exist. The ethnic boundaries of the Midwestern teenager are paper boundaries. Pluralism—the acceptance of many ideas and philosophies, with none being superior to the others—has replaced common beliefs and patterns as the wave of the future. Pluralism will remain, and its waters are much more difficult to navigate than commonality. No wonder many teenagers have lost their direction.

It is my observation that never before have parents of teenagers felt so helpless, but it is also my opinion that never before have the parents of teenagers been so important. More than ever, teenagers need parents. All research indicates that the most significant influence on the life of the teenager comes from parents. It is only when parents become uninvolved that their role of guidance is replaced by the gang, the peer group, or the friend at school. I am deeply committed to the premise that the teenager's best interest is served when parents assume their role as loving leaders in the home.

This book focuses on what I believe to be the most foundational building block of parent-teen relationships—love. I believe that *love* is the most important word in the English language and the most misunderstood word. It is my hope that this book will remove some of the confusion and help parents focus effectively on how to meet their teenager's emotional need for love. I believe that if the need is met, it will profoundly affect the behavior of the teenager. At the root of much teenage misbehavior is a teen's empty love tank. I am not suggesting that parents do not love their teenagers; I am suggesting that thousands of teenagers do not feel that love. For most parents, it is not a matter of sincerity but rather lack of information on how to communicate love effectively on an emotional level.

A part of the problem is that many parents do not feel loved themselves. Their marriage relationship has been sabotaged, and emotional love does not flow freely between Mom and Dad. It was this need to effectively communicate emotional love in a marriage that motivated me to write my original book, *The Five Love Languages: How to Express Heartfelt Commitment to Your Spouse*. This book, which has now sold more than one million copies, has changed the emotional climate for hundreds of thousands of marriages. These couples have learned how to speak each other's "primary love language" and have found that in so doing, they have become effective communicators of emotional love. As an author, this has been extremely gratifying for me, especially in hearing the stories of couples who were estranged from each other but have found renewed emotional love as they have read and applied the principles from *The Five Love Languages* .

I've also been greatly gratified by the response to my later book, *The Five Love Languages of Children,* which I co-authored with Ross Campbell, a psychiatrist with thirty years' experience with children and their parents. Both Dr. Campbell and I are greatly encouraged not only by the number of parents who have used this book to discover the primary love language of their children but also the number of educators who have used this book as a basis for workshops for school teachers who can also learn to effectively fill the love tank of a child. It is many of these parents and teachers who have encouraged me to write this present volume on the five love languages of teenagers. As one mother said, "Dr. Chapman, your book on the five love languages of children really helped us when our children were younger. But now, we have two teenagers and it's just not the same. We've tried to do what we've always done, but teenagers are different. Please write a book to help us learn to love our teenagers more effectively."

This mother was right; teenagers are different, and loving teens effectively takes some new insights. Teens are going through a tremendous transition, and parents who will be effective in loving them must also make transitions in the manner in which they express their love. It is my hope that this book will do for the parents of teenagers what the first book did for thousands of marriages and the second book did for parents of children. If this happens, I will be fully repaid for the energy I have invested in this volume.

I have written primarily to parents, but I believe grandparents and school teachers—indeed all adults who care about teenagers—will become more effective lovers by reading and practicing the principles found in this book. Teenagers need to feel the love not only of parents, but also the love of other significant adults in their lives. If you're a grandparent, remember that teenagers desperately need the wisdom of older, more mature adults. Show them love, and they will listen to your words of wisdom.

In this book you will enter the closed doors of my counseling office and meet scores of parents and teens who have allowed me to share their journey toward understanding and love. Of course, all names have been changed to protect the privacy of these individuals. As you read the candid dialogue of these parents and teens, I believe you will discover how the principles of the five love languages can really work in the lives of your teens and family.

And now a preview of where we're going. In chapter 1, parents will explore the world in which their teenager lives. We will look not only at the developmental changes that take place as your child becomes an adolescent but also at the contemporary world in which the teenager must experience these developmental changes. In chapter 2, we will learn the importance of love in the emotional, intellectual, social, and spiritual development of the teenager. In chapters 3 through 7, we will look at the five languages that communicate love and appropriate ways to speak these love languages to teenagers. Chapter 8 will offer suggestions on how to discover your teen's primary love language, the most effective way to fill their emotional love tank.

Chapters 9 through 12 will explore key issues in your teenager's life, including anger and independence. We will consider how love interfaces with the teenager's understanding and processing of anger; how love fosters independence; the relationship between freedom and responsibility; and how love sets boundaries, boundaries that are enforced with discipline and consequences. In chapter 13, we will explore what is often love's most difficult task: loving when the teen fails. And the final two chapters will deal with the unique application of these love languages for single parents and parents with a blended family.

I believe that if the teenager's emotional need for love is met through the years of adolescence, he or she will navigate the waters of change and come out on the other side of the rapids as a healthy young adult. That's the shared vision of most parents. I believe this is your vision. Now let's plunge into the waters, entering the teen's world and learning the challenge and opportunities to communicate love to our teens.

chapter one

UNDERSTANDING CONTEMPORARY TEENS

Did you know that sixty years ago teenagers did not exist as a separate generational group? The word *teenager* first came into popular use around the time of the Second World War. (See appendix 1 for a fascinating history of the term and a description of the first teenagers.) Though many changes have taken place since the first teenagers arrived formally on the social scene, there are plenty of similarities between the teens of the 1940s and those of the first decade of the twenty-first century.

From those early days of emerging teenage culture to its contemporary counterpart, the underlying themes have been the same: *independence* and *self-identity*. Throughout the years, teenagers in our American society have been active in searching for their identity while trying to establish their independence from parents. Neither of these themes played loudly in the pre-teenage era.

Before the industrial age, teens worked on their parents' farms until they were married and were given or inherited their own acreage. Identity was not something the teen sought; he was a farmer from the time he was old enough to work in the fields. The adolescent boy or girl was a child until he or she married; then the child became an adult.

THE SEARCH FOR
INDEPENDENCE AND IDENTITY

Until the early 1940s, independence was unthinkable until the adolescent was married—and at that juncture, real independence was possible only if the parents were benevolent enough to help financially.

With the coming of industrialization, one's identity became more a matter of choice. You could learn a trade and work in the factory, thus becoming a machinist, a weaver, a cobbler, etc. Independence also was more of a reality because securing a job could mean moving to a neighboring village where, with monies earned, one could establish a separate residence from parents. Thus, the larger cultural changes became the backdrop for an emerging teenage culture.

Since the 1940s, teenagers have followed this paradigm of developing independence and identity, but they have done so in a rapidly changing world. One by one electricity, telephones, automobiles, radios, airplanes, televisions, and computers have expanded the possibilities of developing new styles for seeking independence and identity. The contemporary teenager lives in a truly global society. Interestingly, however, his focus continues to be upon himself—his identity and his independence. More about this later.

The places where the teenager expresses independence and identity have changed through the years, but the means continue to be basically the same: music, dance, fashion, fads, language, and relationships. For example, the musical genre has expanded through the years from big band to rhythm and blues, rock and roll, folk, country, bluegrass, heavy metal, rap, and so forth. Thus, the teen has much more variety from which to choose. But you can be certain that the teen's musical taste will be different from that of his parents; it's a matter of independence and identity. The same principle is true in all other areas of teenage culture.

So what characterizes the contemporary teen culture? How is your teenager similar and different from teenagers of other generations?

SIMILARITIES WITH PAST TEENAGE GENERATIONS

Facing Physical and Mental Changes

The basic challenges facing today's teenager are very similar to the challenges you faced when you were a teenager. First, there is the challenge of accepting and adapting to the changes that take place in the teen's body. Arms and legs, hands and feet are all growing sometimes in a disproportionate rate, producing the reality of "teenage clumsiness," which is sometimes extremely embarrassing to the teenager. Secondary sexual characteristics are developing, which may be both exciting and anxiety-producing. And what parent has not felt the pain as they watched their teenager struggle with that devastating enemy, acne?

These physiological changes produce numerous questions in the mind of the teenager. "I'm becoming an adult, but what will I look like? Will I be too tall or too short? Will my ears protrude too far? Will my breasts be too small? What about my nose? Are my feet too big? Am I too fat or too skinny?" On and on the parade of questions marches through the mind of the developing teenager. The manner in which a teenager answers these questions will have a positive or negative effect upon his/her self-identity.

With this physical growth, there is also an accompanying intellectual "growth spurt." The teenager is developing a new way of thinking. As a child, she thought in terms of concrete actions and events. As a teenager, she begins to think in terms of abstract concepts like honesty, loyalty, and justice. With abstract thinking comes the expanded world of unlimited possibilities. The teen now has the ability to think about how things could be different, what a world without war would look like, how understanding parents would treat their children. The world of expanded possibilities opens all kinds of doors for self-identity. The teenager realizes, "I could be a brain surgeon or a pilot or a garbage collector." The possibilities are unlimited and the teen may envision himself in numerous vocational settings.

Entering the Age of Reason

Adolescence is also the age of reason. The teenager is able to think logically and to see the logical consequences of different positions. This logic is applied not only to his own reasoning but also to the reasoning of parents. This is one reason why a teenager is often perceived to be "argumentative." In reality, he is developing his mental skills. If the parents understand this, they can have meaningful and interesting conversations with their teenagers. If they don't understand this, they can develop an adversarial relationship, and the teenager must go elsewhere to flex his intellectual muscles. With this rapid growth in intellectual development and the gleaning of new information, the teenager often believes himself to be smarter than his parents and in some areas, he may be right.

This advanced level of thinking leads the teenager into a whole new arena of challenges in the field of social relationships. The discussion of "ideas" with his peers and listening to their point of view gives rise to new levels of intimacy on the one hand and opens the possibility of an adversarial relationship on the other. Thus, development of cliques (small, close social groupings) among teens has far more to do with agreement over intellectual ideas than it does with dress and hair color. Teens, like adults, tend to feel more comfortable with those who agree with them and thus tend to spend more time socially in their presence.

Confronting Personal Morality and Values

The intellectual ability to analyze ideas and actions in a logical manner and to project outcomes of certain beliefs gives rise to another common teenage challenge; namely, examining the belief systems with which one was raised and determining if those beliefs are worthy of one's commitment. "Were my parents right in their views of God, morality, and values?" These are heavy issues with which every teenager must wrestle. If parents do not understand this struggle, they will often become a negative influence and actually push the teenager away from the beliefs and values which the parent has earlier taught.

When the teenager questions the parents about basic beliefs, wise parents welcome the questions, seek to give honest answers in a nonauthoritarian manner, and encourage the teenager to continue to explore these ideas. In other words, they welcome the opportunity to dialogue with the teenager about the beliefs that they have espoused through the years. If, on the other hand the parents condemn the teenager for asking questions, perhaps heaping guilt upon him for even thinking that the parents' beliefs may be incorrect, the teenager is forced to go elsewhere to share his questions.

Thinking About Sexuality and Marriage

Another important challenge for the teenager is understanding his own sexuality and learning masculine or feminine social roles. What is appropriate and not appropriate in relating to members of the opposite sex? What is appropriate and inappropriate in dealing with my own sexual thoughts and feelings? These questions, often ignored by parents, cannot be ignored by the teenager.

The teen's emerging sexuality is a part of who he is, and relating to members of the opposite sex is an ever-present reality. Most teens dream of someday being married and having a family. In a recent survey where teens were asked to rank a number of the important issues in their future, "eighty-six percent said that having a stable family will be the most important item on the blueprint of their future lives."[1] Making the journey from early adolescence to that stable marriage and family which the teen desires occupies many hours of teenage thought.

Parents who want to help will use the normal flow of family conversation to address issues related to sexuality, dating, and marriage. They will also make available printed materials which speak on the teenage level and provide practical and sound information. For those teenagers who are involved in church, caring adults and youth ministers often provide sessions relating to sex, dating, and marriage. These classes provide a social context in which teens can learn and discuss this important aspect of teen development in an open and caring way.

Questioning the Future

There is one other common challenge faced by teenagers of the past and present. It is grappling with the question "What will I do with my life?" It involves choosing a vocation, but it is far deeper than that. It is ultimately a spiritual question: "What is worth the investment of my life? Where will I find the greatest happiness? And where can I make the greatest contribution?" As philosophical as these questions may appear, they are very real to our teenagers. More immediately, teenagers must answer the questions, "Will I go to college, and if so, where? Shall I join the military, and if so, which branch? Or shall I get a job, and if so, which job?" Of course, teenagers understand that these choices all lead somewhere. There is something beyond the next step and somehow, the next step will influence where teenagers end up. It is an awesome challenge for young minds.

Parents who wish to be helpful will share something of their own struggle, their own joys, their own disappointments. As a parent, you cannot and should not offer easy answers, but you can encourage the teenager's search and perhaps introduce your son or daughter to people of various vocations who can share their journey. You can encourage your adolescent to take advantage of vocational counselors both at high school and later at the university. But ultimately, you should encourage your teenager to follow the example of Samuel. The ancient Hebrew prophet as a teenager heard God's call and said, "Speak, for your servant is listening."[2] The men and women who have made the greatest impact upon human history have been men and women who had a sense of divine call and who lived out that call in their vocation.

All of the above challenges are similar to the challenges that teenagers in all generations have faced. But the contemporary teenager lives in a very different world from the teenager of the past and certainly a different world from that in which his parents lived when they were teenagers.

FIVE FUNDAMENTAL DIFFERENCES

With all these similarities, let's not forget that a mighty gulf exists between the contemporary teenager and teenagers of the past; that gulf is the modern cultural setting in which teens face the challenges noted above. What are some of these cultural differences?

1. Technology

One of the most observable differences is that contemporary teenagers have grown up in a world of highly advanced technology.

Their parents grew up with the telephone, radio, and network television, but for the contemporary teenager, cable and satellite television have created a much more global world than their parents experienced. A plethora of radio and TV channels provides access to every conceivable type of entertainment within our own culture. But the teenager is not limited to these programmed outlets. Every movie ever produced is available for rental at the local video store and every song ever sung can be purchased on a CD and heard on the teenager's ever-present boom box.

The contemporary teen has also grown up with the computer; they have both come of age together. Millions of teenagers have had their own personal computer as long as they can remember. The Internet superhighway has become a vast thoroughfare with both positive and negative influences upon the contemporary teenager. Besides giving our teens access to previews of upcoming movies, to broadcasts of radio stations across the country, and the ability to download the latest music, it allows them to communicate with friends as if they had instant messengers. In fact, with chat rooms and "instant messaging," the Internet is fast replacing the telephone as the teen's method of communicating with friends and discussing ideas. A recent survey indicated that teenagers use the Internet an average of 8.5 hours a week for chatting and E-mailing, compared with 1.8 hours spent using it for school work.[3] These technological realities put your teenager in touch with the world and the world in touch with your teenager. Thus, the contemporary teenager is exposed to far more cultural stimuli than his parents ever dreamed.

2. Knowledge of and Exposure to Violence

A second cultural difference is that your teenager is growing up with far more knowledge of violent human behavior. Part of this is because of the technological advances, that is, more violence is reported through the media, but a part of it simply reflects our culture's thirst—almost obsession—for violence. Our movies, songs, and novels often rush toward violent scenes. A recent Gallup youth survey found that 36 percent of teenagers had seen a movie or television show containing a lot of violence in the past month.

Interestingly, in 1999 nearly eight in ten teens, 78 percent, told the Gallup organization that they "do not have a problem watching violent movies or television programs." However, 53 percent of the same teenagers agreed that "violence on television and in movies sends the wrong messages to young people." The same survey indicated that 65 percent of the teens surveyed believe that "movies and television have a great deal of influence on the outlook of young people today."[4]

Exposure to violence is not limited to the media and movies. Many contemporary teenagers have experienced violence on the personal level. They have watched their fathers physically abuse their mothers or they themselves have suffered physical abuse from fathers, stepfathers, or other adults. Most teenagers acknowledge that the public school is often the scene of violent behavior.

Some teens are even perpetrators of violence, including homicide. While the overall homicide rate in the United States has remained somewhat steady for the past thirty years, the youth homicide rate has continued to increase. The period of greatest growth was from the mid-1980s to the mid-1990s, when youth homicide increased 168 percent. The FBI reported that there are about 23,000 homicides each year in the United States, and in 25 percent of these killings, the perpetrator is 21 years of age or younger.[5] Violence has always been a part of our culture, but your teenager is far more intellectually and emotionally in tune with this violence than any preceding generation.

3. The Fragmented Family

A third cultural factor that influences the contemporary teenager is the fragmented nature of the modern American family. According to a recent Gallup youth survey, four of every ten American teens (39 percent) are living with only one of their parents. In eight out of ten cases, the absent parent is the father. The same survey indicated that 20 percent of American teenagers live with a stepfather or some other adult male who lives with their mother.[6]

Sociologists have observed "in unprecedented numbers, our families are unalike: we have fathers working while mothers keep house; fathers and mothers both working away from home; single parents; second marriages bringing children together from unrelated backgrounds; childless couples; unmarried couples with and without children; and gay and lesbian parents. We are living through a period of historic change in American family life.[7] Another researcher noted, "The data is not yet in on the residual of this fragmentation, but a sociological view suggests a direct link with many of the social strains we see every day. Some of the attitudes, stress, alienation, . . . and shortened attention spans are directly related to strains of adjusting to new kinds of families."[8]

In addition to the fragmentation of the nuclear family, today's teen is growing up largely without an extended family: grandparents, aunts, uncles, and other relatives. With advanced mobility, more and more nuclear families are living at greater distances from the extended family compared with earlier generations. Also, whereas neighbors once served as surrogate parents, watching out for each other's children, busy neighbors rarely can do that now. Once the local school was more homogeneous and the community offered a safe environment for young people to relate to others. That's far less the case now. All these positive influences beyond the home are fast disappearing.

James Cromer, director of the Yale Child Study Center, sees this breakdown as a factor nearly as critical as the breakdown of the nuclear family. Speaking of his own childhood, Cromer said, "Between home and school, at least five close friends of my parents reported everything I did that was unacceptable. They are not there anymore for today's kids."[9] In the past, teenagers could depend upon extended families, healthy neighborhoods, churches, and community groups. The contemporary teen most often does not have these nets of support.

4. Knowledge of and Exposure to Sexuality

Also vastly different is today's overtly sexual atmosphere in which our teens grow up. The baby boomers of the 1960s rebelled against the traditional sexual mores of their parents, but they remembered what the sexual rules were and sometimes even experienced guilt in breaking them. But the contemporary teenager has grown up in a world without sexual rules. Movies, media, and music all equate sex with love and depict sex as an expected part of a meaningful dating relationship. Thus, vast numbers of teenagers are sexually active. "Survey results vary, but averaging them shows us that between 70–80 percent of American teenagers have had sex by the end of high school."[10]

Teenagers who are not sexually active struggle with thoughts such as *Am I missing out on something important? Is there something wrong with me?* Meanwhile, those teens who are sexually active have other negative feelings: They often feel used, abused, and empty.

The contemporary teen lives in a world where sex is not only an expected part of the dating relationship but living together before marriage is more and more common, and a homosexual relationship is being promoted as an alternate lifestyle. Indeed, the words *bisexual* and *transvestite* are becoming common vocabulary for the modern teen. In a very real sense, sex has become the American goddess, and the shrines and venues for worship are as varied as the mind can imagine. This is the world in which the contemporary teenager must navigate the waters of his/her own emerging sexuality.

5. Neutral Moral and Religious Values

Finally, the contemporary teen is growing up in a world that is truly post-Christian. In the area of religion and morals, there is no sure word. In past generations, most Americans could have defined moral and immoral behavior. These moral judgments were primarily based on the Judeo-Christian Scriptures. This is not true for the contemporary teenager. For the first time in American history, an entire generation is growing up without certain moral values. Values are often neutral; the teen is told what feels good is good. Wrong is relative.

In a revealing survey of older teenagers in the mid-1990s, the Barna Research Group found that 91 percent of teenagers agreed with the statement "What is right for one person in a given situation might not be right for another person in a similar situation." Another 80 percent agreed with the idea, "When it comes to matters of morals and ethics, truth means different things to different people; no one can be absolutely positive that they know the truth." And in a society where truth and integrity were once valued, 57 percent of the teens believed that "lying is sometimes necessary."[11]

The contemporary generation has no clear definition of right and wrong. The reasons behind this growth of an amoral generation were explained by educator Thom Rainer as follows: "The *Builders,* born before 1946, accepted (and still do today) basic Judeo-Christian principles to discern right from wrong. They believe that the Bible is a moral guide for life today. However, the *Builders'* children—*Boomers* and their children *Busters*—withdrew in large numbers from church and other Christian activities." Rainer continued:

> Without the influence of the church, they began to engage in activities clearly defined as immoral by their parents. They did have the absolute standards of their parents' and grandparents' morality, but they accepted them in theory rather than in practice. But the *Bridger* generation (born in the years 1977–1994) had neither a moral standard, such as the Bible, nor a moral example in their parents. Their understanding of right and wrong is fuzzy at best. An entire amoral generation will soon enter adulthood.[12]

The teenage years have always been the time to explore religious beliefs. Teens are asking questions about the religious beliefs—or disbeliefs—of their parents. As in other areas of life, they are seeking to clarify their own identity. The difference in the contemporary world is that because of the global nature of today's world, our teens are exposed to numerous religious beliefs—both by means of modern technology and through friends who are involved in other religious groups.

Religion is important to the contemporary teen. A recent Gallup survey indicated that four out of every five teenagers (79 percent) see religious faith as a significant influence in their lives.[13] A majority of teenagers (64 percent) belong to a church, synagogue, or other organized religious group. One-half of the teenagers (49 percent) say that their life belongs to God or a higher power. Fully one-third of teens (35 percent) say their religious faith is the most important influence in their life and one-third (34 percent) describe themselves as "born-again." Four in ten teenagers (42 percent) told the Gallup group that they had attended services for religious worship the previous week.[14] Today's teenagers are more interested in the experiential, relational nature of religious groups than abstract religious belief. If the group is accepting, caring and supportive, they are drawn to the spiritual group even though they disagree with many of the group's religious beliefs.

PARENTS *CAN* GUIDE

This is the world into which your teenager has come of age. The good news is that contemporary teenagers are looking to parents for guidance. In a recent survey, teens reported that parents have more influence than peers do in the following areas: whether to attend college, whether to attend religious services, whether to do homework, and whether to drink. Parents also had an impact on the teens' job or career plans. Friends had more influence on their decision in terms of immediate issues such as: whether or not to cut classes, who to date, the way they wear their hair, what kind of clothes they wore.[15]

The survey found that when teenagers were asked to report "Who has the greatest influence on your decisions? Parents or friends?" the decisions most heavily weighted toward parental influence were those that appear to have a major effect on what kind of person the teen will be. Yes, your teenager will be influenced by friends on some issues, but parental influence is still the major influence on your teenager's thoughts and behavior. The remaining chapters of this book are designed to help you learn to effectively meet your teenager's need for love and thus lay the foundation for influencing your teen more effectively in all other areas of life.

NOTES

1. *YOUTHviews* 6, no. 8 (April 1997): 3; published by the George H. Gallup International Institute, Princeton, N.J.

2. 1 Samuel 3:10.

3. Linda Temple, "Courting by Computer: On-Line Replacing Phone Lines for Teens in Touch," *USA Today*, 14 April 1997.

4. *YOUTHviews* 6, no. 7 (March 1999): 3.

5. Ames Garbarino, *Lost Boys: Why Our Sons Turn Violent and How We Can Save Them* (New York: Free Press, 1999), 6–7.

6. *YOUTHviews* 5, no. 9 (May 1998): 2.

7. Jerrold K. Footlick, "What Happened to the American Family?" *Newsweek* (Special Edition), Winter/Spring, 1990, 15.

8. Eric Miller with Mary Porter, *In the Shadow of the Baby Boom* (Brooklyn, N.Y.: EPM Communications, 1994), 5.

9. Richard Louv, *Childhood's Future* (New York: Anchor, 1990), 6.

10. Ron Hutchcraft, *The Battle for a Generation* (Chicago: Moody, 1996), 32.

11. George Barna, *Generation Next* (Ventura, Calif.: Regal, 1995), 32.

12. Thom S. Rainer, *The Bridger Generation* (Nashville: Broadman & Holman, 1977), 44.

13. *YOUTHviews* 6, no. 3 (November 1998): 2.

14. Ibid., 6, no. 1 (September 1998): 2.

15. Ibid., 5, no. 1 (September 1997): 1.

chapter two

THE IMPORTANCE OF PARENTAL LOVE

Becky, a mother of two, had all the symptoms of parental trauma. "Dr. Chapman, I'm frightened to death," she said. "My son is twelve; my daughter is eleven. I've been reading books about teenagers and I'm scared. It seems like all teenagers are having sex, using drugs, and carrying guns to school. Is it really that bad?" Becky asked the question during a marriage seminar in Moline, Illinois. Then she added, "I've been thinking that maybe I should home school my children through high school but that also scares me. I don't know if I am ready for my children to become teenagers."

Over the past five years, I have met a lot of parents like Becky. Many parents are reading more books about parenting teenagers. They are hearing more about teenage violence on television. They are reading their local newspaper, and frankly, they are running scared. If you happen to be one of these scared parents or if you are asking yourself, "Should I be scared?" I hope this chapter will allay some of your fears. Anxiety is not a good mental attitude with which to parent teenagers. I hope that this chapter will relieve some of your anxiety and give you more confidence in the positive role you can play in the life of your teenager.

THE GOOD NEWS ABOUT
FAMILIES AND SCHOOLS

Let me begin by reporting that not all of the facts are negative. While it is true that a recent Gallup Youth Survey found that only 57 percent of American teenagers live with both of their parents, it is also true that 87 percent of teens have contact with their fathers even when they are not living together all the time.[1] A solid majority of teens (70 percent) say that they feel "extremely" or "very" close to their fathers.[2] Another recent survey indicated that the majority of teens ages thirteen to seventeen say that they usually have good feelings in school. A sizeable majority of teenagers report that they feel happy (85 percent) and supported at school (82 percent). Nearly as many say that they feel appreciated (78 percent), interested (77 percent), encouraged (76 percent), and challenged (72 percent).[3] Two statistics that should warm the hearts of all education-minded parents are: 97 percent of teenagers will graduate from high school and 83 percent of them consider a college education to be "very important" today.[4]

After reviewing these findings, George Gallup Jr. characterized contemporary youth as being motivated by idealism, optimism, spontaneity, and exuberance. "Young people tell us that they are enthusiastic about helping others, willing to work for world peace and a healthy world, and they feel positive about their schools and even more positive about their teachers." Concerning teens' attitudes toward their future, Gallup concluded: "A large majority of American youth report that they are happy and excited about the future, feel very close to their families, are likely to marry, want to have children, are satisfied with their personal lives, and desire to reach the top of their chosen careers."[5]

Lawrence Steinberg, a senior research associate at the Center for Research in Human Development and Education, is a nationally recognized expert on adolescence. He has noted, "Adolescence is not an inherently difficult period. Psychological problems, problem behavior, and family conflict are no more common in adolescence

32

than at any other stage of the life cycle. To be sure, some adolescents are troubled and some get into trouble. But the great majority (almost 9 out of 10) do not." Steinberg, who is also professor of psychology at Temple University, added: "The problems we have come to see as a 'normal' part of adolescent development—drugs, delinquency, irresponsible sex, opposition to any and all authority—are not normal at all. They are both preventable and treatable. The bottom line is that good kids don't suddenly go bad in adolescence."[6]

The reality is that most of what we read in the newspaper and hear via the media deals with the 10 percent of troubled teenagers, most of whom were also troubled children. You and your teenager *can* have a positive parent/teen relationship. That's what your teenager wants, and I assume that is what you want. In this chapter, we're going to look at what I believe to be the most important aspect of that relationship, namely meeting your teen's need for emotional love. If this need is met, then the teenager will effectively navigate the cultural waters which we talked about in chapter 1.

When teens are secure in the love of parents, they will have confidence to face the negative influences in our culture that would keep them from becoming mature, productive adults. Without the love of parents, the teenager is far more likely to succumb to the evil influences of drugs, perverted sex, and violence. In my opinion, nothing is more important than the parent learning how to effectively meet the teen's emotional need for love.

What do I mean by "emotional love?" Deep within the soul of the teenager is the desire to feel connected, accepted, and nurtured by parents. When this happens, the teenager feels loved. When the teen does not feel connected, accepted, and nurtured, his inner emotional tank is empty—and that emptiness will greatly affect the behavior of the teen. Let me describe each of these in more depth.

THE TEEN'S DESIRE FOR CONNECTION

The Presence of Parents

Much has been written about the importance of the young child "bonding" to the parents. Most child psychologists agree that if this emotional bonding does not take place, the child's emotional development will be plagued with feelings of insecurity. The opposite of connection is abandonment. If the young child's parents are not available because of death, divorce, or desertion, obviously emotional bonding cannot take place. The prerequisite for bonding is the presence of the parents. Bonding requires time together.

In the teenage years, the same principles are true. Parents who are around little because of divorce, work schedules, etc., jeopardize the teenager's sense of feeling connected to parents. It is a simple reality that for a teen to feel connected and thus loved by the parents, they must spend time together. The teen who feels abandoned will wrestle with the question, "What's wrong with me that my parents don't care about me?" If parents wish a teenager to feel loved, they must make time to be with the teenager.

The Connecting Power of Communication

Obviously, physical proximity between parents and teens does not necessarily result in connection. Emotional connectedness requires communication. You may be a stay-at-home mother or a father at home on a two-week vacation and still be unconnected if there is little communication.

I was encouraged recently while examining a research project to find that 71 percent of teens surveyed indicated they eat at least one meal a day with family. But my encouragement was short-lived when I discovered that fully half of all teens surveyed watched television the last time they had dinner with their parents. In addition, one in four said they listened to the radio while 15 percent read a book, magazine, or newspaper while dining.[7] It appears that most parents are not using mealtimes as a means for building connection with teenagers.

In my opinion, the meal table is one of the best places to build emotional connectedness with teenagers. What teenager doesn't love to eat? A little talking with parents is a small price to pay for a good meal. If your family does not fall into the 71 percent who has at least one meal together every day, let me encourage you to work toward this ideal. And for those who are eating but not talking, let me suggest a new guideline for family mealtimes. Announce to the teenagers and younger children that you are starting a new tradition at mealtimes. "First, we talk to God, (yes, teach your children to be grateful for their food), then to each other; after that, if we wish, we can revert to TV, newspapers, and radio."

After someone has volunteered to thank God for the food and the person or persons who prepared it, then each family member shares with the others three things that happened in their lives today and how they feel about them. When one family member is talking, the others are listening sympathetically. They may ask questions to clarify what they are hearing but they don't give advice unless it is solicited by the person who is talking.

This one new tradition may be enough to help you establish and maintain a sense of connectedness with your teenager.

THE TEEN'S DESIRE FOR ACCEPTANCE

The Power of Acceptance . . . and Rejection

A second element of emotional love is feeling accepted by parents. One fourteen-year-old boy said, "The main thing I like about my parents is that they accept me for who I am. They don't try to make me like my older sister." This teenager feels loved, and this love comes from being accepted by his parents.

"My parents like me. I'm OK." These are the messages played in the mind of the teenager who feels accepted. The opposite of acceptance is rejection. Its messages are "They don't like me. I'm not good enough for them. They wish I were different." The child who feels rejected obviously does not feel loved.

Anthropologist Ronald Rohner has studied rejection in more than a hundred cultures around the world. His findings are clear that although cultures differ in how they express rejection, rejected children everywhere are at heightened risk for numerous psychological problems, ranging from low self-esteem, deficient moral development, difficulty in handling aggression to confused sexual identity. Rohner believes that the effects of rejection are so strong that he calls rejection a "psychological malignancy that spreads throughout a child's emotional system, wreaking havoc."[8]

James Garbarino, professor of human development at Cornell University, has spent many years studying the inner life of violent teenagers. He concluded that the feeling of rejection is a major element in the psychological makeup of the violent teenager. Often this rejection grows out of being compared with another sibling. While interviewing one eighteen-year-old from New York who was serving a life sentence for shooting a police officer, Garbarino set two beverage cans on a desktop and said to the young man, "Let's think of this whole desktop as your mother's love. Now, this can is you," he said, holding up one of the cans. "And this one is your brother," gesturing toward the other can. "How full of your mother's love is your can? And how full is your brother's can?"

The young prisoner pointed to his own can, indicating that he received about 20 percent of his mother's love and his brother got 80 percent.

"Now let's use the desk to show being accepted or being rejected." Garbarino then pointed to one end of the desk. "This end means complete acceptance; the other end is total rejection. Choose places for the two cans to show how much your mother accepted you and how much she accepted your brother."

The young man put his can almost all the way to the end of the desk on the side of rejection and put the can representing his brother all the way to the other end of the desk, indicating complete acceptance.

"Ninety percent rejection for you and a 100 percent acceptance for your brother?" the counselor asked.

"Yes," the young man responded.[9] Obviously, the teenager who feels rejected does not feel loved.

Accepting the Teen . . . Correcting the Behavior

Many parents think showing total acceptance is wrong. Bob, a concerned parent of two teenagers, spoke with great candidness when he said to me, "Dr. Chapman, I don't understand how you can accept a teenager when his behavior is despicable. I don't want my teens to feel rejected, but frankly I don't like their behavior and I don't like them when they engage in that behavior. Maybe I am rejecting them, but in my heart that is not what I feel. I feel love and concern. I don't want them to destroy their lives."

Bob was speaking for thousands of parents who have not yet

learned how to communicate acceptance while at the same time correcting the misbehavior of their teen. We will explore this further as we get into the five love languages and also in chapter 12, where we deal with discipline.

For the moment, let me seek to clarify our goal by using a theological illustration. Paul, a first-century apostle of the Christian faith, said of God "He made us accepted in the Beloved."[10] He was alluding to the central Christian doctrine that the God who is holy has accepted us who are unholy because He sees us as being a part of Himself because we have accepted His Son—the Beloved. Since we have accepted His Son, God has accepted us. Paul's idea is that though God is not always pleased with our behavior, God is always pleased with us because we are His children. As parents, this is what we are trying to do—to communicate with our children that we are happy to be their parents without respect to their behavior. It is what we typically refer to as unconditional love.

The idea of unconditional love is, "I love you, I care about you. I am committed to you because you are my child. I don't always like what you do, but I always love you and care about your well-being. You are my son or daughter and I will never reject you. I will always be here doing what I believe is best for you. I will love you no matter what."

Ken Canfield, president of the National Center for Fathering, said, "Never forget the great question of adolescence: 'Who am I?' Your teenager will have to answer that question for himself. What he wants to hear from you is 'Whoever you end up being, I still love you.'" Then Canfield noted a great fear every teen has: "Never forget the great fear of adolescence—'Am I normal?' The likely answer to that question is 'Yes.' But what the teenager wants to hear from his dad is 'Even if you were abnormal, I'd still love you.'"[11]

Canfield was talking about unconditional acceptance, unconditional love. I will give other suggestions later, but let me give here a simple approach that may greatly affect the way your teenager hears your verbal messages of guidance or correction. Before you give your profound statement of what you wish your teenager would do, always preface it by these words. "I love you very much. I will love you even if you don't follow my advice but because I love you, I must give you my advice." Then share your words of profound wisdom.

Your teenager needs to hear that you accept him even when you don't approve of his behavior. Wrap these words in your own personality. If you are theatrical, you may say, "Would my son, whom I love very much and whom I will always and forever love, like to hear the profound advice of his father?" "Would my beloved daughter, whom I will always cherish, like to hear the hidden thoughts of her father which may have the potential of greatly enhancing his daughter's life?" Find a way to say it that feels comfortable to you, but say it, and say it often.

THE TEEN'S DESIRE FOR NURTURE

The third aspect of loving your teenager is giving him or her nurture. Nurture has to do with feeding the inner spirit of your teen. We nurture plants by enhancing the soil in which they are planted. We nurture teenagers by enhancing the climate in which they grow. Teenagers who grow up in a warm, caring, encouraging, positive emotional climate are more likely to produce beautiful flowers and luscious fruit as they reach maturity.

Avoid Abuse

The opposite of nurture is abuse. An abusive atmosphere is like spraying poison on the soul of a teenager. Teenagers who receive hostile, cutting, harsh, or demeaning words from their parents will eventually make it to adulthood, but the scars of verbal abuse will be evidenced for a lifetime. Parents who indulge in physical abuse by slapping, shoving, pushing, beating, or shaking their teenager may well harm the young person's physical development, but far more tragically will malign the teen's emotional development, which as an adult will make their lives far more difficult.

Few things are more detrimental to the teenager's developing psyche than abuse. Teenagers draw conclusions based on what they observe and what they experience at the hands of their parents. Research indicates that most teenagers who turn violent have themselves been traumatized by abuse and are starved for love. Garbarino describes violent boys in this manner: "They take drugs. They engage in violence. They steal. They gorge themselves on sex. They join gangs and cults and when no one is watching or listening to them, they suck their thumbs and cry themselves to sleep."[12] Behind many violent teenagers is an abusive parent. Love does not abuse; love nurtures.

Be a Nurturing Parent

To nurture your teenager first requires that you nurture yourself. If parents are going to create for the teenager a supportive and positive climate in which he or she can accomplish the developmental tasks of adolescence, we will have to grow in the areas of our own emotional weaknesses. The fact is that many parents of teenagers did not grow up in nurturing families; consequently, they have developed negative patterns of responding to teenagers which come across as abusive. If you see this in yourself, the first step is to deal with your own pain and learn to process your own anger.

This may involve reading books on resolving anger,[13] joining support groups through your local church or community center, or going for personal counseling. It is never too late to deal with the dark side of your own history. Your teenagers deserve your best and your best is not possible until you have dealt with your past.

Nurturing parents have a positive attitude. I do not mean that they deny the realities of life, but they choose to see the hand of God behind the scenes of human events. They look for the sun behind the clouds and they communicate this spirit to their teenagers. Nurturing parents are encouraging, looking for the positive things their teenagers do and say and commending them.

Nurturing parents are caring parents, constantly looking for ways to enhance the lives of their teenagers. In the chapters that follow, we will look at the five love languages and help you to discover the primary love language of your teenager. Speaking this language is the most powerful way to nurture your child's inner spirit and to enhance his life.

Recognize that Nurture Affects Every Area of a Teen's Life

One of the reasons emotional love is so important for your teenager is because it affects every other aspect of the teenager's life. When the teenager's love tank is empty, he feels that "no one really cares about me." Motivation for learning is dissipated. "Why should I study at school? No one cares what happens to me anyway." Statements like this are often heard by high school guidance counselors.

An empty love tank also affects the teen's ability to empathize with others. When the teen does not feel loved, he will have greater difficulty appreciating how his negative actions might affect someone else's feelings. Research indicates that most violent juvenile delinquents display very little empathy.[14] Empathy is one of the foundations for what Daniel Goleman calls "emotional intelligence." He defines emotional intelligence as the ability to read emotions in others, to communicate effectively in the non-verbal realm, to handle the ups and downs of daily life, and to have appropriate expectations for relationships.[15] Thus, lack of emotional intelligence affects the teen's ability to relate positively to others.

Lack of empathy, in turn, affects the teenager's development of the conscience and moral judgments. It is during the teenage years that the standard for one's conscience is being internalized. In the childhood years, standards have been given by parents. Now the teen is wrestling with his/her own concept of what is moral and immoral. If, because of lack of emotional love, the teenager is not able to empathize with others, there will be little sense that it is wrong to hurt others. In the realm of spirituality, if the child's emotional need for love has not been met, then the theological idea of a loving God will have little meaning to the teenager. This is one reason why teenagers who are starved for emotional love will often turn away from the parent's religious beliefs and practices.

In summary, the teenager's intellectual, emotional, social, moral, and spiritual development are greatly enhanced if the teenager has significant amounts of emotional love. Conversely, the teen is greatly impaired in all of these areas if the emotional need for love is not met. That is why I choose to devote this entire book to what I believe to be the most important aspect of parenting your teenager, namely meeting his/her need for emotional love.

THE MOST BASIC NEED: FEELING LOVED

Sociologists, psychologists, and religious leaders all agree that the most fundamental need of the teenager is to feel emotional love from the significant adults in his life. David Popenoe, professor of sociology at Rutgers University and co-chair of the Council on Families in America, wrote, "Children develop best when they are provided the opportunity to have warm, intimate, continuous, and enduring relationships with both their fathers and their mothers." Psychologists Henry Cloud and John Townsend add, "There is no greater ingredient of growth for your youngster than love." And in *Lost Boys,* James Garbarino asked: "What tools does a boy have to make sense of his life if he has no sense of being loved and appreciated?"[16]

When the religious leaders of that day asked Jesus of Nazareth, "Which is the greatest commandment in the law?" the founder of the Christian faith replied, "'Love the Lord your God with all your heart and with all your soul and with all your mind.' This is the first and greatest commandment. And the second is like it: 'Love your neighbor as yourself.' All the Law and the Prophets hang on these two commandments."[17] Thus, Jesus summarized all the teachings of the Old Testament books of law and the words of the Jewish prophets in these two commandments. I would like to suggest that the teenager living in your house is your nearest neighbor.

FINDING LOVE IN ALL THE WRONG PLACES

The reality is that if parents and other significant adults do not meet a teen's need for love, the teenager will go looking for love in all the wrong places. After sixteen-year-old Luke Woodham killed his mother and then opened fire at his high school in Pearl, Mississippi, killing three and wounding seven on October 1, 1997, he later told an ABC News correspondent that he felt so isolated and rejected in his community that he was easily drawn into a group of boys who were self-proclaimed Satanists. He said, "My whole life I felt outcasted, alone. Finally, I found some people who wanted to be my friends." Garbarino concluded, "Emotionally needy boys who are rejected by teachers and parents are prime targets for anti-social older youth and adults. These negative role models recruit vulnerable boys, and they exchange self-affirmation for loyalty to the anti-social cause. Many violent and troubled boys have stories of how they were befriended by older boys who accepted them in return for their involvement in criminal enterprises."[18]

Research has also shown that one reason teenage girls have babies is their deep desire to have someone who will love them.

Having a baby often turns these girls' lives around because not only do they have someone who is totally dependent upon them but they have someone whom they can love. Loving and being loved motivates them to other productive steps such as continuing education and/or working hard to take care of their baby.[19]

After years of trying to understand violent and delinquent teenagers, Garbarino concluded, "Nothing seems to threaten the human spirit more than rejection, brutalization, and lack of love."[20]

Nothing is more important in parenting teenagers than learning how to effectively meet the teen's need for emotional love. What you are about to read in the next five chapters will introduce you to the five basic love languages—the five most effective ways to keep full the emotional love tank of your teenager. Then I will address the matter of discovering your teen's primary love language, the one language that is most effective in meeting his/her emotional need for love. As I have shared this material in parenting lectures across the country, many parents have found that the application of these truths has radically changed the behavior of their teens and has given the parents feelings of deep satisfaction that whatever else they are doing as parents, they are being effective in meeting their teens' most important emotional need. That's my desire for you as well.

NOTES

1. *YOUTHviews* 5, no. 8 (April 1998): 1; published by The George H. Gallup International Institute, Princeton, N.J.

2. *YOUTHviews* 5, no. 9 (May 1998): 2.

3. *YOUTHviews* 6, no. 8 (April 1999): 3.

4. *YOUTHviews* 5, no. 7 (March 1998): 2.

5. *YOUTHviews* 5, no. 6 (February 1998): 5.

6. Lawrence Steinberg and Ann Levine, *You and Your Adolescent* (New York: Harper & Row, 1990), 2.

7. *YOUTHviews* 5, no. 2 (October, 1997): 1, 4.

8. As quoted in James Garbarino, *Lost Boys: Why Our Sons Turn Violent and How We Can Save Them* (New York: Free Press, 1999), 50.

9. Ibid., 51.

10. Ephesians 1:6, NKJV.

11. Ken Canfield, *The Heart of a Father* (Chicago: Northfield, 1996), 194–95.

12. Garbarino, *Lost Boys,* 158.

13. Those who struggle with unresolved anger may profit from reading Gary Chapman, *The Other Side of Love: Handling Anger in a Godly Way* (Chicago: Moody, 1999).

14. Garbarino, *Lost Boys,* 138.

15. Daniel Goleman, *Emotional Intelligence* (New York: Bantam, 1995), 25–35.

16. David Popenoe, *Life Without Father* (New York: Free Press, 1996), 191; Henry Cloud and John Townsend, *Boundaries with Kids* (Grand Rapids: Zondervan, 1998), 46; and Garbarino, *Lost Boys,* 154.

17. Matthew 22:35–40.

18. Garbarino, *Lost Boys,* 168.

19. Ibid., 163.

20. Ibid., 132.

chapter three

LOVE LANGUAGE #1: WORDS OF AFFIRMATION

Fifteen-year-old Brad was in my office at his parents' request. His feet fit loosely into his earth-colored sandals. His multi-pocketed pants hung precariously on his thin frame. His tee shirt read "Freedom is having all the jelly beans you want." I was not at all sure that he wanted to be in my office, but I was pleasantly surprised that Brad listened carefully to my inquiries and shared freely his thoughts and feelings. (I've had other teenagers in my office whose answer to every question was "It's OK.")

Brad's parents had complained that he had become extremely rebellious toward them, that he had lashed out in anger several times, and had even threatened to leave home. It was this threat that motivated them to insist that he talk with me. The thought of Brad leaving home had traumatized them, and to use his father's words, "He's the kind of kid who would do it. He's never met a stranger. He would find someone to take him in. But the thought terrifies us."

"We've tried to talk to Brad," his mother continued, "but it seems we always get into an argument and one of us ends up losing control and saying things that we don't mean. We later apologize and try to go on, but Brad seems so unreasonable every time we don't agree with him."

After a brief introduction, I assured Brad that my role was not to tell him what to do but that I did hope I might help him understand his parents a little better and perhaps help them understand him. I indicated that his parents "seemed concerned" and that is why they had asked the two of us to get together. He nodded in an affirming manner. Wanting to connect with Brad, I decided to begin with the present rather than probing the past. I said to Brad, "Your parents tell me that you are thinking of leaving home. I was wondering if you could tell me a little bit about that."

"I'm not going to leave home," Brad said, shaking his head from left to right. "I said that one night when I was really mad and they weren't listening to me. Sometimes I do think about leaving home, but I don't think I'd ever do it."

"What do you think about when you think about leaving home?" I inquired. "What do you envision your life would be like if you weren't living with your parents?"

"I'd be free to do what I want to do," Brad said. "I wouldn't have to argue with them about every little thing. That's what I don't like about living at home, all the arguments."

I was beginning to sense that negative words were very painful to Brad, which led me to guess that his primary love language was *words of affirmation*. Typically when teenagers are deeply hurt by negative words, it is an indication that affirming words speak most deeply to the teen's emotional need for love.

"Do you feel that your parents love you?" I asked. Brad paused a moment and then said, "I know they love me but sometimes I don't feel loved, especially in the last few years."

"When you were little, how did your parents show their love to you?" I asked.

"They told me how great I was," he said with a chuckle. "Now I think they have changed their minds."

"Do you remember some of the positive things they told you?"

"I remember one time when I was playing little league football, my dad told me that I was the best player he had ever seen. He said that I could play pro football someday if I wanted to."

"Do you play football in high school?" I asked. Shaking his head in an affirmative manner, Brad then admitted he was playing but dismissed his chances to go farther in the sport. "I'm OK but I'm not that good." When I asked him to recall positive things his mother said to him as a child, Brad replied, "Mom always said 'I love you, I love you, I love you.' She always said it three times really fast. Some times I thought she wasn't sincere but mostly I knew she was."

"Does she still say those words to you?" I asked.

"Not lately," he said. "All she does now is criticize me."

"What does she say when she criticizes you?" I asked.

"Well, last night she told me that I was irresponsible and that if I didn't change, I would never make it in college. She tells me I'm sloppy and disrespectful."

"Are you?" I inquired.

"I guess I'm sloppy," he said slowly, "but I wouldn't be disrespectful if they weren't on my back all the time."

"What else do your parents criticize you about?" I asked.

"Everything. They say I spend too much time on the telephone, too much time with my friends. I don't come home when they think I should. I don't call them when I'm late. I don't spend enough time on homework. They say I don't take school seriously. Like I said, everything."

"So with all of these criticisms, how do you feel toward your parents?"

"Some days I'd just like to get away from them," Brad said. "I just get tired of the constant hassle. Why can't they let me be who I am? I don't think I'm all that bad. I wish they would just back off."

"What would you do if they backed off?" I inquired. "I don't know," Brad said. "Just be a normal teenager, I guess. I'm not going to do something stupid like drugs or getting some girl pregnant or blow some kids away with a shotgun. I think my parents watch too much violence on television. They watch the *crazies* and think all teenagers are like that. I'm not crazy. Why can't they trust me?"

RUNNING ON EMPTY

After three more sessions with Brad, I concluded that he was a pretty normal teenager who was living with an empty love tank not because his parents did not love him but because his parents had stopped speaking his primary love language, *words of affirmation*. In his childhood, they had often affirmed him verbally. Their words of affirmation were vivid memories, but now, in his mind, all of that has changed. What he heard was negative words and what he felt was rejection. His love tank had been full as a child but as a teenager, he was running on empty.

After thoroughly hearing Brad's story, I shared with him my assessment. I explained to him that all of us have an emotional love tank and when that love tank is full—when we really feel loved by the important people in our lives—the world looks bright and we can discuss our differences in a positive way. But when the love tank is empty and we feel rejected rather than loved, it becomes extremely difficult to discuss differences without stooping to argument and slander. I also told Brad that his parents had their own emotional love tank and that my guess was that they were also running on empty. In the early years, he had probably spoken their love languages and they felt his love; but now their emotional tanks were empty.

"When parents have empty love tanks," I said, "they often exhibit unhealthy behavioral patterns toward their teenagers." I assured Brad that I believed all of this could be changed and that his relationship with his parents could return to being positive and supportive. I suggested that the next three years of his life could be the best three years and that when he was ready to leave for college, he might even "miss" his parents. Brad laughed and said, "I'd like that!"

I assured Brad that I would seek to help his parents understand my assessment of the situation, and I challenged him to express his love for his parents in spite of negative feelings he had toward them at the moment. I explained that his growing independence from his parents was best fostered in a climate of love rather than hostility. "Love is a choice," I said, "and I think that if you will choose to love your parents and express it in their primary love languages, you can be a part of the solution. Remember love, not hate, equals peace."

Brad nodded, smiled, and said "Yeah, man!" (It was one of those affirming moments when I realized that I was still able to communicate with a teenager.)

"In about six weeks, after I've spent some time with your parents, I want us to get together again and see how things are going," I said to Brad.

"OK," he replied, as he opened the door and left my office with his pantlegs dragging on the floor.

What I sought to communicate to Brad's parents in the three sessions we had together is what I'd like to communicate to you in the remainder of this chapter. I was deeply sympathetic with Brad's parents, as I am with thousands of parents of teenagers who face similar struggles. Brad's parents, like most of you who are reading this book, were conscientious parents. They had read books on parenting, attended parenting seminars, and shared their parenting experiences with their peers. In fact, they had been excellent parents the first twelve years of Brad's life. But they were caught off guard when the teenage years rolled around. When childhood flowed into the white waters of adolescence, their parenting canoe was dashed against the rocks and they found themselves struggling for survival.

TREATING TEENS AS TEENS

Many parents believe that when their children become teenagers, they can continue to parent in the same manner that has served them well in the child's preschool and elementary school years. But this is a serious mistake because the teenager is not a child. He/she is in transition toward adulthood. The melody playing in the mind of a teenager is independence and self-identity. This melody must be harmonized with all the physiological, emotional, intellectual, spiritual, and social changes that are taking place inside the teenager, which we discussed in chapter 1. When parents do not account for this new song that is being played in the teenager's mind, they set the stage for conflict between parent and teenager.

Parents who treat the teenager in the same manner in which they treated the child will not experience the same results they received earlier. When the teenager does not respond as the child responded, the parents are now pushed to try something different. Without proper training, parents almost always revert to efforts at coercion which lead to arguments, loss of temper, and sometimes verbal abuse. Such behavior is emotionally devastating to the teenager whose primary love language is *words of affirmation*. The parents' effort to verbally argue the teenager into submission are in reality pushing the teenager toward rebellion. Without realizing it, the parents are removing the teenager's emotional support system and replacing it with verbal warfare. Consider the change as your teen sees it: As a child, he felt the warm loving security of his parents but as a teenager, verbal grenades explode in his soul and his love tank is ruptured. As parents, our intentions still may be good, but the results are definitely bad. Unless we parents change course, we will most certainly end up with a rebellious teenager and often an estranged young adult.

But this need not happen. Thousands of parents have done what Brad's parents did—realized they needed a midcourse correction and took action. The first step for Brad's parents was to recognize what had happened. I explained to them that, in my opinion, Brad's primary love language was *words of affirmation* and that in the earlier childhood years, they had filled his love tank by giving him many affirming words. However, in the turbulence of the teenage years, they had replaced affirming words with condemning words, accepting words with words of rejection, and in so doing they had not only emptied Brad's love tank, they had filled it instead with resentment.

The lights came on, and Brad's father said, "Now I understand what has happened. It seems so clear. But how do we turn it around?" I was glad he asked because the parent who wants to learn, can!

MAKING THE CHANGE
TO AFFIRMING WORDS

I suggested that the first step was a cease fire: stop the condemning, negative bombshells. Second, they should call for a family conference and openly share with Brad their deep regret that even though they were sincere parents and had nothing but his best interest in mind, they realized they had gone about parenting him in the wrong way. They could further say that they had a lot to learn about parenting during the teenage years, that they sincerely wanted to learn and more than anything, they wanted him to know that they loved him no matter what he did, and that they would always love him.

"I encourage you to tell Brad that you care first and foremost about his well-being and that you intend to eliminate critical, condemning, demeaning, and harsh words from your vocabulary.

"Be honest with Brad. Tell him that you won't be perfect in doing this over the next few months, but when you fail, you will sincerely apologize because that is not your intention. You may want to say to him, 'We still recognize that we're your parents. and we want to help you through these teenage years to mature adulthood. We plan to be there for you when you need advice, and we intend to continue to set guidelines that we believe are for your benefit.'"

Then I told Brad's parents to be careful not to argue about these guidelines. "Let him know you want to learn to work with him in open communication and negotiation. Tell him, 'Brad, we want to treat you as the emerging young man you are; your ideas and feelings are important. We know this will take time and all of us will stumble occasionally in the process, but we're committed to being the parents you deserve.'"

His parents did just that. Later they told me that this family conference was the turning point in their relationship with Brad. They felt that Brad genuinely forgave them for their failures, although he was not overly optimistic about their abilities to change. They understood this and acknowledged that this would be difficult, but they were committed to growth in their parenting abilities.

I know that some of you are thinking, "But if we are not going to verbally condemn our teenager's wrong behavior, then how are we going to discipline them?" As one mother said to me, "Dr. Chapman, surely you are not suggesting that we simply let teenagers do whatever they want to do?" I responded "Certainly not." Teenagers need boundaries. Parents who love them will see that they live within the boundaries. But there is a better way to motivate teenagers to do so than by yelling cruel, bitter, condemning words when they misbehave. We will discuss this more thoroughly in chapter 12 when we discuss the relationship between love and responsibility. What we are talking about in this chapter is how to keep the love tank of the teenager full. Harsh, condemning, argumentative words are obviously not the way to do it. Negative, condemning words are harmful to any teenager, but they are devastating to the teenager whose primary love language is words of affirmation.

Most teenagers are struggling with self-identity. They are comparing themselves with their peers physically, intellectually, and socially. Many are concluding that they simply do not "measure up." Many feel insecure, have little self-esteem, and blame themselves. If there is a stage of life where humans need more affirming words, it would certainly be during the teenage years. Yet this is the very stage at which parents often turn to negative words in their efforts to get the teenager to do what parents believe is best. I cannot overemphasize the need for parents to give teenagers affirming words. Even if your teen's primary love language is not words of affirmation, she will appreciate your affirming statements. The ancient Hebrew proverb was right. "Death and life are in the power of the tongue."[1]

HOW TO AFFIRM YOUR TEENAGER

How then do we speak words of life to our teenagers? Let me suggest some ways to water the soul of your teenager with words that affirm.

Words of Praise

First, there are words of praise. Praise has to do with recognizing your teenager's accomplishments and commending her. All teenagers do some things right. Look for these noble actions and reward them with verbal praise. Two factors are important in giving words of praise to teenagers. *First and foremost is sincerity.* With a teenager, "flattery will get you nowhere." Contemporary teens are looking for authenticity in adults. They are sick of politicians who speak out of both sides of their mouths. They are looking for adults with integrity. You may have gotten away with flattery when she was three, but it will not work when she is thirteen. To tell a teenager, "You did a good job cleaning your room," when in fact she did not, is a slap in the face to your daughter's intelligence. She is smarter than that. Don't play games with her.

That brings me to *the second important factor in praising teenagers: Praise specifics.* Sweeping general statements of praise such as "You did a good job cleaning your room" are seldom ever true. The truth is far more often found in the specifics. "You did a good job of getting the coffee stain out of the carpet." "Thanks for putting the dirty clothes in the hamper; it was a real help when I did the laundry this morning." "Thanks for raking the leaves out of the side yard Saturday. It really looks nice." These are the kinds of specific praises that ring true with the teenager. Train yourself to look for specifics.

Bob's son Barry plays on the high school baseball team. Recently he had a particularly bad day. In batting and in fielding, it seemed like everything went wrong. But there was one play where Barry was perfect. He was at his third base position with a runner on first and one out. When the batter sent a sizzling ground ball to third base, Barry scooped it up, made a perfect throw to the second baseman, who in turn made a perfect throw to first base, and the inning was over. It was the only play in the whole game where Barry performed well, and his team lost the game. Barry rode home on the bus with the team. His dad and younger brother drove home in the car, but when Barry walked in the house several hours later, his younger brother met him at the door and said. "Dad said, 'It's the greatest play he's ever seen.'"

"What are you talking about?" Barry asked.

"Your double play," his younger brother replied.

Barry's dad heard the conversation, turned the TV off, and walked into the room. "That's right," he said. "I'll remember that play the rest of my life. I know you guys lost. I know you had a rough evening, but I'm telling you—that was the most spectacular play I've ever seen! That ball was hot, but you played it like a pro. It was exciting. I'll never forget it."

Barry walked into the kitchen for a drink of water. His dad walked back to the family room, but in the kitchen Barry was drinking more than water. His love tank was filling up as he thought about the words of his father. Barry's father had mastered the art of looking for specifics and praising teenagers.

It takes effort, especially for parents who tend to be negative themselves, but any parent can learn to locate specific actions worthy of praise and use them as occasions for words of affirmation.

However, *there is a third aspect of giving praise: When you can't praise results, praise efforts.* For instance, your thirteen-year-old has mowed the grass. It's not as perfect as if you had mowed it. You have a little more experience than he. But most of the grass is cut, and your teenager invested two hours of life laying the grass low. Get hold of yourself, don't point out the grass that was missed. You can do that next week before he starts mowing again. Now is the time to say, "Nathan, you're really coming along in your grass mowing skills. I really appreciate your hard effort. I want you to know it is a real help to me and I appreciate it." Nathan walks away and somehow mowing the grass seems worthwhile. His love tank is filling up as he senses he is important to his father and his work was noticed.

Someone asks, "But won't he always be a mediocre grass mower if I don't point out the grass he missed?" My response is, "It is a matter of timing." After two hours of lawn mowing, no one is encouraged to hear that his job was not done perfectly. To do so is almost surely to make the teenager hate mowing grass. When his efforts are rewarded with praise, he feels appreciated and motivated to mow the grass again. He is even open to instruction as he begins next week on how he can do an even better job.

(To the parents who are reading this, I would like to suggest that the same principle is true in your marriage relationship. Reward each other for effort rendered rather than pointing out the imperfections of the completed task. Try it. It works. I promise. For example, the husband spends three hours washing the car. His wife comes outside, points out a spot he missed. Prediction: that's the cleanest car she'll see for awhile. Or, the wife fixes a meal for her husband. He sits down at the table and says "Did you forget the slaw?" Prediction: I hope he likes fast food restaurants. He's going to spend a lot of time there the next three months. Case closed. Reward for effort, not perfection.)

Teenagers need to hear words of praise from parents. There are always teenage actions worthy of praise. Some parents are so focused on the teenager's failure to reach their expectations that they cannot see the teenager's positive actions. That's narrow, negative tunnel vision. Focusing on the negative has been the downfall of many parents and has resulted in an empty love tank for many teenagers. No matter what is going on in the life of your teenager that brings you pain, disappointment, or anger, continue to look for those actions worthy of praise, and give your teenager affirming words.

Words of Affection

Another important way to express words of affirmation to a teenager is to express verbal affection. Whereas praise focuses on the positive behavior of a teenager, affection focuses on the teenager himself/herself. It is verbally expressing positive regard for the teenager as a person. The most common statement of verbal affection is the simple words, "I love you." These three words are always appropriate, though there may be a brief stage in which the teenager does not wish to hear you say these words in the presence of his peers. If your teenager makes this request, by all means honor it. When spoken in private, however, these three words are always appropriate at every stage of teenage development.

In fact, teenagers who do not hear the words "I love you" from parents will often experience deep emotional pain in adulthood. During the past few years I've been privileged to speak at a number of marriage enrichment conferences for professional athletes. One of my saddest experiences has been to look into the eyes of a pro athlete—I'm talking about macho of the macho—and to see the tears form in his eyes as he said to me, "Dr. Chapman, I've never heard my father say the words 'I love you.'" I wanted to take him in my arms and say, "Here, let me be your father. I love you." I can say the words and I can hug him (though with the football players, I cannot get my arms around them), but my hug and my verbal affirmation can never take the place of the words of a father. There is a void in the soul of the man or woman who has never heard the words "I love you" from a father and mother.

Usually mothers speak these words freely to their teenage sons and daughters. Fathers are often reluctant to do so. Sometimes fathers have never heard the words themselves and thus they have difficulty speaking what they have never heard. It doesn't come naturally for them. If you happen to be one of these fathers, I want to encourage you to break the chains of tradition, look your teenage son or daughter in the eye, place your hands on their shoulders and say, "What I am about to say to you is extremely important to me. I want you to hear me carefully." Then with your eyes looking into their eyes say the words, "I love you very much" and then embrace them. Whatever the experience means to you, I can assure you that your words will ring in the heart of your teenager forever. Now that the dam is broken, the waters of love are flowing. Say the words again and again and again. Your teenager will never tire of hearing them and your own love tank will be replenished when you hear your teenager say the same words to you.

Of course, there are other ways to verbally express affection. Vicki Lansky, author of *101 Ways To Tell Your Child I Love You,* told about the time her thirteen-year-old daughter Dana was feeling blue and she wanted to cheer her up. Mrs. Lansky said, "I really enjoyed you today." Why did she say "enjoy" rather than "love"? Lansky explained, "Using the word *enjoy* rather than the word *love* really made the difference." Several times after that her daughter would ask, "Did you enjoy me today, too, Mommy?"[2] Make up your own synonym and try it on your teenager. Here are some examples to get you started.

"I relish being with you."

"I adore you."

"I feel proud when I think about you."

"You are my sunshine."

"If I could choose any teenager in the world, I would choose you."

"You are so wonderful."

"I wake every morning and think 'What a privilege to be your father/mother.'"

"Yesterday I was sitting at my desk thinking 'I really miss my daughter.'"

"I love it when you are around."

If you are poetic, you may even say, in all sincerity, "You are like a river of joy in my life" and know that your daughter will bask in that sentiment.

Now, think up a few of your own and write them in a notebook and periodically sprinkle them in along with your "I love you's." If your teenager is accustomed to hearing "I love you," then one of these optional statements of affection may fill your teenager's love tank more effectively.

Verbal affection can also focus on various attributes of the teen's body or personality. "Your hair looks like sunshine today" may be especially affirming to a sixteen-year-old who is wondering if she "looks OK." "Your eyes are beautiful" may be the words that return to the heart of the seventeen-year-old who has just been dumped by her boyfriend. "You are so strong" may be the words that change the mood of a fifteen-year-old son who is overly concerned about facial blemishes. Look for physical characteristics of your teenager that you can verbally affirm. It is an effective way of expressing verbal affection.

These words of affection may also focus on the teenager's personality. "I am so happy that you have such an outgoing personality. I know that you think of yourself as being shy, but I've observed that once you start talking to someone, you open up. It's just like the floodgate's open and you start talking freely."

Here are other expressions that show love for who your teenager is.

"You are so steady. I like the way you think before you speak."

"Your bubbly personality makes so many people happy."

"You may be quiet, but when you speak, you say something."

"One of the things I really admire about you is that you are dependable. When you give your word, I can count on it."

"I am so happy that I can trust you. Other mothers tell me that they cannot trust their daughters, but I trust you explicitly."

"I love the way you encourage people. I observed you last night talking with Tim after the game was over. You have a real gift of encouragement."

Such statements of affection speak deeply to the inner spirit of teenagers. They give your son and daughter a sense of being valued, admired, loved.

For some parents, such verbal expressions of affection will not come easily. I challenge you to keep a notebook. Write down the examples I have given above, read them aloud several times in private. Make up your own statements of affection and periodically share one with your teenager.

Speaking Affirming Words in Front of the Family

Try affirming your teenager in the presence of the entire family. Give words of praise and appreciation in the presence of younger or older siblings. (I don't suggest you do it in the presence of the teen's peers.) Words of affirmation often speak louder when given in the presence of others. For example, the family is having dinner when Jeremy's father says, "I said this to Jeremy earlier in private but I want to say it in front of the whole family. I was proud of him last night. He had reason to be angry with the official's call but he showed tremendous sportsmanship in the way he responded and I'm proud of him." Little Ellie says, "Yeah. Let's hear it for Jeremy." Everybody claps. Jeremy has been emotionally affirmed and the rest of the family has been reminded of the importance of character.

Or, Dad says about his daughter, "Did everyone see my Meredith tonight? She stepped up to the foul line, made both shots and won the game. Yeah!!" Meredith not only had the satisfaction at the game; she relives the satisfaction and feels emotionally affirmed by the family. This may speak even more deeply to Meredith's emotional need for love than if her father had limited his comments to a private encounter between the two of them.

Words of affirmation is one of the five primary love languages. All teenagers need words of affirmation. In the midst of the insecurity of the teenage transition, affirming words are often like rain on the desert soul of a teenager. For those teenagers for whom words of affirmation is their primary love language, nothing is more important emotionally than the affirming words heard from parents.

What Teens Say

Listen to the following statements by teens who feel loved when they hear their parents speaking words of affirmation.

Matt, a seventeen-year-old senior and member of the wrestling team: "When I win, nothing is more important than hearing my father say, 'Great job, Son.' And when I lose, nothing is more helpful than hearing him say, 'You gave him the best wrestle he's had in a long time. Wait till next time.'"

Bethany, age thirteen: "I know my mother loves me. She tells me all the time. I think my dad does, too, but he doesn't say it."

Ryan, age fifteen, who lives in Chicago's inner city: "I don't have a dad except these guys at the center. But I know my mom loves me. She tells me how proud she is of me and encourages me to make something of myself."

Yolanda, age eighteen: "I'm going off to college in a few months. I think I am the luckiest girl alive. My parents both love me. Even through the difficult teenage years, they have always encouraged me. My dad says, 'You're the greatest,' and my mom says, 'You can be whatever you want to be.' I just hope I can help some other people the way they have helped me."

Judith, age fourteen and an eighth grader: "My mom left when I was four years old, so I don't remember her, but later my dad married my stepmother. I consider her my mother. Sometimes when I get down on myself she tells me how much she loves me and she tells me good things about myself that I sometimes forget. I couldn't make it without her."

For these and thousands of other teenagers, the love language of *words of affirmation* speaks deeply. When parents speak such words regularly, the teen's emotional tank will remain full.

NOTES

1. Proverbs 18:21, NKJV.
2. Anne Cassidy, "Fifteen Ways to Say 'I Love You,'" *Women's Day,* 18 February 1997, 24.

chapter four

LOVE LANGUAGE #2: PHYSICAL TOUCH

There's undeniable emotional power in touching those we love. That's why parents are encouraged to hold and cuddle infants, kissing them on the face and stroking their skin. Hugging three-year-olds or letting them sit on your lap while you read a story is a powerful way of filling a child's love tank. On the other end of life, physical touch is also an emotional communicator. Who has not walked the hallways of "homes for the elderly" and seen senior adults sitting in wheelchairs, extending a hand which desires to be touched? And, of course, in marriage lovers embrace and kiss.

But what about teenagers? Are they different? Does physical touch communicate emotionally to the teenager? The answer is yes and no. It all depends on when, where, and how you touch the teenager.

For instance, a hug in the presence of the teenager's peers may stimulate embarrassment rather than love and may well motivate the teenager to push the parent away or say, "Stop it." However, massaging the teenager's shoulder muscles after he/she comes home from a game may deeply communicate emotional love. Trying to touch a teenager when the teen is in an "anti-social mood" will almost always annoy the teenager. But touching after a disappointing day at school will be welcomed as true parental love.

Teenagers are different. You cannot continue to give the same kind of touches in the same places and in the same manner that you gave when they were children. Again, parents must remember the teenager's theme is independence and self-identity. Thus, parents must ask, "Does my proposed touch threaten my teen's sense of independence? Does it enhance positive self-identity?"

Remember, the teen desperately needs to feel your love. *Physical touch* is one of the five basic languages of love, but you must speak the language of physical touch at the appropriate time, in the appropriate place, and in an appropriate manner. If your teenager's primary love language in childhood was *physical touch,* the love language will not change during the adolescent years. However, the dialect in which you speak that language must change if you want the teenager to feel loved. Let's examine each of these.

THE APPROPRIATE TIME FOR TOUCHING

The ancient Hebrew book of wisdom says, "There is a time for everything . . . a time to embrace and a time to refrain [from embracing]."[1] Coaches often remind their athletes, "Timing is everything." Similarly, parents of teenagers must learn the art of appropriate timing. Good actions taken at the wrong time often backfire. This is a difficult task for two reasons. First, timing is largely determined by the teenager's mood. And second, the teen's mood is not always apparent. Sometimes it is after parents "make their move" and lovingly touch a teenager that they discover the teenager is in an "anti-touch mood." But "difficult" does not mean impossible.

Wise parents will study their teenager. They will learn to pick up on the teenager's mood by his behavior. One mother said, "I can tell whether my son wants to be touched by the way he closes the door when he enters the house. If he slams the door, it's a 'Don't touch me' mood. If he takes time to quietly close the door, he is saying 'I'm open to a touch, Mom.'" Another mother said, "I can tell when my daughter doesn't want to be touched by the distance she stands from me when she talks. If she stands on the other side of the room while talking, I know she doesn't want to be touched. But if she comes up and stands close to me, I know she's open to a loving touch."

Teenagers communicate mood by their body language—how close they are to you, or whether their arms are folded, for example. The astute parent will observe this body language and learn the appropriate times for touching a teenager. It is not necessary to understand why the teenager is in the "Don't touch me now" mood. What is important is to recognize it and respect it.

It is almost always inappropriate to seek to touch a teenager when he or she is angry. When your teen daughter, for instance, is angry with you or someone else, she won't want to be touched. She is angry because in her mind someone "did me wrong." Anger is the emotion that pushes people away from each other. If you attempt to touch a teenager when she is angry, you will almost always be rebuffed. To an angry teenager, physical touch comes across as an effort to control. It strikes at the teenager's need for independence. Thus, the teenager pulls away from your touch. We will discuss how to process teen anger in a later chapter. What we are saying here is that it is usually inappropriate to use the love language of physical touch when a teenager is angry.

On the other hand, there are many appropriate times for touching teenagers. One such occasion is when your teenager has succeeded in a major accomplishment. It may be a victory on the athletic field, a successful piano recital, an exceptionally well-executed dance performance, the completion of a major paper for school, the passing of an algebra exam, the securing of a driver's license, etc. These are the times when teenagers are usually open to loving physical touch from parents. The thrill of accomplishment has thrust them down the road of independence and self-identity. Your celebration of their successes by verbal affirmation and physical touch will be received as further evidence of your recognition of their emerging maturity.

Conversely, times of failure in the teenager's life are also times for expressing the love language of physical touch. The teenager is down on himself because he flunked the calculus exam, his girlfriend just ditched him, or he just had a fender bender. Your teenage daughter is feeling in the pits because her best friend has a date for Friday night and she does not, or worse yet her boyfriend has just broken up with her and started dating her best girlfriend. These are occasions when teenagers are open to the love language of physical touch.

In the normal flow of daily life, if the teenager is in a good mood, he/she is typically open to some form of physical touch as an expression of love. If the teen is in a bad mood, he will be annoyed by physical touch. Thoughtful parents will respect the mood of their teenager and will seek to give physical touch only at appropriate times. Sometimes we learn by trial and error but if we think, we can learn even from our mistakes.

Here is the experience of one mother. "When Julie turned thirteen, I thought she was on drugs. Her behavior changed radically. In all of her childhood years, she was a "touchy-feely child." I hugged and kissed her all the time and often gave her back rubs. But when she turned thirteen, I found her pulling away from me, not wanting me to touch her. I thought something terrible had happened to our relationship. I later realized that she was a normal teenager. I have now learned when Julie is in the mood for touching and when she is not.

"Once in awhile, I misread her and she jerks back from my hugs. But most of the time, I connect because I've chosen the right time. Julie is fifteen and one-half now, and I feel good about our relationship. I think her primary love language is physical touch. I know she needs it. I just want to continue to be sensitive to do it at the right time."

THE APPROPRIATE PLACE FOR TOUCHING

As there is a time for touch and a time not to touch, there is also a place to touch and a place not to touch. I'm talking here about geography, not sexuality. We will deal with that later. The ten-year-old welcomed his mother's embrace after the little league football game was over. He rushed to wherever his mother was standing and waited for her positive words and affirming touch. But at sixteen when the varsity game is over, he will not be looking for Mom and he hopes that she will not be looking for him. He will be celebrating his independence and self-identity with his teammates and friends. They can slap him on the back, beat him on the head, give him "high fives," but when his mother approaches, his thought is, *Please,*

Mom, don't even think about it. In most public settings, teenagers do not want to be hugged or touched affectionately by their parents.

This is especially true in the presence of their peers. The teen's self-identity is tied up with that of his friends. When Mom or Dad enters that world and expresses physical affection, it threatens the teenager's self-identity and strikes at his desire for independence. As one teenager said, "It makes me feel like they think I'm still a kid." A good rule of thumb is never to touch a teenager in the presence of his/her friends unless the teenager initiates it by touching you.

Sometimes teenagers are open to physical touch in the presence of extended family members such as grandparents. If you are bragging to the grandparents about the teenager's accomplishments, then a pat on the back at the end of your speech may be accepted by the teenager. Don't assume this to be true, however. Watch your teenager's response and don't pursue touching if they give you the clue to "back off."

Then where is the appropriate place to speak the love language of physical touch to teenagers? Typically in the privacy of your own home or when you are with the teenager alone. When given in private or in the presence of immediate family members, physical touch can be an effective communicator of emotional love. Remember, for some teenagers, physical touch is their primary love language. For these teens it's extremely important that parents learn the appropriate time and place to express love.

Fourteen-year-old Jacob said, "I love going on camping trips with my dad. That's when I feel closest to him." When I asked, "What do you like most about camping with your dad?" Jacob replied, "When we arm wrestle at night by the fire. I especially like it when I beat him." Emotional love is coming through to Jacob by the language of physical touch. Independence and self-identity are being encouraged, especially when he wins.

Fifteen-year-old Jessica said, "Mom and I are really close. I don't think I'd make it without her hugs. School has been hard this year but I always know that when I get home, I'll get a hug from Mom." Jessica's mom has discovered her primary love language and is speaking it in the privacy of their home. Remember, though, when speaking this love language, always do so at the appropriate time and in the appropriate place. Otherwise, it will not be interpreted as love.

THE APPROPRIATE MANNER FOR PHYSICAL TOUCH

Be Flexible

Here we are talking about not only the kinds of touches we give but the manner in which we give them. There are numerous ways in which to express affection by physical touch. Hugs, kisses, back rubs, pats, tender touches, massages, and arm wrestlings are all appropriate ways to speak the language of physical touch to a teenager. However, the process is not as simple as it sounds. Teenagers are individuals. They don't all like the same kinds of touches. Some teens like back rubs and others don't. Some like for you to play with their hair and others don't. Your teen is unique, and you will have to learn not only the love language but the dialects in which he or she best receives love.

If your teen doesn't enjoy shoulder rubs, it would be a mistake to force such touch upon her simply because you like shoulder rubs. We must not force our own love language on the teenager; rather, we must learn the teen's language. What makes it even more complicated is that the kinds of touch you gave when your teenager was a child may not be the kinds of touch your teenager appreciates as a teen. Parents are often frustrated by this. They think they have discovered the child's primary love language and they have learned how to speak it. Now the teenager is drawing back from the same kinds of touch that earlier she enjoyed. A major reason is the teen's quest for independence and self-identity. When you touch your teenager in the same manner that you touched him when he was a child, these touches may stimulate feelings of dependence and insecurity—the exact opposite of what the teenager wants to feel. Thus, the teenager draws back from these "childish" expressions of love.

Sometime ago I shared this insight at a parenting workshop. I could see the lights come on in Brad's mind. At the break time he came up to me and said, "Now I understand it. My son Matt is now fifteen. When he was young, I used to give him back rubs all the time. He loved it. For the past two or three years, he has not let me give him a back rub. I've felt like he was pulling away from me. I couldn't understand why he had changed so much. Now I see that the back rubs remind him of childhood. He is on a course toward independence and doesn't wish to return to childhood. It all makes sense now."

I suggested to Brad that he find new ways of expressing the love language of physical touch to Matt. "Slap him on the back, tap him on the shoulder, trip him when he walks by your chair. If he falls, wrestle him on the floor. You will see his love tank start filling up because you are treating him like the emerging man he is, rather than like the child he used to be. You are fostering his sense of independence rather than sabotaging it." Brad has learned an important lesson about loving teenagers.

If your teenager says, "I don't like that" in response to your efforts to physically touch her, then back off and find another method of physical touch. Don't force a particular kind of physical touch upon your teenager because you think "she should like it." The whole concept of the five love languages is learning to speak the other person's language, not your own. What makes your teen feel loved is the key question. If physical touch is her primary love language, then you must find the particular kinds of touch that communicate love to her. The process of loving a teenager is complicated by the parents' own preferences. Some parents have never "tripped" their teenager and cannot imagine doing so as an expression of love. Others have never "elbowed" their teen. I'm not suggesting that all teenagers like these dialects of physical touch. What I am suggesting is that you discover the kinds of physical touch that your teenager appreciates and speak that dialect regularly.

Obviously, the emotional climate in which you give physical touch is extremely important. If you trip your teen when you are angry, it is not an expression of love. If you slap him on the shoulder because you are frustrated with his behavior, he will not feel loved. The mother who withholds hugs from her daughter because she doesn't like her choice of friends runs the risk of losing her daughter. As parents we are responsible for our own attitudes. If we express love to our teenagers only when they are doing things which please us, we have left the high road of unconditional love and have entered the treacherous world of manipulation.

Use Physical Touch Gently to Correct

The good news about the love language of physical touch is that it can be easily spoken even when your teen's behavior is not pleasing. You can even express your displeasure with the teen's behavior at the same time you are expressing love by physical touch. Marcia is touching her teenage daughter's arm and saying, "I am very upset with the fact that you came home an hour late last night. I understand that you were having a good time with your friends and didn't notice what time it was. But do you understand how troublesome that is to me? We've always agreed that if you are going to be late, you will call me so I won't be worried about you."

Now she turns and faces her daughter. Placing both hands on her daughter's shoulders she says, "Darling, I love you so much. I don't want to make your life miserable. I just want to know that you are all right." Marcia is loving her daughter in an extremely effective manner while at the same time addressing her concerns.

The language of physical touch spoken at the right time in the right place and in the right manner speaks deeply to the teenage soul. Physical touch says "I recognize you as a person of importance. I'm with you. I care about you. I love you." Every teenager needs to hear the language of physical touch. If they don't hear it from parents, they will seek it elsewhere.

A Word to Fathers

There is a tendency on the part of the fathers of this generation to withdraw physical touch from their emerging teenage daughters, particularly when the daughter approaches puberty. Some don't know how to respond to their daughters' ongoing physical change; others think their daughters don't want touch since they are no longer girls. Still other fathers fear someone may accuse them of sexual touches or even abuse. Whatever the reason, withholding physical touch is a serious mistake. The teenage daughter needs to feel good about herself as a female. She needs to sense that she is attractive to the male gender. The father's role is to give her this sense of well-being about herself. Appropriate physical touch is a vehicle for doing this. If the father withdraws physical affection from the daughter, she is far more likely to become sexually active at a younger age.

Fathers, I strongly encourage you to continue to speak the love language of physical touch as your daughter enters her teenage years. She needs those appropriate touches as she develops her independence and self-identity as a woman.

INAPPROPRIATE PHYSICAL TOUCH

I wish I did not have to write the next few paragraphs. I wish that the terms *physical abuse* and *sexual abuse* were not so commonplace in our society. The reality is that a significant minority of teenagers do experience abuse from their parents. The more dramatic cases, we see on the evening news. But most teenagers suffer silently and sometimes those closest to them are not aware of the abuse.

Physical Abuse and Anger

Physical abuse is causing physical harm by beating, hitting, kicking, etc., out of anger rather than play. The key word is anger. Some parents of teens have never learned to handle anger in a constructive manner. When they are angered by the teen's behavior, the flow of vicious words are followed by physical violence. Slaps, pushes, shoves, choking, holding, shaking, and hitting are all abusive behaviors to teenagers. Where this occurs, we can be certain that the teenager's love tank is not only empty, it is riddled with holes. Positive words and expressions of physical affection which follow such angry outbursts will always appear hollow to the teenager. The teenage heart does not easily recover from such physical abuse.

The parent who wishes his teenager to feel loved after such angry episodes must not only render a sincere and honest apology to the teenager, but he/she must seek help in breaking these destructive patterns and learning positive anger management skills. This is best done through reading books,[2] attending support groups, and/or professional counseling.

Explosive anger will not simply go away with the passing of time. The parent must take initiative to change these destructive outbursts. Nor will the teen's emotional pain subside merely with the passing of time. If the parent does not render a genuine apology and change patterns, the teen will most assuredly continue to feel unloved by the parent who abuses her. Ironically, the teenager often feels unloved by the other parent as well. The teen reasons "If they loved me, they would not allow this abusive behavior to continue. They would protect me." If you are married to a persistently abusive spouse, I would encourage you to go for personal counseling and gain the emotional strength and knowledge as to how you can take constructive steps to protect yourself and your teenager. You are not serving the cause of love when you continue to allow such abusive behavior to continue. You need the help of a trained counselor or pastor to help you become a positive change agent in your family.

Sexual Abuse

Sexual abuse is taking advantage of your parental role to obtain sexual favors from your teenager to satisfy your own sexual desires. Sexual abuse is most often perpetrated by fathers, stepfathers, or a mother's boyfriend. Such abuse is normally focused on teenage girls. Although homosexual abuse does sometimes occur in the nuclear family, it is not nearly as common as heterosexual abuse. Often the parental sexual abuser will seek to convince the teenager that his sexual overtures are expressions of love for the teenager. This message will not "ring true" with the teenager. Something deep within the teenager says, "This is not right."

However, the teenager is often reluctant to discuss the sexual experience with the other parent or another adult. Sometimes, teenagers are kept silent by shame, but the most common constraint is the emotion of fear. Often they have been threatened by the parental abuser. One fifteen-year-old daughter said, "My father told me that if I told my mother or anyone else about what was going on between us, he would deny it and my mother would believe him and not me. He would see to it that I was punished for lying." A seventeen-year-old girl when asked why she did not tell her mother that her stepfather had been sexually abusing her since she was thirteen responded, "If I told my mother, I knew my stepdad would kill me. He told me often it would be easy to get rid of me. I knew he was serious and I didn't want to die." It was not until her stepfather was in prison for another criminal offense that she finally shared with a counselor what had been going on between her and her stepfather.

It should be obvious to all that sexual intimacy with a teenager on the part of a parent figure is not an expression of love to a teenager. It is in fact self-gratification—the opposite of love. The teenager will feel used and abused. Such abuse over a period of time breeds bitterness, hatred, and often depression in the teenager. Sometimes these emotions erupt in violent behavior. We see it on the evening news. The girl down the street murders her stepfather and everyone wonders what happened to such a nice girl. Sexual abuse breeds hurt and anger and drastically affects the teenager's emotional, social, and sexual development.

Dealing with Sexual Abuse

If you are involved in gaining sexual gratification from a teenager who lives in your house, the first step is to acknowledge the wrongness of such behavior. The second step is to make an appointment with a professional counselor, share the problem, and begin the process of trying to heal the relationship with your teenager. Yes, such a bold step will be costly, may bring embarrassment, may disrupt your marital relationship, and may create emotional stress for you. But failure to do so will be more costly in the long run.

I'm fully aware that most sexual abusers will not take the advice I have just given. Therefore, the other parent must press the issue. Of course, often the other parent is not aware of what is going on. Sometimes they have closed their eyes to revealing clues and have plugged their ears to the teenager's efforts to tell them. Such insensitivity for whatever reason is treason to your teenager. I urge you to listen and probe any statement from your teenager which even faintly resembles a plea for help. And I urge you to keep your eyes open to any evidence that inappropriate behavior is taking place between your spouse and your teenager.

Please be aware that sometimes your teenager will deny it when you ask a straightforward question. Again, that denial is often based on shame and fear. Don't take your teen's immediate response as the final word on the situation. If you have reason to believe that there is inappropriate sexual behavior between your spouse and your teenager, I urge you to contact a professional counselor, share the evidence you have, and let the counselor help you take appropriate steps. Sexual abuse is devastating to your teenager's well-being. If you know of such abuse and do not deal with it, your teenager will not only feel abused by the perpetrator but abandoned by you. Yes, dealing with the abuse will be costly, perhaps embarrassing, and may even destroy your marriage or relationship with the abuser but it is the only alternative if you love your teenager.

With proper counseling and spiritual help, there can be healing even after such devastating abuse. But without such emotional and spiritual guidance, your teenager may never experience a healthy adulthood. Many of the troubled young adults in our society can trace the roots of their trouble to sexual abuse when they were teenagers. Not all this abuse was perpetrated by parents or parental figures. Often it was perpetrated by extended family members: aunts, uncles, cousins, or adults the teenager met at school, church, or in other community settings. Most homosexual abuse of teenagers takes place outside the nuclear family. If parents become aware of such abuse, it should immediately be reported to the local mental health/social work authorities. Teenagers should not be left to fend for themselves in the shark-infested waters of Western society's sexual confusion. Parental love impels us to do all that we can to help our teens develop a positive sexual identity and to keep them shielded from adults who would seek to abuse them for their own personal sexual gratification.

The encouraging news is that most parents are not physically or sexually abusing their teenagers. Most parents are loving their teenagers by speaking the love language of physical touch. A recent survey of American teenagers ages thirteen through seventeen found that 75 percent believed that fathers should hug their teenagers at least once a week. And 55 percent of the same teens said that their own fathers did so.[3]

What the Teens Say

Physical touch is one of the primary emotional love languages. Teenagers need to be touched by parents if they are to feel loved. For some teenagers, physical touch is their primary love language. It speaks more deeply and quickly than the other four. Listen to the following teenagers for whom physical touch is their primary love language.

Victoria, sixteen, who lives with her single-parent mother: "I love it when Mom gives me back rubs. All my problems seem to go away when Mom rubs my back."

Joel, age seventeen: "I know my dad loves me. He is always picking on me. He elbows me when we are watching a game together. He hits me on the shoulder and trips me when I walk by. Sometimes I'm not in the mood to be touched and Dad respects that. But the next day he bumps me when I walk by. I love it!"

Meredith, who's fifteen: "My dad doesn't hug me as much as he used to. I don't know if he thinks that I'm an adult now and don't need it. But I miss his hugs. They always make me feel special."

Barrett, who has had a rough year with algebra: "The best part of homework is when Mom comes by and rubs my shoulders. I forget all about algebra. It relaxes me. When she walks away, I feel better."

Jessica, age seventeen: "I know that sometimes I'm hard to live with. My parents have put up with a lot of my moods. I guess it's just being a teenager, but when they hug me or even touch my arm, I feel like everything is going to be OK. It's like a calming thing. I know that they really love me."

NOTES

1. Ecclesiastes 3:1, 5.

2. For practical help on anger management, see Gary Chapman, *The Other Side of Love: Handling Anger in a Godly Way* (Chicago: Moody Press, 1999).

3. *YOUTHviews,* 6, no. 8 (April, 1999): 1.; published by The George H. Gallup International Institute, Princeton, N.J.

chapter five

LOVE LANGUAGE #3:
QUALITY TIME

At 11:45 P.M. I stepped into the room of my teenage son. I had spent the day counseling and felt physically and emotionally spent. I anticipated a brief "goodnight, I love you" experience. Instead, my son said, "Dad, I don't understand girls." I sat on the floor, leaned against the side of his bed and asked, "What brings you to that conclusion?"

That was the beginning of a two-hour conversation. Derek was seventeen years old at the time. He is now thirty-one. He still doesn't understand girls. Neither do I. But we've always been close enough to talk, and I think that is what's important.

To give your teenager *quality time* is to give your teenager a portion of your life. *Quality time* means giving the teenager your undivided attention. At the moment, nothing else matters. Quality time is a powerful communicator of emotional love.

Unfortunately the love language of quality time is much more difficult to speak than the love language of words of affirmation or physical touch for one simple reason. It takes more time. A meaningful touch can be given in a second; words of affirmation can be spoken in less than a minute. But quality time may require hours. In today's hurried world, many parents of teenagers find it difficult to speak the language of quality time. Consequently, many teenagers live in houses filled with gadgets but have love tanks that are empty. They often feel like they too are simply a part of their parent's collection of things.

Busy parents who want their teenagers to feel loved must *make* time to give their teenagers focused attention. Psychiatrist Ross Campbell wrote, "Without focused attention, a teenager experiences increased anxiety, because he feels everything else is more important than he is. He is consequently less secure and becomes impaired in his emotional and psychological growth."[1]

TOGETHERNESS

The central aspect of *quality time* is togetherness. I do not mean proximity. Being in the same house with your teenager is not *quality time*. When you are in the same room with your teenager, you are in close proximity, but you are not necessarily together. Togetherness has to do with being in touch with each other. Father and son watching a sports event on television or in the stadium may or may not experience togetherness. If the teen walks away from the experience feeling lonely and thinking *Sports are more important to my father than I am,* then togetherness did not occur. But if the teen gets the message, "The most important thing about this game is being with you. I love it when we do things together," the father and the son have connected. And the son will walk away feeling loved. The focus of this chapter is to help you experience togetherness when the two of you are together.

What does it mean to be "in touch" with your teenager? Essentially it means that the teenager is feeling that he is the focus of your attention. This does not mean that every time you are together you must have long in-depth conversations. However, it does mean that the parent must intentionally seek to communicate by eye contact, words, touch, and body language that the teen is more important than the event.

Fifteen-year-old Clint illustrated this when he said, "My father thinks he is doing me a favor when he takes me fishing. He calls it "our buddy time" but we don't ever talk about us. Our conversations are about fishing and nature, but I don't care about fishing or nature. I wish I could talk to my father about my problems, but he doesn't seem interested in me." I knew Clint's father and I can tell you assuredly that he thought he was doing a wonderful thing by taking Clint fishing. He had no idea that they were not "in touch."

The problem was his focus was on the activity rather than his son. He was shocked to learn later in our counseling session that his son actually walked away from the fishing experience feeling empty and rejected. Clint's father had a lot to learn about speaking the love language of *quality time.*

QUALITY CONVERSATION

Like words of affirmation and physical touch, the love language of quality time also has many dialects. One of the most common dialects is that of quality conversation. By quality conversation, I mean dialogue between parent and teen where each is free to share their experiences, thoughts, feelings, and desires in a friendly, accepting atmosphere. It requires that parents learn to speak "with" their teens rather than "at" their teens.

A CHANGE IN OUR COMMUNICATION STYLE

Quality conversation is quite different from the first love language. Words of affirmation focus on what we are *saying,* whereas quality conversation focuses on what we are *hearing.* If the parent is going to express love by means of quality time and is going to spend that time in conversation, it means the parent will focus on drawing out and listening sympathetically to what the teenager says. The parent will ask questions—not in a badgering manner but with a genuine desire to understand the teen's thoughts, feelings, and desires. Most parents will have to work at this because it is a change in communication style.

When our children were little, we issued instructions and commands, but if we continue this pattern of communication during the teenage years, the teenager will say, "You are treating me like a child." And he will be correct. We must now learn to treat our child as a teenager, remembering his emerging independence and encouraging his developing self-identity.

This means that we must allow our teenager to think her own thoughts, experience her own emotions, have her own dreams, and be able to share these with us without receiving our unsolicited assessment. We must learn to help her evaluate her ideas, understand her emotions, and take realistic steps toward accomplishing her dreams. And we must learn to do this in a friendly, encouraging atmosphere of dialogue rather than the dogmatic statements of monologue. For most parents, this is one of the greatest challenges of parenting teenagers. Many parents have become exasperated in the process of learning.

"I don't know how to parent a teenager," Marlene told me. "I thought I was doing fairly well until Katie turned sixteen. Now I wake up to discover that I am 'stupid, not in touch with the real world,' and trying to control her life. I feel totally frustrated and unappreciated by my daughter. Everything I say is wrong. I don't know how to talk to her anymore."

I had known Marlene for a number of years and knew that her communication style was what I called "the babbling brook" (whatever comes in the eye gate and the ear gate comes out the mouth gate, and normally there is not sixty seconds between the two). Whatever Marlene saw, heard, or felt she expressed freely and without reflection as to whether others were interested in hearing her thoughts, feelings, and impressions. Katie, who had accepted this as normal in her childhood years, was now trying to discover her own identity and establish a measure of independence from her mother. She no longer accepted her mother's word as "the gospel." She now had a few thoughts of her own and she expressed them as freely as her mother.

I knew that for Marlene, the learning curve was going to be steep. But I also knew that if she didn't learn a new pattern of communicating with Katie, she was going to lose the warm relationship she had in earlier years. Marlene had to learn to "slow the flow" of her own words, and she had to learn the new art of active listening and sympathetic dialogue.

GUIDELINES FOR QUALITY CONVERSATIONS

Here are eight guidelines for better listening and true dialogue. The first five have to do with learning to actively listen to your teenager. Good listening must precede steps 6 through 8. These guidelines helped Marlene learn about quality conversation. Practice them and your conversations with your teen will improve.

1. *Maintain eye contact when your teenager is talking.* This keeps your mind from wandering and communicates that the teen has your full attention. Refrain from rolling your eyes in disgust, closing your eyes when they give you a low blow, looking over their head, or staring at your shoes while they are talking.

2. *Don't listen to your teenager and do something else at the same time.* Remember *quality time* is giving someone your undivided attention. If you are watching, reading, or doing something else in which you are keenly interested and cannot turn from immediately, tell your teenager the truth. A positive approach might be "I know you are trying to talk to me and I'm interested. But I want to give you my full attention. I can't do that right now but if you will give me ten minutes to finish this, I'll sit down and listen to you." Most teenagers will respect such a request.

3. *Listen for feelings.* Ask yourself, "What emotions are my teenager experiencing?" When you think you have the answer, confirm it. For example, "It sounds like you are feeling disappointed because I forgot . . ." That gives the teen a chance to clarify his feelings. It also communicates that you are listening intently to what he is saying.

4. *Observe body language.* Clenched fists, trembling hands, tears, furrowed brows, and eye movement may give you clues as to what the teen is feeling. Sometimes body language speaks one message while words speak another. Ask for clarification to make sure you know what she is really thinking and feeling.

5. *Refuse to interrupt.* Research has indicated that the average individual listens for only seventeen seconds before interrupting and interjecting his own ideas. Such interruptions often stop the conversation before it gets started. At this point in the conversation, your objective is not to defend yourself or to set the teen straight; it is to understand the teenager's thoughts, feelings, and desires.

6. *Ask reflective questions.* When you think you understand what your teenager is saying, check it out by reflecting back the statement (as you understand it) in a question: "What I hear you saying is. . . . Is that correct?" Or, "Are you saying . . . ?" Reflective listening clears up misunderstandings and your perception of what the teen is saying. Remember, you are trying to answer the questions "What is my teen thinking? What is my teen feeling? What does my teen desire of me?" Until you have clearly answered those questions, you are not ready to share your ideas.

7. *Express understanding.* The teen needs to know that she has been heard and understood. Suppose as a parent you ask the reflective question, "What I hear you saying is that you want to go to the beach with three of your friends, that you want to drive your car because they do not have drivers licenses, and that you would like for me to pay for gas and lodging because none of you have enough money. Is that what you are asking?" If the teenager responds "Yes," then you can express understanding of their request: "I can see how you would find that very desirable. I'm sure you would have a good time at the beach." In expressing understanding, you are affirming the teen's sense of worth and you are treating the teen as a person who has desires. Now you are ready for step eight.

8. *Ask permission to share your perspective.* "Would you like to hear my perspective on the idea?" If the teen says "Yes," you proceed to share your thoughts, ideas, and feelings. If the teen says "Not really," then the conversation is over and the trip to the beach goes unfunded. If you have expressed understanding of the teen's thoughts, feelings, and desires, there is every likelihood that the teenager will be open to hear your perspective. Even though she may not agree with you, she will listen.

TOWARD A BETTER RELATIONSHIP

Some parents find the idea of asking permission to share their perspective offensive. "Why should I have to ask my teen permission to speak?" one father asked. The question is not whether the parents have the right to speak to the teenager, they do. The question is "Do you want your teenager to listen to what you are saying?" Asking permission recognizes that she is an individual and has the choice of hearing what is in your heart and mind or not hearing it. You are recognizing your teen as an individual. You are creating the climate for sympathetic dialogue. Parents certainly have the freedom to preach their sermon without asking permission, but teenagers also have the freedom "to tune parents out" if they choose. Many will do so because they feel they are being treated as a child. When you ask permission to share your perspective, the teen feels that she is being treated as a maturing young person.

Parents still have the final word in such matters as paying for a beach trip or for that matter in allowing the teen to go to the beach at all. It is not a matter of parental authority; it is a matter of parent-teen relationships, or how you will express your authority. You can always lord it over your teenager as a tyrant. This will almost certainly result in your teenager feeling rejected and unloved. On the other hand, you can relate to your teen as a loving parent who recognizes the teenager's transition into adulthood and seeks to foster a healthy, loving transition.

It will be obvious that such quality conversations will take time. Twice as much time will be spent in listening to the teenager as in talking. The dividends, however, are enormous. The teen feels respected, understood, and loved—the dream of every parent. Such dreams do not come true by simply doing what you've always done. It comes by learning new patterns of communication which are more appropriate during the years of teenage development.

LEARNING TO TALK

Talking is an important part of meaningful dialogue with your teenager. However, the manner in which you talk is extremely important. Effective talking focuses on sharing your own thoughts, feelings, and desires, not on attacking those of the teenager. Parents create an adversarial relationship when they begin their talking by condemning the teenager's perspective on the subject. Far better to take the positive approach of sharing your perspective: your thoughts, your feelings, your desires.

Speaking "I" Statements

The simplest way to learn this approach to talking is to begin your sentences with *I* rather than *you:* "I think . . . , I feel . . . , I want . . ." These are statements of self-revelation; they are informing the teenager of what is going on inside of you. Conversely, "*You* are wrong, *you* don't understand, *you* are misreading the situation, *you* are being unreasonable, *you* are making my life difficult" are statements of blame and accusation. They almost always lead to one of two responses: explosive argumentation or withdrawal and depression, depending upon the teenager's basic personality.

You statements stop the flow of dialogue; *I* statements open the road to further discussion. It may take some time for you to learn this new way of talking. If you find yourself beginning your sentences with *you*, stop. Tell your teenager that you are trying to learn a new way to talk and that you'd like to try that sentence again. Rephrase the sentence, starting with *I*.

For example, if you hear yourself saying, "You make me angry when . . ." you should stop and say, "Let me try that again. I feel angry when . . ." Then you say to your teenager, "Do you understand why I'm trying to learn a new way to talk? I don't want to condemn you; I want to understand you. At the same time, I want you to understand my feelings and thoughts." Most teenagers will appreciate parents' efforts to learn new patterns of communication.

Teaching Instead of Preaching

Another important principle in talking with teenagers is to teach rather than preach. I grew up in the rural South where teachers and preachers were highly respected. The difference between the two was not in content, for the secular and sacred were intricately woven together, even at school. Nor was the difference in geography. It is true that the preacher preached at church and the teacher taught at school, but it is also true that the teacher often taught at church and the preacher sometimes preached at school. The difference was in the manner of delivery. The preacher was forceful in delivery— speaking loudly at times and softly at others, sometimes crying, sometimes laughing, but always passionate and dogmatic. The teacher, on the other hand, used a conversational tone, taught the content more "matter of factly"—passionate, I'm sure, but never overtly so. Parents of teenagers who wish to be effective communicators must emulate the teacher rather than the preacher.

The raised voice and theatrics on the part of parents typically causes teenagers to turn elsewhere for advice. On the other hand, parents who learn to share ideas in a reasoned and calm manner will often find teenagers asking for their advice. I do not mean that parents cannot be dogmatic about deeply held beliefs. I mean, rather, that their dogmatism must be tempered by an openness to other's opinions, especially those of their teenager. "Let me tell you what I've always believed about that and tell you why I believe it to be best and then give me your feedback. I'd be interested in your observations." Such an approach allows the parent to express strong beliefs but also makes it easy for the teenager to share his thoughts, even if they are divergent from those of the parent. It is this kind of climate the parent must seek to create.

Remember, teenagers are beginning to think abstractly and in logical sequence. They are examining the beliefs with which they grew up and are deciding their own value systems. Parents who wish to influence this process must learn to be teachers rather than preachers. Learn the art of asking questions. Parents who learn how to ask questions will keep their teenagers talking. I don't mean badgering questions, such as, "Where did you go, how long did you stay, who was with you?" I mean questions that solicit the teenager's thoughts, such as, "How do you think most teenagers reacted to the burning of the American flag last week by the students at the university?" Listen attentively and you will hear not only the observation of your teenager about his peers but you will also discover his/her thoughts on the subject. Keen interest in the teenager's opinions solicited by thoughtful questions may also lead the teenager to ask for your opinions. Questions beget not only answers but other questions.

Offering Reasons

One other idea about talking to teenagers: Replace "Because I said so" with "Let me tell you why." Teenagers are interested in reasons. They are developing their own ability to reason, and they respond to the person who has logical reasons for his beliefs or opinions. The parent who reverts to pure authority without expressed reasons stops the flow of sympathetic dialogue with the teenager. The teenager feels rejected by the parent and the love tank is empty.

The parent who learns the art of effectively listening and talking to teenagers is the parent who will most effectively communicate love on an emotional level. Quality conversation is one of the most powerful ways to communicate such love.

QUALITY ACTIVITIES

Teenagers are creatures of action. Many of the parent's best quality conversations will take place in association with some activity. Some of these activities are a part of the normal flow of life—school, athletics, music, dance, drama, community, and church. In all of these arenas, teenagers are active. Parents who wish to spend quality time with teenagers will find these venues offer many opportunities. In the younger teenage years, there are all the hours spent enroute to and from such activities. These times in the car need not be riddled with arguments if parents follow the eight guidelines listed above for talking and listening. Often the events themselves offer opportunities for expressing quality time with your teen. When your teenager understands that you are at the event because you want to see them perform, you are interested in their pursuits, that nothing is more important to you this afternoon than attending their event, it speaks volumes to the teenager.

One fourteen-year-old said, "My dad always attends my concerts. He is not a musician, but he encourages me. I feel so fortunate." Another teenage daughter in the same orchestra said, "I know my dad loves me, but he never leaves work to attend my concerts. He makes time to play golf with his buddies, but he never makes time for me." The second teenage daughter believes intellectually that her father loves her but is living with an empty emotional love tank. Teenagers know that giving your time to attend one of their activities is giving them a part of your life, and it communicates deeply your love for them. Conversely when parents do not make time to attend the events in which their teenagers are involved, the message is "You are not as important as other things."

Teenagers do better in the normal challenges of teenage development if their parents are involved with them in the normal flow of life. It is interesting that when five thousand adults were asked, "What did you least appreciate from your parents as a teenager?" the number one response was, "They were not involved in my life."[2] The fact is teenagers want their parents to be involved in their lives. Such involvement not only creates memories for the future but deep bonds of love in the present. Helping with homework, attending activities, driving your teens to the mall and shopping with them all create opportunities for quality time with teens. Parental involvement says, "Your interests are important to me."

THE RIGHT ENVIRONMENT FOR QUALITY TIME

Parents may also learn to create environments for *quality time* with teenagers by planning and executing events outside the normal weekly routines. This requires time, money, and effort, but the dividends are enormous. Camping or hiking trips, rafting, kayaking, or other water events, attending sports, musical, or theatrical events in a distant city, or visiting places of historical interest are but a few ways to create environments for spending *quality time* with your teenager.

Choose Events Your Teen Likes

The key to creating successful environments is to begin with the interests of your teenager. Planning a trip based on your own interests rather than the teenager's interests is planning for a bad experience. Discover your teenager's interests and be creative in planning environments that will motivate your teenager to spend *quality time* with you.

I remember when our seventeen-year-old son Derek got involved in learning about Buddy Holly, the 1950s singer-musician who died young in a plane crash. I made a trip to the library and read everything I could find about Buddy Holly. I read the lyrics to his songs. Later I engaged Derek in conversation about Buddy's lyrics. He was surprised that I even knew the lyrics. Some time later, I scheduled a marriage seminar in Fort Worth, Texas, and asked

Derek if he would like to go with me. "After the seminar," I said, "we will drive out to Lubbock and discover the roots of Buddy Holly." I'll never forget the look in his eyes when he said, "Oh, Dad. I'd love to do that." (I had no idea how far it was from Fort Worth to Lubbock.) Talk about quality time, we had it.

All across west Texas, we talked about what we expected to find in Lubbock. We talked about Derek's own history and the possibilities of his future. We saw the oil wells, barbed wire fences, railroad tracks, and tumbleweed. But mainly, we talked. Periodically we stopped, got outside the car, and took in the silence of west Texas.

When we arrived at Lubbock, we went to the chamber of commerce and received four pages of information on Buddy Holly. We went to the house where Buddy Holly was born. (The house was actually gone, but we took a picture of the lot where Buddy Holly's house used to stand.) We drove to the radio station where Buddy Holly played his first record. They actually invited us inside and showed us the turntable on which his first record was played. We went to the house where Buddy Holly lived when he cut his first record. I took a picture of Derek in the front yard. The homeowner came outside to greet us. We told her what we were doing and she said, "It's all right. They do it all the time." We went to the club where Buddy Holly played his first gig. (It is now a used car lot but the rusty sign still hangs outside—"Cotton Club.") We went to the high school which Buddy Holly attended and I took a picture of Derek leaning against the cream-colored brick building. We went to the little Baptist church where Buddy Holly was married and where his funeral was conducted. The youth director's father had been the youth director when Buddy Holly was living. Now the younger youth director told us all about the wedding, all about the funeral.

Then we drove to the edge of town, to Buddy Holly's grave. We saw the marble stone and the bronze guitar. I walked away to give Derek some private time; then slowly we walked to the car and drove away. With Lubbock in our rearview mirror, we discussed Buddy Holly: What would have happened if Buddy had not been killed in the plane crash at such an early age? What were Buddy's religious beliefs? Since some people die young, what are the important things about life? We talked and talked, and talked all the way back to Fort Worth. That was a *quality time* experience that neither of us has ever forgotten.

Imagine our surprise some years later when we were on another quality time experience in London to discover the musical "Buddy." All the actors were British, speaking with Texas accents. It was fabulous! Then I remember a little later when Derek got into Bruce Springsteen. I won't bore you with the details, but we went to Freeport, New Jersey, and discovered the roots of Bruce.

Create an Environment for Quality Time

Seeking to tap into Derek's interests, I planned a trip for us every year during his teenage years. I highly recommend it as a means for creating an environment for *quality time*. Even now Derek often looks back and reminisces about our *quality time* trips together. We are forever bonded by those memory building quality-time experiences.

I would encourage you to think of creating a quality-time experience with your teenager. It need not be as expensive or extensive as London, Lubbock, or Freeport. It can be as brief and inexpensive as traveling to a town thirty miles away to experience together something in which your teenager is interested. Planned activities provide an opportunity to speak the love language of quality time. Even if your teen's primary love language is not quality time, such activities will let you know your teen better, create meaningful and lasting memories, and let your teen know you love him.

"MY TEENAGER WON'T TALK"

One common complaint among parents is that when their child becomes a teenager, they stop talking. "My teenager won't talk. So why even try to have a quality conversation?" It is true that adolescents have a greater need for privacy than younger children. Having thoughts and feelings of their own that differ from those of parents is a part of becoming independent. There are times when teenagers don't want to talk about it because they want to work it out for themselves. On those occasions, parents are unwise to pressure the teen to talk. What we do need to do is to let the teen know that we are available if they want to talk.

Sometimes teenagers do not want to talk with parents because when they have tried to talk, it ended in the teenager feeling put down or rejected. As parents, we must listen to what we say and how we say it. The teenager comes home discouraged from a failure at school. They begin to share it with a parent and the parent says, "What did you do wrong this time?" The conversation is over, and the teenager walks away feeling misunderstood.

Sometimes parents offer empty reassurances. "By this time next week, you won't even remember what happened today." At other times we are often too quick to give advice. "Moping around won't help. Why don't you go jogging?"

These are the kind of responses that close the flow of communication. Such statements communicate a "know it all" attitude. They express no empathy for what the teenager is feeling at the moment. Some teenagers don't talk because they know these are the kind of responses they will receive.

As parents, we can help open the door of communication if we are sensitive to the teenager's moods. "Looks like you had a hard day today. Want to talk abou it?" is an invitation that many teens will accept. "You look excited tonight. Did something good happen today?" makes it easy for the teenage daughter to talk. Sympathetic listening (which we discussed above) and nonthreatening questions will create a climate that makes it easier for your teenager to talk. Remember, your teenager has the right to keep her thoughts and feelings to herself. Sometimes that will be her choice. Attempting to make her talk on these occasions is denying her individuality and independence from you. Let her know that you are available to talk if she wants to.

Sometimes teenagers are willing to talk but not at the times the parents prefer. Sometimes teenagers want to talk at their own convenience. This is often late at night and in the privacy of their own rooms or in the den after everyone else has gone to bed. Thoughtful parents will take advantage of these opportunities when they arise. Two extra hours of sleep will make little difference in the parent's overall well-being, but two hours of *quality time* with the teenager may make the difference between the teenager going to bed with a sense of love rather than loneliness and rejection.

"MY TEENAGER DOESN'T WANT TO SPEND TIME WITH ME"

Recognize His Need for Friends

Another complaint parents voice when trying to maintain quality time is, "My teenager doesn't want to spend time with me." Of course, during the teenage years your son or daughter will develop deep friendships with those outside the family. Sociologists refer to this as the teenager's peer group. Dr. Eastwood Atwater defines the peer group as "people who regard one another as equals because of their age, grade, or particular status."[3] Dr. Atwater also indicates that peer groups play four primary roles in the teenager's life. These are:

1. The group helps the teen transition to adulthood by providing a social-emotional support group.
2. The peer group provides standards that the teenager can use to judge their own behavior and experiences.
3. It provides opportunities for developing interpersonal relationships and developing social skills.
4. It provides a context in which the teenager can develop his/her sense of self-identity.[4]

Hanging out with friends after church, school, or other activities, going to movies or the mall, spending the night with each other, talking on the telephone or sending E-mail messages are activities that automatically increase when a child becomes a teenager. "Adolescents' newfound peer groups help to satisfy their need for companionship and fun, along with emotional support, understanding, and intimacy," notes counselor Gary Smalley. "They still need these things from their families and other adults as well, but it's vital in their development to receive these things from friends."[5]

Parents often misinterpret the adolescent's heightened interest in friends as disinterest in the family. They assume that a fifteen-year-old would not be interested in going hunting with Dad or shopping with Mom or on a family picnic. However, research shows that most teenagers would like to spend more, not less, time with their parents than they presently spend.[6]

Consult Your Teen When Planning

A part of the problem is that parents sometimes plan activities without bringing the teenager in on the planning. Consequently, the teen has something exciting planned with their peer group and does not want to go with the parents. The parents interpret this as rejection or lack of desire to be with the family. However, if the parents would have recognized the teenager as a person (independence and self-identity) and consulted with the teenager at the planning stage, the teenager may have been very interested in accompanying the family. It is when we treat our teenagers as children and make plans *for* them rather than treating them as emerging independent persons that we get the impression that they don't wish to be with the family.

Seventeen-year-old Brandon said, "My parents tell me that they are hurt because I don't want to go with them when they plan trips for us. The problem is they don't ever consult my schedule. They make plans and announce them to me on the day before we are supposed to leave. I have things already planned with my friends, and my parents get upset because I don't want to break those plans and go with them."

Consider Your Teen's Interests

Another reason teenagers are sometimes reluctant to respond to parents' planned activities is that parents fail to take into account the teenager's interests. What parent has not been through the following routine? Mom says, "We're going down to see Uncle Bob and Aunt Clara on Saturday and we would like for you to go with us." The teen replies, "I don't want to go." Mom: "Why?" Teen: "It's boring down there. There's nothing to do." Mom: "You could spend time with your cousin. You enjoy being with each other." Teen: "Mom, he's a kid. I'm a teenager now. It's not the same."

If parents are in touch with the teenager's interests, with a little thought they can plan into such a trip some activity that would be of interest to the teenager and make the trip more appealing. I'm not saying that teenagers should never be forced to accompany the family in a visit to relatives. I am suggesting that if such a trip is forced upon the teenager, you cannot expect it to be a quality time experience for the two of you. Far better to work with the teenager's interests and schedule, planning activities together that will be meaningful for both of you.

What the Teens Say

Let me repeat what I said at the beginning of this chapter. The love language quality time is much more difficult to speak than words of affirmation or physical touch. But quality time is one of the five love languages. For some teenagers, it is their primary love language. Without *quality time* with parents, these teenagers will not feel loved even though the parents may be speaking other love languages. It is essential for these teenagers that parents make time to give the teenager focused attention. Listen to the following teens for whom *quality time* is their primary love language.

Marissa, age fourteen, and a would-be fisherman: "I love it when my dad takes me with him when he goes fishing. To be honest with you, I really don't like those smelly things. But I like being with Dad. We talk about all kinds of things and I really love getting up early. It's the best time I have with him."

Kyle, age sixteen, and the proud owner of his first driver's license: "Now that I can drive, I like going places without my parents. But I also like doing things with them. I really like it when Dad and I can do things together. Some of my friends don't have fathers. I think I'm really fortunate."

Monica, age fourteen, lives with her mother and has little contact with her father. "What I like about Mom is that we can talk about everything. We don't keep secrets. I feel really close to Mom. She has helped me with a lot of problems. I know I can always tell her what's bothering me and she will help me."

Jennifer, age eighteen, is getting ready to go to college in the fall. "I think the thing I'm going to miss most when I go to school is my talks with Mom and Dad. Sometimes, they are late at night and long but I know they are always there for me. I won't have that at college. I know we can talk on the phone but it won't be quite the same."

NOTES

1. Ross Campbell, *How to Really Love Your Teenager* (Wheaton, Ill.: Victor, 1983), 33.

2. Gary Smalley and Greg Smalley, *Bound by Honor* (Wheaton. Ill.: Tyndale, 1998), 98.

3. Eastwood Atwater, *Adolescence* (Englewood Cliffs, N.J.: Prentice Hall, 1996), 198.

4. Ibid., 201–202.

5. Smalley and Smalley, *Bound by Honor,* 107.

6. Lawrence Steinberg and Ann Levine, *You and Your Adolescent* (New York: Harper & Row, 1990), 13.

chapter six

LOVE LANGUAGE #4:
ACTS OF SERVICE

I think the thing that made me feel most loved was the way my parents worked so hard to help me with everything." Mark had just started his first full-time job and was contemplating getting married soon. As he talked about his teenage years, he began recalling specifics. "I remember all the meals Mom made even though she worked outside the home, and the time Dad helped me with the old clunker we bought together when I was sixteen. The little things, the big things—they did so much to help me."

Now twenty-four, Mark continued to reminisce. "I realize it now more than I did then. But even at the time, I knew that they were working hard to help me and I always appreciated it. I hope I can do the same for my children someday."

Mark was describing parents who spoke the love language *acts of service.*

Parenting is a service-oriented vocation. The day you decided to have a child, you enrolled for long-term service. By the time your child becomes a teenager, you have been speaking this language for thirteen years. If you want to feel really good about yourself, take a few minutes and calculate the number of diapers you changed, meals you prepared, clothes you washed, folded and/or ironed, Band-Aids you applied, toys you repaired, sheets you tucked, hair you washed and combed, etc. Please don't show this list to your teenager. But in the privacy of your bedroom read it aloud, especially on the days when you are feeling like a parental failure. There is the solid, irrefutable evidence that you have loved this child.

However, your child has now become a teenager, and you must learn some new dialects if you are to effectively speak the love language acts of service. There are no more diapers but there are plenty of buttons to replace, dresses to make or mend, meals to prepare, bicycle tires to replace, cars to tinker with, shirts to wash and iron (forget the ironing, wrinkled is "in"), uniforms to bleach, personal taxis to drive (at least until they are sixteen in most states), etc.

THE POWERFUL LANGUAGE OF SERVICE

All of this hard work takes on a dimension of nobility when you understand that such acts of service are powerful expressions of emotional love to your teenager. Some parents have slipped into performing these routine acts of service out of a sense of parental duty. They are blinded by the trees and cannot see the forest. My hope for these parents is that the following pages will blow away the clouds of the mundane and allow the sunshine of genuine love to create a brighter vision for parenting teens. The fact is that acts of service casts one of love's brightest rays.

History is replete with examples of men and women who learned how to speak the love language known as acts of service. Who does not know of Mother Teresa? Her name is synonymous with acts of service. In Africa, there was Albert Schweitzer and in India, Mohandas Gandhi. Most people who have studied closely the life of Jesus of Nazareth, the first century founder of the Christian faith, agree that His life can be summarized by His simple act of washing the feet of His disciples. He Himself said, I "did not come to be served, but to serve, and to give [my] life as a ransom for many."[1] He instructed His followers, "Whoever wants to become great among you must be your servant."[2]

True greatness is expressed in serving. Acts of service freely given from parents to teenagers are true expressions of emotional love.

SERVICE FREELY GIVEN

Because service to a child is constant for so many years and takes place in and around so many other obligations, parents can forget that the daily and mundane acts they perform are expressions of love with long-term effects. At times, parents can even feel more like slaves than loving servants, put upon by spouse, children, and others. However, if parents assume this attitude, the teenager will sense it and will feel little love from the acts of service.

Loving service is not slavery. Slavery is imposed from the outside and is done with reluctance. Loving service is an internally motivated desire to give one's energy to others. Loving service is a gift, not a necessity, and is done freely, not under coercion. When parents serve their teenagers with a spirit of resentment and bitterness, the teens' physical needs may be met but their emotional development will be greatly hampered.

Because service is a daily occurrence, even the best parents need to stop for an attitude check now and then to be sure that their acts of service are communicating love. I remember Cameron telling me, "My dad will help with my homework if I insist. But he makes me feel guilty and undeserving. I usually don't ask for his help." Those acts of service by Dad don't communicate love. Mothers can also communicate little love in their service. "I wish Mom would help me on my school projects but I feel like she is too busy," said Julia, now in her first year of high school. "When I do ask her, I feel like she is only doing it to get me off her back." If parental acts of service are to be heard as love in the soul of the teenager, they must be freely given.

MANIPULATION IS NOT LOVE

It is possible to use acts of service as a means of manipulating your teenager. "I will drive you to the mall to meet your friends if you will clean up your room." This is an effort to strike a deal with the teenager, to make a contract: "I will . . . if you will. . . ." I'm not suggesting that we should never seek to make contracts with our teens, but we must never view this as an expression of emotional love. Your driving the teen to the mall is payment for the services rendered; namely, cleaning the room. It is a bartering system to get the teenager to do something you find desirable; it's not an expression of love.

If your acts of service are always tied to the teen's doing something you desire, you are practicing manipulation. Manipulation is never an expression of love. Love cannot be earned. It is a gift freely expressed. We are to love our teenagers unconditionally. Perhaps they are not pleasing us in all their behavior. We can still speak the love language acts of service. In fact, the teenager will feel more deeply loved when she knows that your love is unconditional.

That system of trying to change your teen's behavior by promising to do something you know she wants you to do is called by psychologists *behavior modification*. It has to do with rewarding the teen for what the parent considers good behavior by doing something the teen desires or withholding something when the teen fails to comply with the parent's wishes. This method of parenting was popular during the 1970s but, in my opinion, is not the healthiest way to parent children and is certainly not the best way to relate to teenagers.

I'm not saying that behavior modification should never be used as a parenting style. It may be helpful particularly in breaking ingrained patterns which the parent considers to be irresponsible behavior. Sometimes the reward offered will be enough to motivate a teenager to change behavior that she would not normally be motivated to change. Unfortunately, this behavior change is not always permanent unless you continue to give rewards. (More about this in chapter 12 when we talk about love and responsibility.)

On the other hand, parents must also be warned that teenagers will sometimes try to manipulate you by acts of service. If there is something they want you to do for them, they may offer to do something that they know you have requested in the past. Sixteen-year-old Bradley said, "If I want Mom to do something for me, all I have to do is offer to clean my room. She'll do anything I want." Bradley has learned to manipulate his mother. If the mother feels that what Bradley is asking is for his good, she may agree to his contract. But parents should never agree to do something that they believe is unwise simply because the teen is agreeing to do something they desire.

Some teenagers are master manipulators. "If you love me, you . . ." is the ultimate statement of manipulation for the teenager. The teen is using the parent's desire to be a good parent as a tool to get parental approval of his desires. The best parental response is "I love you too much to do something I believe is detrimental to you no matter how much you want it." Manipulation has nothing to do with love and everything to do with control. It is not a good approach for parent-teen relationships.

RECIPROCAL LOVE

Modeling and Guiding

Conscientious parents of teenagers have two main desires: to love and to be loved. We want our teens to feel our love in order to keep their love tanks full, but we also want them to learn how to love others. Parents sometimes ask, "If I continue with acts of service to my teenager, how will he learn to do things for himself and how will he learn to serve others?" The answer to that question is found in modeling and guiding. We model unconditional love when we do things for the teenager that we know they would like for us to do so long as we believe these actions are good for the teenager. However, we must choose these acts of service wisely. Otherwise, we create a dependent teenager who takes but never learns to give. For example, cooking a meal is an act of service, but teaching a teenager how to cook a meal is an even greater act of service. Obviously it is easier to prepare the meal yourself than it is to teach a teenager to prepare the meal. Which is the greater act of love? Obviously, the latter.

A rule of thumb is that you do acts of service for your teenagers that they cannot do for themselves. When they are young, you wash the clothes for them; when they are teenagers, you teach them how to wash the clothes. Parents who don't learn this distinction may actually cripple the teens' maturity in the name of love. This does not mean that you would never do the laundry for them. It does mean that you will not always do the laundry. Instead, you will go beyond modeling to guiding your teen toward independent actions and maturity.

Guiding the Right Way

I think it is helpful for parents to verbally explain to teenagers what they are doing. Mom says to Patrick, age thirteen, "Now that you are a teenager, I want to share some personal thoughts with you. When you were little, I did lots of things for you because I loved you very much. I fixed all of your meals, I did your laundry, I cleaned up your room, etc. I could go on doing all of these things for you until you graduated from high school, but that would not be the loving thing to do. Because I still love you very much, I am going to teach you to do these things for yourself. I don't want you to finish high school and leave home and not have the skills to make it on your own.

"I've made a list of the things I want to teach you, Patrick. I want to show it to you and give you the opportunity to add to the list the things you would like to learn. I also want you to choose the order in which you would like to learn them. I will not push you beyond your limits but as you are ready, I want to teach you these skills."

Patrick's mother has explained her plan for loving him by acts of service. And Patrick probably will respond positively to the plan because Mom has let him be a part of choosing the things he would like to learn and the order in which he would like to learn them. Patrick and his father could also make a similar list of things his father would like to teach him and things he would like to learn from his father.

The teenager who has parents who will take this approach is a fortunate teenager indeed. He will not only feel loved by the parents, but will grow up to be a responsible adult who knows not only how to take care of himself, but also how to love others by acts of service.

In this approach, parents are not only speaking the love language acts of service, they are also guiding the teenager in learning the necessary skills to serve others effectively. This guidance will require both teaching and training. *Teaching* is the Greek word that emphasizes giving instruction by use of words. *Training* is the Greek word that emphasizes learning by doing. In the Greek approach to parenting, these were the dual wheels of parenting. Parents who follow this approach will give verbal instructions regarding a particular skill. They will demonstrate how it is done, then they will give the teenager hands-on experience in doing it himself.

For example, the father who wants to teach his son to wash the family car and later perhaps his own car begins with some verbal instructions. "One of the things you will want to always remember is to hose the car first in order to remove sand particles so that the car is not scratched as you soap it. Once you've done this, you will want to begin with the top of the car and work your way to the hood, trunk, and sides of the car, washing only one portion at a time and rinsing it quickly so that the soap does not dry and streak the car." Then the father demonstrates what he has just said, allowing the teenager to help with the process. Perhaps they will wash the car together for a couple of weekends. Then the father allows the son to wash the car by himself. After that, they may wash the car together, the father may wash it alone, or the son may wash it alone, depending on their desires. When the son washes the car alone, the father expresses praise and appreciation. The teenager has learned not only how to wash the car but how to love the father.

Helping Your Teen's Sense of Identity and Independence

In today's hurried society, some parents have failed to teach their teenagers the fundamental skills of maintaining life. Consequently, many of these teenagers later find themselves married only to discover that neither they nor their spouse know how to clean a commode, vacuum floors, cook meals, or do laundry. They are totally inept in the basic skills of serving each other. Their parents failed to teach them how to speak the love language of acts of service.

It will be obvious that making the shift from doing things for the child to teaching the teenager how to do things for himself will require much time and energy on the part of the parent. However, few things are more important to the teen's emotional and social well-being. If the teen learns to do acts of service, he will feel good about himself; thus, his self-identity will be enhanced. As the teen serves people outside the family, he will receive positive feedback. Everyone likes the person who serves others. Thus, the teen's self-identity will be further enhanced.

Furthermore, in learning such skills, the teen is able to maintain life on his own; thus, he has a greater sense of independence. Parents are making a powerful contribution to the teen's developmental maturity. Parents who fail to do this will have teenagers who become bored with life, have little sense of accomplishment, have low self-esteem, and will struggle in social relationships. I cannot overemphasize how important it is for parents of teenagers to love their teenager enough to teach them the skills of serving others. When parents fail to do this, teenagers will inevitably feel cheated by their parents. Love feeds children when they are little but teaches them to feed themselves when they are teenagers.

FOCUSING ON ACTS OF SERVICE

Two Effective Family Games

In *The Five Signs of a Loving Family,* I presented practical ways to foster an "attitude of service" in your family. I suggested two games that can be played daily in every family.[3] I believe that teenagers will respond positively to these games. The first is called *"I Really Appreciate That!"* This game helps you begin by affirming the acts of service that are already evident in your family relationships. While you are sitting around the table or sitting in the den, each family member completes the following sentence. "One way in which I served you today is . . . " The sentence may be completed by such statements as "cooking this meal, washing the dishes, vacuuming the floors, taking out the trash, mowing the lawn, picking up the mail." As each family member completes the sentence, the family member who was being served will reply, "I really appreciate that." The game is a positive way of reminding family members of the acts of service which are already going on in the family. It is also a way of affirming acts of service by expressing appreciation.

A second game is entitled *"Do You Know What I Would Like?"* In this game, each family member gives a request to another family member by asking, "Do you know what I'd like?" and then making a specific request for a service. For instance, Mom says, "I'd like for you to fix me some pancakes and sausage Saturday morning." Julie, who received the request, responds, "I'll try to remember that." Note: The person who is being asked to perform the service does not promise to do it but promises to try to remember it. That person then has a choice to do it or not to do it. Remember, all true service must be given freely. Efforts at coercion or manipulation are not love.

Both of these games may be played with teenagers as well as younger children. If they are played in a spirit of family fun and with a nonjudgmental and nondemanding attitude, they can help foster an attitude of service in the family.

Filling Scott's Love Tank

For some teenagers, acts of service is their primary love language. When parents express love by acts of service, the teenager's love tank is filled quickly. Scott was one such teenager. Upon his sixteenth birthday, his parents had bought him a car, which in their words "was the worst thing we could have done." Six months later, he was in my office because his parents threatened to take away his car if he didn't come (a perfect example of manipulation, but probably the only way Scott would have come to see me). Scott's parents had seen me the week before and shared their concerns. Since getting the car, Scott had been totally irresponsible. He had already received two traffic tickets for speeding and had been cited in one "fender bender" accident.

His parents indicated that Scott's attitude was "very belligerent" toward them. "Now that he has a car, he doesn't want to spend any time at home," his father said. "He works at a fast-food restaurant two hours each afternoon in order to pay for his gas. Then he wants to spend the rest of the afternoon and evening with his friends. He eats at the restaurant so he doesn't feel the need to come home for dinner. We have threatened to take the car away, but we don't know if that is what we should do.

"Actually, we don't know what to do. That's why we came to see you." Both of Scott's parents were highly motivated individuals. They both had good careers, and Scott was their only child.

In my conversations with Scott over the next few weeks, I discovered that he had little respect for his parents. "They are both into their careers," he said. "They don't really care about me." I discovered that his parents typically did not arrive home from work until 6 or 6:30 P.M. Before Scott had his car and part-time job, he would normally arrive home from school about 3:30, do his homework, and talk on the phone with his friends. When his parents arrived, they had dinner together. "Most of the time, they picked up food on the way home. Mom doesn't like to cook, and Dad doesn't know how. After dinner, they checked to make sure I had finished my homework. Then Dad worked on his business stuff and watched television. Mom did some reading and made some phone calls.

"I usually went to my room and surfed on the Internet and talked with my friends on the phone," Scott continued. "It was boring. There was nothing for me to do."

In further conversations with Scott, I learned that on numerous occasions, he would ask his parents to help him with various projects, but in his opinion "they never had time." "When I was thirteen," he said, "I asked my Dad to teach me how to water-ski, but he told me it was too dangerous and I was too young. When I wanted to learn to play the guitar, he said I didn't have any musical ability and it would be a waste of money. I even asked Mom to teach me how to cook. She said she would but she never did."

It was obvious to me that Scott felt cheated by his parents. They had fed him, housed him, and clothed him, but they had not spoken to his inner need for emotional love. It appeared to me that acts of service was his primary love language, but that his parents had never learned how to speak his dialect. They had served him by providing basic physical needs, but they had not been sensitive to his interests and thus had made little effort to foster the required skills in developing these interests. Consequently, Scott felt rejected and unloved. His behavior was simply a reflection of these emotions.

I wish I could say that things turned around quickly for Scott and his parents. But in reality, things got worse before they got better. I shared my observations with Scott's parents and I think they understood and made some sincere efforts to try to connect with Scott. But he was not very responsive. Most of their efforts were rebuffed. His attitude seemed to be that what they were doing was too late and too little.

An entire year passed before significant change took place. I visited Scott in the hospital after an automobile accident in which he suffered a broken hip, a broken leg, and a crushed ankle. He had just begun his senior year of high school; now, during his time of recuperation Scott finally reconnected emotionally with his parents. They apologized for having failed to meet his needs in the earlier years, and Scott admitted that he had shut them out of his life because he felt so rejected by them.

With this emotional reconnection, things improved significantly over the next year. While Scott was in a cast, his parents had ample opportunities to express love by acts of service but more importantly, they discovered Scott's present interests and took steps to help him develop these interests. Scott's senior year in high school was, as he put it, "the worst and best year of my life." Scott experienced great physical pain, but he also rediscovered genuine emotional closeness with his parents. He lived at home the next two years and attended a local college, which also provided numerous opportunities for his parents to express *acts of service*. Both of his parents became very involved in helping him with school projects. He and his father spent many weekends on the lake. Scott was no longer interested in water-skiing, but he did learn to drive his father's boat and he became proficient on the Jet Ski. With college, Scott's interests expanded, and his parents stayed in touch with those interests and took every opportunity to serve him by helping him explore his interests. Scott is now twenty-seven, married, and is speaking acts of service to his own son.

Scott's parents, as many parents, were very sincere. They loved their son incredibly, but they had failed to discover and speak his primary love language. When they finally discovered it and tried to speak it, Scott did not respond immediately. This is typical when a teenager has felt alone and rejected for a period of time. However, parents must not give up. If they are consistent in making attempts to speak the teenager's primary love language, that love will eventually pierce the emotional pain of a teenager and they can reconnect emotionally.

What the Teens Say

This reconnection will be the turning point in their relationship if it is followed by consistent efforts to speak the teen's primary love language. Listen to the following teenagers whose primary love language is acts of service.

Gray, age thirteen, lives with his mother and younger sister. His father left when Gray was seven. "I know my mom loves me because she washes my messy clothes, fixes supper every night, and helps me with my homework even when I don't ask her. She works hard as a nurse so we can have food and clothes. I think my dad loves me but he doesn't do much to help."

Krystal, age fourteen, is the oldest of four children. "I know my folks love me because they do so many things for me. Mom takes me to cheerleader practice and to all the games. Daddy helps me with my homework, especially my math, which I hate."

Todd, age seventeen, has his own lawn service in the summer and has bought his first car. "I've got the greatest dad in the world," he said. "He taught me how to mow grass, start a business, and make money so I could buy a car. Last week, he showed me how to change the spark plugs."

Kristin is thirteen. "I know my mom loves me because she takes time to teach me everything. Last week, she got me started on needlepoint. I'm going to make my own Christmas presents this year."

NOTES

1. Matthew 20:28.
2. Matthew 20:26.
3. Gary Chapman with Derek Chapman, *The Five Signs of a Loving Family* (Chicago: Northfield, 1997), 35–36.

chapter seven

LOVE LANGUAGE #5:
GIFTS

I had an afternoon break during one marriage seminar held in a memorable setting, the NATO Air Base in Geilenkirchen, Germany. For most of the troops, it was a minimum two-year assignment so spouses and families lived on the base. During this afternoon, I spotted thirteen-year-old Alex, who was sitting at a picnic table doing his homework. He looked like a typical American teenager: crew cut, blue jeans, and a well-worn, faded green sweatshirt. I had the feeling he wouldn't mind being disturbed, so I introduced myself and engaged him in conversation.

In due time, I commented on the St. Christopher medallion that was hanging on the chain around Alex's neck. "My dad gave that to me on my thirteenth birthday in March," he said. "Dad said that when he had to be away on duty, he wanted it to remind me of him. I wear it all the time."

"Who was St. Christopher?" I inquired.

"I'm not sure," he said, "some saint in the church who did a lot of good."

I could tell that for Alex, the medallion had little religious significance. But on the emotional level, its worth was priceless. It was a constant reminder of his father's love. I had the sense that if thirty years from now I happen to encounter Alex again, he will still be wearing the St. Christopher medal around his neck.

WHAT MAKES A GIFT A GIFT?

Gifts are visible, tangible evidence of emotional love. It is important to understand the essential nature of a gift. The Greek word from which we get our English word *gift* is *charis,* which means grace or an undeserved gift. By its very nature, a gift is not something that the teenager deserves; it is given because the parent desires to share unconditional love with the teen. Some parents fail to realize this; they think they are giving gifts to their teenagers when in reality they are simply paying them for a service rendered. When that happens, they are not really speaking the love language called *gifts.*

For instance, Beverly told her fifteen-year-old, Amanda, "If you will go clean your room, as soon as dinner is over, we will go to the mall and I will buy you that dress you want." In reality, she was either trying to manipulate Amanda to do what she wanted or she was bartering a deal with Amanda: "If you will . . . then I will give you a dress." Or perhaps she was sick and tired of Amanda's harassment about the dress, and this was her way of caving in to the harassment while trying to get a little work out of Amanda in the process. At any rate, the dress will not be a gift. It will be payment for Amanda's cleaning her room. It was set up that way by Beverly. She may think she is expressing love to Amanda by giving her a dress, but Amanda will accept the dress as something she deserves, not as a gift.

For some parents, almost all of what they call "gifts" are in fact efforts at manipulating the teenager, bartering for something they desire, or payment for the teenager's work. The only time some teenagers receive true gifts is at Christmas and on their birthday. Other than that, the parents' gifts are not gifts at all. Don't misunderstand me; I'm not suggesting that parents should never repay teenagers for services rendered. I am simply saying that these payments are not to be considered gifts. The teenager could probably work out a similar deal with some adult down the street. Even if the parent gives them a better deal than they could get down the street, it is still a deal and not a gift.

It might help to ask yourself, "What is the last genuine gift I gave to my teenager?" Once you have the gift in mind, ask yourself "Did I require anything of my teenager before I gave her the gift?" If so, then mark it off, because it was not a genuine gift. Start over and try to find the last gift you gave your teenager. Some parents will find it was last Christmas or the last birthday.

Teenagers are not opposed to this deal-making with their parents. In fact, many of them are happy to make deals. It has become their accustomed way of getting what they want. If they can't get it by verbally harassing the parent, then they will get it by "cutting a deal" with the parent. This is the standard method of operation in many homes, but it has nothing to do with gift giving.

THE GIFT AND THE CEREMONY

Another important aspect of gift giving is that it should be done with some measure of ceremony. Think back on a significant gift you have received in the past. What was the gift? Who gave it to you? How was it wrapped? How was it presented to you? Was the presentation of the gift accompanied by words, touches, or other expressions of love? Chances are the more effort the giver put into packaging and presentation, the more love you felt. The purpose of gift giving is not simply to get an object from one person's hand to another. The purpose is to express emotional love. We want the person to sense deeply "I care about you. I think you are important, I love you." These emotional messages are enhanced when attention is given to the ceremony accompanying the passing of the gift.

Parents of teenagers will do well to remember this. When we diminish the ceremony, we diminish the emotional power of the gift. Johnny requests a pair of tennis shoes. Mom or Dad drives Johnny to the mall, buys the shoes. Johnny wears them as he leaves the store, and that's that. No ceremony at all. Many teenagers have become accustomed to this procedure. Such gifts communicate little emotional love. If all gifts are given in this manner, it creates an entitlement mentality in the teenager's mind. "I'm a teenager. My parents owe it to me to get me whatever I want." There is little appreciation on the part of the teenager and the gift has little emotional meaning.

However, if the shoes are taken home, wrapped in a creative manner, and presented in the presence of other family members as an expression of love for the teenager, accompanied by words of affirmation and physical touch, the gift suddenly becomes a strong vehicle of emotional love. If you have been a no-ceremony gift giver, let me suggest that you announce to your teenager that you have chosen to bring more celebration into the life of your family and that there will be a new way of giving gifts in the future. Your teenager may laugh or even be annoyed by your early efforts to change the pattern, but I can tell you he will soon come to view your gifts in a different light. And he will learn how to speak the love language of giving gifts, which will serve him well in adulthood.

GIFTS AND MATERIALISM

I am often asked by sincere parents, "If I give too many gifts to my teenagers, will I not foster the spirit of materialism that is so prevalent in our culture?" That is a very real danger in our society. Ours is largely a materialistic society. The bumper sticker reads: "He who dies with the most toys wins." Adults and teenagers alike are busy collecting toys. If we have the latest, the best, the most technologically advanced, then we are successful. While adults are collecting bigger and multiple houses, more expensive cars, more sophisticated appliances, boats, planes, and the latest model personal computers, teens are collecting faster cars, more powerful audio systems, designer clothes and shoes, CDs, and buying into the latest fad to prove that they are not like their parents. We are all marching to the beat of the same drummer. We are simply collecting different toys.

As parents, we are wise to ask, "Is this what I want to teach my teenagers?" We must also ask, "Is this what I want to do with my own life? Is there something more to life than acquiring and playing with my toys?" Most adults believe that there is, but many are not able to delineate for themselves or others what it is.

I believe the answer lies in two arenas. First, learning to enjoy the ordinary and second, learning to share it with others. For thousands of years men and women lived without the "toys"—the thousands of products—made possible by the industrial and technological revolutions of the nineteenth and twentieth centuries. Without these toys, people enjoyed the ordinary things of life—eating, sleeping, working, music, art, and interacting with nature. Second, they shared this ordinary life with others. Not only was there a sense of connectedness within the extended family, but there was also a sense of community with neighbors. For many, this sense of connectedness also extended to God. God was seen as the Creator and Sustainer of all that existed and the source of moral law that regulated man's relationship with man.

Materialism in the Western world began when man came to believe that by his own efforts he could accomplish utopia. Industrial and technological advances convinced man that he no longer needed law, and that moral laws were not divine but could be manipulated by man. Human reason replaced God, and the products of man's hand became his idols. Materialism, then, is the worship of these idols. The fundamental weakness of worshiping idols is that when you most need them, they are not there. When human relationships are fractured by man's inhumanity to man, when drugs and sexually transmitted diseases destroy our teenagers, when divorce destroys our marriages and disease destroys our bodies—then the toys we have gathered around us speak no word of comfort or meaning. Our idols have deserted us.

Many adults in our society are concluding that materialism is a poor substitute for the simple fundamentals of enjoying the ordinary aspects of daily life and sharing these joys with others. Many are looking again to the spiritual rather than the material to answer the deep longings of the human heart for ultimate meaning in life. If those are your conclusions, then certainly you would be concerned about fostering the spirit of materialism by the overuse or misuse of gifts. This does not mean that we can escape the world of machines and technology. It does mean that the gifts which we choose to give and the manner in which we give gifts will be influenced by our commitment to these deeper realities.

Let me suggest two areas which I believe parents must consider in speaking the love language of gifts.

GIVING MONEY

The Value of Money

First is the matter of giving money. The reality is that in Western society teenagers are major consumers, major spenders in a multibillion dollar market. Advertisers direct huge chunks of their advertising budget toward teenagers. Where do teenagers get all this money? By and large, the money comes from their parents. One might think that if gifts is one of the primary love languages and if parents are giving all this money to their teenagers, then the teenager's love tank should be full. The problem with this reasoning is twofold. First, most of that money is not given as a gift; it is structured into the family's method of operation and is simply expected by the teenager. Second, because the teenager has not worked to secure the money, the teen places little sense of value on the money. Thus, receiving it from parents does not communicate love at a deep emotional level. So how are parents to address the issue of giving money to their teenagers?

I believe we approach the problem in two ways. One, we must encourage the teenager to work for money. This is the only way the teen will come to have any sense of the value of money. If the teen works for the $50 he is about to spend on this piece of designer clothing, he or she has some sense of the effort that went into attaining this object. It forces the teen to ask, "Is this object worth the effort?" Thus, the teen becomes a discerning consumer. If the teenager must work for money, it also forces the teen to make choices between material objects. If one cannot have everything, then one must make some discerning judgment about what is most desired. This also prepares the teen for the real world of adult living.

If the parent is concerned that after-school work will keep the teenager from enjoying sports, drama, music lessons, dance, gymnastics, or other pursuits, then perhaps the parent can consider paying the teenager for her effort in these venues at the same pay scale of the local fast-food restaurant. All of these pursuits require diligent effort, fully as much as the effort put in the part-time after-school job. Paying a teenager for these efforts has much the same benefits as a part-time job. The point is that unlimited money is not to be given by the parent nor expected by the teenager if we want our teenagers to avoid the dangers of materialism.

Giving Money for Specific Purposes

The second approach is that when the parent chooses to give money, they give it for specific purposes, such as to pay for a sports camp or church camp, to attend a concert, or to pay for a class in photography, art, and so forth. Then they can present it as a gift, following the guidelines mentioned above; namely, given unconditionally, given with ceremony, accompanied by affirming words, physical touch, and as often as possible, done in the presence of other family members.

Since the teenager has worked and now knows something of the value of money, the gift of money can be appreciated on an emotional level. The teenager has some idea of how long it takes to make the money the parent is now giving her as a gift. Thus, there can be genuine appreciation on an emotional level.

When parents freely dish out money—$20 here, $40 there, $100 here—without following these guidelines of effective gift giving, their gifts of money may be little appreciated and fail to meet the teenager's emotional need for love. I am convinced that most parents of teenagers have never learned how to make the gift of money an effective vehicle of emotional love. I believe the suggestions given above will help parents do this far more effectively.

GIVING GIFTS

Consider Your Teen's Welfare

When it comes to giving gifts other than money, I believe the parent must do so with due consideration. Remember, the purpose of a gift is to communicate emotionally "I love you" to the teenager. Therefore, the parent must ask, "Am I convinced that this gift is for the well-being of my teenager?" If the answer is no, then the parent cannot conscientiously give that gift to the teenager. Obviously this would rule out giving illegal drugs to our teenagers, but it may also rule out a number of more conventional gifts. It has become commonplace in middle-class America for many affluent parents to give a car to their sixteen-year-old. I'm not suggesting that this is always bad for the teenager. What I am suggesting is that parents need to ask the question "Is the gift of a car good for my teenager?"

There are many factors in answering that question. One is the level of maturity and responsibility of the teenager himself. Some teens are not emotionally ready for a car at age sixteen. Some teens have not demonstrated a sufficient level of responsibility in other areas that warrant the giving of a car.

Assuming the parent concludes that the car itself would be good for the teenager, the second question is "Is giving the car to the teen the best way? Would it be better if I required the teen to work to pay for all or part of the car? Would this tend to foster responsible use of the car more than if I simply gave the car?" These are the kinds of questions that thoughtful parents seek to answer. There is no one pattern that is best for all parents and all teenagers. However, parents who do not give thought to these questions will likely make unwise decisions in whether or how they give a car to their teenagers.

Similar questions arise when we talk about giving our teenager a college education. Is it simply to be expected that if the parents can afford it, it is their responsibility to pay for the teenager's college education? Again the question is "What is best for the teenager?" Parents want to do the loving thing—to look out for the interests of the teenager. Is it more loving to let the teenager pay for part of his college experience? If the parents choose to pay for all educational expenses, what can or should be expected of the teenager? Should we be thinking in terms of an unconditional gift or should we be thinking in terms of teaching the teenager responsibility? This may not be the time for an unconditional gift of $40,000 per year for the next four years. This may not be the time for speaking the love language of gifts, but rather a time for the teenager to learn to speak acts of service; or maybe there needs to be a combination of the two love languages. What is important is that we know what we are doing and why we are doing it.

If I choose to give the teenager an unconditional gift—all expenses paid, first year of college no matter how they respond, then that's my choice. But perhaps I should limit that gift to one year while I observe the teenager's response to the educational process rather than giving her an unconditional gift of four years.

If as a parent I understand what I'm doing and why I'm doing it, I am less likely to be disappointed in the long run. If, however, we handle these issues of car and college without thought, we set ourselves up for disappointment. How many parents have said later, "I gave him four years of college, no strings attached, and he has little appreciation for my gift." Chances are the parents violated the principles of conscientious thought in the giving of such gifts. The teenager sometimes reasons, "I didn't have to go to college. They said they wanted me to go to college. So I found it boring and partied. They are the ones who told me to do it. Why should they be upset?" With little appreciation for the effort parents expended to pay for college expenses, the teenager walks away not only unappreciative, but now feeling rejected by the parents. His love tank is empty, and the parental gift is ineffective.

Consider Your Teen's Interests

Another aspect to be considered in giving gifts to teenagers is the teenager's own areas of interest. Think back to the gift you received from someone in the past for which you had little use and no desire. You realize that the giver may have spent considerable monies for the gift. You appreciated their thought, but the gift itself was meaningless. It is possible for us to give similar gifts to our teenagers. If we want our gifts to be emotionally effective in communicating love to our teenagers, then we must consider our teenager's interests. Rather than buying something that strikes your own fancy, why not buy something which strikes the fancy of your teenager?

This can be done in a very overt manner. Simply say to your teenager, "If I should decide to buy you a gift this month, would you make me a list of two or three things you would like to have? Be as specific as possible. Give me trade names, colors, etc." Most teenagers will be happy to oblige. (Most wives wish their husbands would ask this question periodically). If the information your teen gives is ambiguous, there is nothing wrong with asking the teenager to accompany you to the mall and show you precisely what gift he or she would like to have if you should decide to give something. Go back later and purchase the gift and follow the guidelines of packaging and presentation discussed above. Why would you want to buy a CD that your teenager will never play, a shirt he will never wear, or a dress she will find hideous?

PRIVATE AND TREASURED GIFTS

Not all gifts should be given in front of the family. The value of some gifts are enhanced by a private presentation. When Shelley was sixteen, I invited her to take a walk with me in the village of Old Salem (a restored Moravian village in our city). The walk was not unusual for us, for we often took walks together through the village. But on this occasion, we sat by the small fish pond and I presented her with a golden key on a gold chain. I gave her what I thought was a beautiful speech about how much I valued her and how happy I was with her accomplishments in life. I told her that the key was a key to her heart and body and that my desire was that she would keep herself pure and someday, present the key to her husband.

To say the least, it was a tender moment for both of us. To her own chagrin, a few years later, she lost the golden key; but the memory of my presentation was hers forever. The physical gift was gone but the symbolism behind the gift was carried in her heart and mind through the years. She now has a little girl of her own, Davy Grace, and I wouldn't be surprised if someday Davy receives a golden key from her father.

Not only are there *private gifts,* but there are *treasured gifts.* Every family has some of these. They are not necessarily gifts of great monetary value, but they are treasures because of what they mean to the family. The treasure may be a ring, necklace, knife, book, pen, Bible, stamp collection, or anything else that has special significance to the parent. These may have been items that have been passed down from former generations or they may simply be items that are purchased for the explicit purpose of giving them to the teenager. They are the kind of *gifts* to which we attach emotional value.

Such gifts may be given in private or in the presence of other family members. But they should definitely be given with ceremony including speeches about the significance and symbolism of the gift

114

and accompanied by warm verbal and physical expressions of affection for the teenager.

These treasured gifts become symbols of love in the heart of the teenager for years to come. When the teenager is going through periods of emotional upheaval, these gifts sit in their rooms as reminders of the genuine love of parents. Often when the teenager looks at the treasure, the affirming words of parents come back. The warm affection of love is relived by the teenager. Every teenager needs a few of these treasured gifts.

COUNTERFEIT GIFTS

There is one kind of gift that no teenager needs. It is what I call *counterfeit gifts*. These are gifts designed to take the place of true love. They are given by busy and sometimes absentee parents—parents who are so caught up in the busyness of life that they have little time for speaking the love language of quality time, acts of service, words of affirmation, or physical touch, so they try to make up for this deficit by giving the teenager gifts—sometimes expensive gifts.

One single mom said, "Every time my sixteen-year-old goes to visit her father, she comes home with a suitcase full of gifts. He is not willing to help me with her medical and dental bills, but he always has money for gifts. He seldom calls her on the phone and only spends two weeks in the summer with her. But somehow the gifts are supposed to make everything all right." This kind of gift giving on the part of non-custodial parents has become commonplace. The teenager typically receives the gifts, expresses verbal appreciation, and goes home with an empty love tank. When gifts are given as a substitute for genuine love, the teenager sees them as the shallow counterfeit they are.

This phenomena happens not only where parents are divorced but often when both parents are living in the same house with the teenager. It occurs most often when both parents have demanding vocations. They are awash in money but bereft of time. The teenager fixes his own breakfast, goes off to school, returns, unlocks the door, walks into an empty house, and does what he wishes until his parents return home depleted of energy. The family eats a fast meal together which was purchased at a fast-food restaurant, each goes off to their own computer, and tomorrow the process will be repeated. In this kind of family, often counterfeit gifts are given regularly. The money is laid down freely, gifts are quickly purchased, and the teenager has all that he desires, except the love of his parents. Such counterfeit gifts will never fill the love tank of the lonely teenager, nor will they ultimately remove the guilt of the uninvolved parent.

This is a good time for me to restate what I said at the beginning of our discussion of the five love languages. Teenagers need to receive love from parents in all five love languages. To speak only the primary love language of the teenager and ignore the other four is not the message of this book. What I am trying to say is that the primary love language of the teenager will speak more deeply and will more quickly fill the emotional love tank. But it must be complemented by speaking the other four languages as well. Once the teenager is receiving a sufficient amount of love in his/her primary love language, then the other love languages become even more meaningful. On the other hand, if the parent ignores the primary love language of the teenager, the other four are not likely to fill the teenager's love tank.

If the primary love language of your teenager happens to be receiving gifts, then the principles of this chapter will be extremely important for you. In many ways, this is the most difficult of the love languages. Few parents actually speak this language fluently. Many parents bungle in their efforts to communicate love emotionally by giving gifts to their teenagers. If you even suspect that your teenager's primary love language is gifts, I suggest that you not only reread this chapter but that you discuss it thoroughly with your spouse and that together you evaluate your past patterns of gift giving.

What the Teens Say

As you seek to identify weaknesses in your pattern of giving gifts and to implement some of the positive suggestions contained in this chapter, you will learn how to speak the love language of giving gifts effectively. In the next chapter, I will share with you how to discover your teenager's primary love language. But first, listen to these teenagers who indicate that their primary love language is receiving gifts.

116

Michelle, fifteen, was asked how she knew her parents loved her. Without hesitation, she pointed to her blouse, skirt, and shoes. Then she said, "Everything I have they gave me. In my mind, that's love. They have given me not only the things I need, but far more. In fact, I share things with my friends whose parents can't afford them."

Serena is a senior in high school. In speaking of her parents, she said, "I look around my room and I see constant reminders of my parent's love. My books, computer, furniture, clothes have all been given to me by my folks over the past few years. I still remember the night they gave me my computer. My father had already connected it and my mom had wrapped it in golden paper. When I cut the ribbon, the computer screen read, 'Happy Birthday, Serena. We love you.'"

Ryan, age fourteen, said, "I guess the reason I know my parents love me is that they have given me so much. They often surprise me by giving me things that they know I would like to have. It's not just what they give me, but it's the way they do it. My family makes a big deal out of giving gifts, and it doesn't even have to be my birthday."

Jeff is seventeen and proud of a certain car. As he explained, "This car is a collection of my family. My dad and I bought the car 50–50, but everything else I received as gifts. The mats on the floor were given by my sister to celebrate my buying the car. Mom and Dad gave me the stereo on my seventeenth birthday. The wheel covers, my mom gave me one each week for four weeks, always on a different night of the week so I would be surprised."

Sean is fifteen and in the eighth grade. He has had a lot of physical problems and has missed a lot of school. "I know I have a lot of problems. Most guys my age are playing ball and stuff. In school, I'm a year behind most guys my age. But as I see it, I'm the luckiest guy alive. My parents love each other, love me, and love my sister. They are always surprising me with things. I'm a computer geek but somehow my dad finds out about new programs before I do. When I see a candle burning on the table, I know that after supper, there is going to be a celebration. Usually, Dad has found a new program for me so we have a party and celebrate."

chapter eight

DISCOVERING YOUR TEEN'S PRIMARY LOVE LANGUAGE

I don't know how I can ever determine her primary love language," Muriel said about her fourteen-year-old daughter, Kayla. "It seems like it changes every day. What she seemed to like yesterday she withdraws from today. She seems so moody, I never know what to expect."

Discovering the primary love language of teenagers is not as easy as discovering the primary love language of younger children. Our teens are just like Kayla—in a state of radical transition. When a person is in a state of transition—things in their external world are changing while their inner world of thoughts, feelings, and desires are in a state of disequilibrium—the person responds differently.

Think of yourself the night before you're leaving on an extended trip. Think about how you respond to the normal behavior of your spouse and children. Chances are your response is shorter, more to the point; you may feel agitated or even explosive. These are not your normal response patterns but if someone was trying to determine your primary love language, they would likely be misled by your responses.

THE CHALLENGE

Moody Teens

Most teenagers are in this state of disequilibrium for several years. Sometimes, this emotional instability is more intense than at other times; that is why we often observe that teenagers are unpredictable in how they will respond in a given situation. As adults, we assume that if a fellow employee responded positively last month to my pat on the back, he will have a similar response this month. While that is usually true with adults, it is not true with teenagers. The teenager's response is greatly influenced by his moods, and these moods are fluctuating, often several times within a day. The loving expression he accepted after breakfast may be rejected after dinner.

Since the teenager is in transition, attitudes quickly change, often driven by changing emotions. Desires also fluctuate greatly. Yesterday the most important thing in the world was getting a specific brand of basketball shoes. Your teenager was so insistent that you dropped your own plans for the evening and went to the mall. Two days later your teenager is leaving for the basketball court wearing a pair of old well-worn basketball shoes, and you are shaking your head saying to yourself, "I don't understand this kid." Muriel's experience with Kayla reflects the typical frustration of relating to a normal teenager, who may not seem normal at all.

Independent Teens

In addition to the teen's fluctuating moods, desires, and behavior, that developing sense of independence is another reason parents find it difficult to determine the teenager's primary love language. We have alluded to this reality several times in the preceding chapters. The normal process during adolescence is the breaking away from parents and establishing a personal identity. The word *adolescence* itself means "breaking away." Kayla no longer wants to be known as Muriel's daughter. She is trying to establish an identity apart from her mother. Gaining independence is a step toward developing this self-identity.

Because self-identity is also in process, Kayla is trying to decide if she wants to be known as "Kayla the basketball star, Kayla the honor roll student, Kayla the caring friend, Kayla the girl with short blond hair, Kayla the dancer, etc." Because Kayla has not determined which or how many of these identities she wishes, she often fluctuates between any one of these self-identifying characteristics. When she thinks of herself as Kayla the basketball star, she may not want quality time with her mother. But when she thinks of herself as Kayla the caring friend, she may be very responsive to quality time. Thus, the teenager's emerging independence and developing sense of self-identity often makes the task of determining her primary love language extremely difficult.

Withdrawing or Angry Teens

Sometimes it seems the teenager draws back from all expressions of love. You give him an affirming word and he says, "Don't get mushy" or "You are embarrassing me." You try to hug him and he shoots out his fingers like a prickly cactus. You give him a gift and receive nothing more than a mechanical "Thank you." You ask if you can take him out to dinner and he responds, "I'm having dinner with my friends." You ask if you can sew the buttons on his jacket and he responds, "Don't need buttons." You try all five love languages and are rebuffed.

Sometimes the teenager draws away from parental love because of unresolved anger between the parent and teenager. (We will discuss this in chapter 9.) But most often, the teen's rejection of all expressions of parental love can be explained in terms of the teen's fluctuating moods, thoughts and desires, emerging independence, and developing self-identity. In short, the teenager is simply being a teenager.

Fortunately, most teenagers do have moments of sanity when they will respond to parental expressions of love. It is not a lost cause. You *can* determine the primary love language of your teenager.

HAS THE CHILD'S LOVE LANGUAGE CHANGED?

I am assuming that a number of parents reading this book also read my book, *The Five Love Languages of Children*. Perhaps when your teenager was a child, you determined his/her primary love language and spoke it fluently for a number of years. Now you're wondering, "Has my child's love language changed?" The good news is that your child's primary love language did not change when he or she became a teenager. I know that some of you are saying, "But I'm doing the same thing I did when he was a child, and now he is not responding." I understand and I am going to address that reality in a moment. But first, let me affirm that the primary love language does not change when the child becomes a teenager.

Why Teens Seem to Change Their Primary Love Language

There are several reasons why parents sometimes assume that the primary love language has changed. *First, the teenager may be drawing back from the love language that earlier seemed to fill his/her love tank.* This resistance can be explained by the reasons we have just discussed: fluctuating moods, thoughts, and desires, emerging independence, and developing self-identity. In fact, the teen may temporarily draw back not only from his primary love language but from all expressions of love.

There is a second reason the teenager's primary love language may seem to have changed from that of his childhood. When a person is receiving enough of their primary love language, then *his secondary love language becomes more important.* Fifteen-year-old Jared is a toucher. His parents learned when he was ten that his primary love language was physical touch. Both of his parents found that language easy to speak so from childhood, they have spoken Jared's primary love language. Lately Jared has complained, "You know, I work hard around here but nobody ever appreciates it." Jared is asking for words of affirmation. This is not the first time his parents have heard this complaint. His parents are wondering if Jared's love language has changed. The reality is that for Jared, words of affirmation is his strong secondary love language. If his parents want to effectively meet Jared's need for emotional love, they must give Jared more words of affirmation while they continue to speak his primary love language: physical touch.

The third possibility is that parents misread the child's love language originally. This is not uncommon because parents tend to see their children through their own eyes rather than the child's eyes. It is easy to think that because our language is physical touch, that will be true of our child. We tend to believe what we want to believe rather than what is true from the child's perspective. As long as the parents expressed their love to the child in all five languages, the child may have received enough of his or her primary love language and the love tank may have stayed full. However in the teenage years because the parents felt rebuffed, they may have drawn back from speaking one or more of the languages while still focusing on what they believed to be the teenager's primary love language. In this case the teenager's primary love language has not changed. The problem was an incorrect diagnosis originally.

Time to Learn a New Dialect

Now what about the parent who said, "But, I'm doing the same thing I did when he was a child but now he is not responding?" This was the experience of Patsy. "I've known for a long time that Teddy's primary love language is words of affirmation. I've always verbally affirmed him but now that he's fourteen, he is saying to me, 'Mom, don't say that. Mom, stop saying that. Mom, I don't want to hear that.' It's very confusing to me," she said.

"Tell me some of the words of affirmation you give Teddy," I inquired of Patsy.

"I say things like, 'You are the greatest. I'm so proud of you. You are so smart. You are so good-looking.' Things I've always said."

Therein lies the problem. Patsy is speaking the same words she has always given her son. Seldom do teenagers want to continue hearing the same dialects as when they were children. Since these were the words they heard as children, they associate these words with childhood. They are trying to be independent and don't want to be treated as children.

Parents who want teenagers to feel loved must learn new dialects. I suggested that Patsy eliminate the dialects she had used through the years and come up with new verbal expressions of love, using more adult words, such as "I admire the strong stand you took for racial equality. . . . I appreciate your hard work on the lawn. . . . I trust you because I know you respect the rights of others." These statements express high regard for the teenager but don't have the ring of childishness. I also suggested that she might want to start calling him Ted instead of Teddy. She looked shocked and said, "You know, Teddy has been telling me the same thing. It's hard to call him Ted when I've called him Teddy all his life." I knew that Patsy had some hard work ahead of her, but I also was confident that she would make the changes.

Roger also demonstrated the need for learning new dialects when he told me about his son's new responses as a teenager. "For a long time, I've known that Brad's love language is acts of service," Roger said. "When he was younger, he would bring me his toys to fix. I think he believed that I could fix anything. When he walked away with a repaired toy or a homework assignment completed, I could tell he felt loved because of the twinkle in his eye. However, since Brad has become a teenager, I'm noticing that he is not asking for my help very much. The other day he was working on his bicycle. When I offered to help, he said, 'Thanks, Dad, but I can do it.' He seldom ever asks for my help with his homework anymore. I don't feel as close to him and I wonder if he feels close to me."

If Brad's love language is acts of service, he may not be feeling his father's love as much as he did earlier. However, it is obvious he does not want from Roger what he wanted as a child. He has learned to do things for himself, which feeds his emerging independence and maturing self-identity.

What Roger must learn is how to speak new dialects of acts of service. I suggested that he look for things that Brad does not yet know how to do and offer to teach him how. Obviously, Brad wants to do things for himself. This enhances his sense of maturity. If Roger offers to teach Brad how to clean a carburetor, how to replace spark plugs, how to realign brakes, how to build a bookcase or anything else in which Brad expresses interest, he will likely find that Brad is very open to receiving acts of service. His emotional closeness with Brad will be enhanced. And Brad will feel secure in the love of his father.

Learning new dialects may be difficult. All of us are creatures of habit. To continue to express love to our teenagers in the same ways we did when they were children is very natural. It seems comfortable to us. Learning new dialects means effort and time, but if we want our teenagers to feel loved, we must be willing to expend the energy to learn new dialects of their primary love language.

FINDING YOUR TEEN'S PRIMARY LOVE LANGUAGE

If this book is your first exposure to the love language concept—you didn't look for his primary love language when he was a child—and you haven't a clue to that love language now that he's a teenager, let me suggest three steps. First, ask questions; then make observations; and third, experiment. Here are approaches for each of these steps.

1. Ask questions.

If you wish to know what is going on inside the teenager's mind, one of the best ways to find out is to ask questions. "Forget that," one father said. "No matter what question I ask, I get one of three answers: 'I don't know'; 'OK'; or 'Whatever.' These three answers are used to explain anything, everything, and nothing." I understand the frustration of this father and it is true that teens sometimes *grunt* instead of talk, but the reality is that the only way to know for certain what a teenager is thinking and feeling is if the teenager chooses to reveal those thoughts and feelings.

Teenagers are more likely to reveal if they are asked questions. Not many teenagers initiate a conversation by saying, "Let me tell you my thoughts. Let me tell you my feelings." On the other hand, they are very likely to say, "Let me tell you what I want." Teens are much freer to share their desires than they are their thoughts and emotions. Often these are locked within the mind until the parent asks the right question.

In your effort to discover your teenager's primary love language, questions may be your greatest ally. Margo said to her fifteen-year-old daughter, Kerstin, "I've been reading some books on parenting. I realize that I'm not a perfect parent. My intentions have been good but sometimes I have done and said things that have hurt you. On the other hand, I'm not always certain that you feel I'm available to you when you need me. I want to ask you a serious question. From your perspective, what would make our relationship better?"

erstin's response was one that Margo will always remember.

n, if you really want to know, I'll tell you, but don't get mad at me. When I try to talk with you, I never feel like I have your full attention. You're always doing needlepoint, reading a book, working on the bills, watching TV, washing clothes, or doing something else.

"You are always doing something. I feel like I am bothering you when I try to talk. I wish that sometimes you could just sit down and talk with me without doing something else."

Margo asked for it and Margo got it. The answer to her question revealed Kerstin's primary love language—she was crying for *quality time*, undivided attention.

Margo's husband Mark asked a different question of their six-teen-year-old son, Will, but he found the same openness exhibited by Kerstin. One night while driving his son to an athletic event, Mark began, "Lately I have been thinking about some changes I need to make in my life. More specifically, I've been thinking about how I can be a better husband to your mother and a better father to you and Kerstin. I'd like to have your input, so I want to ask you this question. If you could change anything about me, what would you change?"

Will thought for what seemed like an eternity to Mark but eventually he said, "In a lot of ways you are a good dad. I appreciate your hard work and the things you give me. But sometimes I feel like I don't ever please you. No matter how hard I work, what I get is crit-icism from you. I know you want me to do my best, but when you constantly criticize me, I feel like giving up."

Fortunately, Mark was sincere in asking his question and he was in a listening mode. He responded, "What I hear you saying is that I give you too much criticism and often don't express appreciation for the hard work you do" to which Will responded, "Yeah. I don't mean that you shouldn't ever criticize me, Dad, but once in awhile it would be nice to know that I did something that pleased you." Inside Mark was reeling from Will's statements, so he said simply, "I appreci-ate your sharing that. I'm going to give some thought to it and I'm going to work on it." Then he reached over and patted Will on the back as they drove into the parking lot of the sports arena.

All that evening, the word *criticism* kept running through Mark's mind. He wasn't aware that he criticized Will that much. In fact, he didn't really see it as criticism. *Yes, I do correct Will,* he told himself. *I pointed out the spots Will missed when he washed the car. And I reminded him that the recycle bin needed to be taken to the street,* but criticism? Mark was carrying on a dialogue in his own mind while he and Will watched the game. *Yes, criticism. That's what Will hears, criticism. That he never pleases me; that what he does is never good enough.* Mark had almost forgotten that he had originally asked the question in hopes of discovering some clue to Will's love language.

All of a sudden, it dawned on him that Will had revealed his love language: words of affirmation. He wanted to be appreciated. *What I've done,* Mark told himself, *is to give him negative, critical words rather than positive, affirming words. No wonder I've sometimes felt that Will did not want to be with me.* Mark promised himself that he would talk to Margo and ask her to help him recognize times when he gave Will critical words and to help him learn how to affirm Will verbally. Mark felt a tear forming in his eye. He brushed it away and as the crowd around him roared, he turned to Will and said, "I love you, man. I really enjoy being with you."

Will hit his dad on the shoulder, smiled, and said, "Thanks, Dad." Then they both joined the roaring crowd.

With one question, Mark had discovered his teenager's primary love language.

There are other questions that parents can ask that may stimulate information from the teenager which will reveal the teen's love language. "Who would you say is your best friend?" When the teen says "Paul," then you ask. "What does Paul do that makes you feel he is your best friend?" Your teen responds, "He listens when I talk and tries to understand." Your teen has just revealed that quality time is his primary love language.

You might ask your daughter, "If you wanted to show your grandmother that you really loved her, how would you do it?" Such questions may reveal the teen's primary love language. They also create an atmosphere for further communication between parent and teen.

I do not suggest that you explain the five love languages to your teenager and ask her, "So what is your primary love language?" First of all, such a question may come across as a game you are playing with the teenager. Remember, the teen is looking for authenticity, sincerity. She is not into playing games. Second, if the teenager genuinely understands the love language concept, she may choose to use it as a means of manipulating your behavior. What parent has not heard a teenager say, "If you loved me, you would ..."? On rare occasions, what the teenager is requesting reveals his or her primary love language, but far more likely it is an effort to satisfy a momentary desire. Once granted by the parent, the teenager seldom feels loved. Almost any question is better than the question "What is your primary love language?"

2. Make observations.

Consciously *observe the behavior of your teenager.* Look for ways in which he expresses love or appreciation to others. Keep notes on what you observe. If you find that five times in the last month, your teenager has given a gift to someone else, there is a good chance that your teenager's love language is gifts. Most people have a tendency to speak their own love language. They do for others what they wish others would do for them. This is not always true, however. For example, sometimes a teenage son will give gifts as expressions of love because his father emphasized gift giving. He remembers his father's words, "Son, if you want to make a woman happy, give her flowers." So he gives gifts not because that is his own love language but because he has learned to speak that language from his father.

Observe also the complaints of the teenager. What a person complains about is a clue to his or her primary love language. This was seen earlier in Will's response to his father when he said, "But sometimes I feel like I don't ever please you. No matter how hard I work, what I get is criticism from you. I know you want me to do my best, but when you constantly criticize me, I feel like giving up." Will's complaints reveal that his love language is words of affirmation. He was complaining not only about his father's criticisms, but also that he seldom gives compliments.

Typically when teenagers complain, parents get defensive. The teenager says, "You have no right to go in my room and move my things around. Now I can't find anything. You don't respect my personal

128

property. It's not right." Many parents respond, "If you would clean your room, I wouldn't have to go in your room. But when you don't clean it, then I'm going to clean it." The conversation now moves to a full blown argument, or it is dropped and both walk away in silence.

However, if the parent would observe the complaints of the teenager, the parent may find that these complaints fall into a pattern. This is not the first time the teenager has complained about someone "moving my things." It may be that the primary love language of this teenager is gifts. Keep in mind that almost everything in a teenager's room was a gift. For this teenager, there is a special place for each gift and when someone moves the gift, it is like moving an expression of love.

It's important to look for patterns of complaints. When several of the complaints fall into the same category, they likely reveal the teenager's primary love language. Observe the following complaints. "You don't ever help me with my homework anymore. That's why I make poor grades. . . . If you would take me to the game, I could make some friends and wouldn't have to sit around the house all the time. . . . I couldn't clean behind the desk because you weren't here to help me move the desk. . . . If you would fix my bicycle, I could ride to school." This teenager's primary love language is probably acts of service. Each of the complaints is asking the parent to do something for the teenager.

Observe also the teenager's requests. What a person requests most often indicates her primary love language. Renee is saying to her mother, "Mom, can you and I go to the walking trail this afternoon? I want to show you some flowers I discovered down by the lake." Renee is requesting quality time. If she often requests activities which put her and her mother together alone, her love language is *quality time*. Similarly, when thirteen-year-old Peter asks, "Dad, when are we going on another camping trip?" or "When can we go fishing again?" or "Can we throw the ball now?" he is revealing that his primary love language is *quality time.*

If parents will observe how the teen expresses love and appreciation to others, what the teen most often complains about, and what the teen most often requests, chances are the parent can discover the teenager's primary love language.

3. Experiment.

A third way to discover a teenager's primary love language is to experiment by focusing on one of the five love languages each week and observing the teenager's response. Spend a week giving the teenager more *physical touches* than normal. Seek to touch them several times a day. The next week, draw back from touching and give them *words of affirmation*. Spend some time each day coming up with new expressions of affirmation that you will give your teenager that evening. The following week, seek to do as many *acts of service* as you can for your teenager, especially things you know the teenager would like for you to do. Fix a special meal, iron that hard-to-iron shirt. Give extra help on algebra. Wash the dog for your teenager (with a positive attitude). Do as many things as you can for your son or daughter.

The following week, make an effort to give the teen *quality time*. Take walks together, play ball with each other. Do with the teen those things he has requested. Spend as much time as you can doing things together. Have as many in-depth conversations as the teen will allow. Give the teen your focused attention.

The last week focus on *gifts*. From a list you have accumulated, purchase some of the key items your teenager has requested. Wrap them with colorful paper, present them to the teen in front of other family members. Make a big deal of it. Have a party every night.

During the week that you are speaking your teenager's primary love language, you will see a difference in your teen's countenance and attitude toward you. The love tank is being filled and the teenager is responding far more warmly to the parent than normal. The teenager is also probably wondering what has happened to you—why you are being so abnormal. You don't have to explain yourself fully. Just tell the teen you have been working at being a better parent.

Another experiment is to give the teen choices between two options and keep a record of their choices. For example, a father says to his thirteen-year-old son, "I have two hours free this afternoon. Would you like to fly your kite together or go to the store for batteries for your new camera?" The choice is between a gift and quality time. The father does what the son chooses and keeps a record as to whether he chose the gift or quality time. Three or four days later, the father gives the teenager another choice. "Since you and I are the only ones at home tonight, would you rather we eat out (quality time) or that I fix your favorite pizza (acts of service)?" Next week the father says. "If you were feeling discouraged and I wanted to make you feel better, which would you prefer? That I write you a note reminding you of all the positive things you have done or would you rather I give you a big bear hug?" The choice is between words of affirmation and physical touch.

As you keep a record of the teenager's choices, they will likely fall into a pattern which will reveal the teen's primary love language.

Once you have discovered your teenager's primary love language, you will want to learn as many dialects (different ways of speaking this language) as you can. And you will want to speak this love language regularly, keeping in mind that the teenager may sometimes draw back even from his primary love language. Respect the teenager's wishes. Never force expressions of love on an unwilling teenager. For example, if you know your teenager's primary love language is physical touch but when you put your arm on your teenager's back, he jerks away, that is not the time to try to give him a bear hug. That's the time to walk away and respect the fact that for the moment, the teenager does not want to be touched.

Try a different kind of touch the next day. When the teenager is in the mood for physical touch, pour it on. It's all right if you wind up wrestling on the floor so long as the teenager is interacting positively with you. If you speak the teenager's primary love language as often as you are allowed, the teenager's love tank will be full. But if you withdraw from physical touch because you don't like the awkwardness of being rebuffed, in time the teenager's love tank will empty and the teen will come to resent the parent. To effectively love a teenager, parents must speak the teen's primary love language regularly and in whatever dialects communicate love to the teenager.

SPEAKING *ALL* FIVE LANGUAGES

The Benefits to Your Teen

Let me emphasize what I said earlier. I am not suggesting that you speak only the primary love language of your teenager. Teenagers need to receive love in all five love languages, and teens need to learn to speak all five love languages. They learn best by seeing it modeled in the parents. What I am suggesting is strong doses of the teen's primary love language and speaking the other four as often as possible. If the teenager has a clear secondary love language, the parent will also want to give heavy doses of that language. As the parents speak all five love languages to the teenager, the teenager is learning how to speak those languages to others.

This is exceedingly important to the teen's future relationships. In the future, the teen will have neighbors, work associates, friends, dating partners, and most likely a spouse and later children to whom they will need to speak love and appreciation. If teenagers become fluent in speaking all five love languages, their relationships with people will be greatly enhanced. If, on the other hand they are limited to speaking only one or two of the love languages, their relationship potential will be diminished. There will be certain people with whom they will not connect emotionally. These people may be significant people, people with whom they would like to have a meaningful and lasting relationship. It should be clear that it is to the advantage of the teenager to learn to give and receive love in all five love languages. The teen who learns to speak the love languages fluently will have a decided advantage in all future relationships.

For the parent who has not learned to speak all five love languages, this may prove to be a formidable challenge. I suggest you read again the chapters on each of the five languages, especially those that are difficult for you to speak. Note the ideas on how to speak the particular language and practice speaking it not only to your teenager but to other family members as well. Eventually you can learn to speak each of the love languages. Few things are more rewarding than expressing love to others in a language that meets their need for emotional love.

The Benefits to Your Marriage

In their efforts to more effectively love teenagers, some couples have found their own marriage reborn. They have realized that for years they have failed to speak each other's primary love language. It is never too late to learn. Couples who have learned to speak each other's primary love language have seen the emotional climate of their marriage radically changed in a brief period of time.

One husband said, "Dr. Chapman, we have been married for thirty-three years. The last twenty-five years have been utterly miserable. A friend gave me a copy of your book, *The Five Love Languages.* When I read it, the lights came on. I realized that I had not spoken my wife's language and she had not spoken mine for all these years. I shared the book with her, we discussed it and agreed to begin speaking each other's primary language. If anyone had told me that our marriage could be turned around in two months, I would never have believed them. But within two months, I had warm feelings for her and she had warm feelings for me. Our marriage has been totally changed. We can't wait to share this with our married children."

Since love is our most basic emotional need, when that need is met by another person, we have warm emotional feelings toward that person. The emotional climate of marriage and family life *can* be greatly enhanced when members of the family learn and speak each other's primary love language.

chapter nine

LOVE AND ANGER: HELP FOR PARENTS

Teenagers get angry with parents, and parents get angry with teenagers. Sometimes both say and do things that hurt the other very deeply. Ambrose Bierce once said, "Speak when you are angry and you will make the best speech you will ever regret."

Most parents and teenagers have made a few of the kind of speeches that Bierce described. We wish we could pull the words back. We wish we could undo the painful action. Mismanaged anger is behind many of the broken relationships between parents and teens.

How does all of this relate to love? In the minds of most people, love and anger are antonyms—they just don't seem to go together. In reality, they are opposite sides of the same coin. Love seeks the good of the other person and so does rightly directed anger. We experience anger when we encounter what we perceive to be wrong behavior on the part of others. Parents get angry with teenagers when the teen does or says something which the parents consider to be irresponsible behavior. Teenagers get angry with parents when the parents' behavior is considered to be unfair or self-serving.

The purpose of anger is to motivate us to take loving action; that is, to do something to try to turn the teenager or parent in the right direction. Unfortunately, many of us have never learned how to take such loving action, and we end up taking destructive action. Sometimes in our response to anger we end up making the situation even worse. The purpose of this chapter is twofold: to help parents manage their own anger in a loving way and to give parents practical ways of teaching their teenager to handle anger positively.

THE NEED TO MANAGE OUR OWN ANGER

We are not likely to teach our teenagers what we have not learned ourselves. Many parents can identify with Marvin, an Idaho potato farmer, who once said to me, "I never experienced intense anger until I got married. And I never experienced superintense anger until I had teenagers." Though we experience anger in all arenas of life, some of our most intense anger is toward family members, and particularly teenagers.

Why Teens Anger Us

Why do we often experience more anger toward our teenagers than we do our younger children? Primarily because of the changes that are going on inside the teenager, which we have discussed in earlier chapters. The teen's increased intellectual abilities to reason and think critically about issues allow him to question our judgment in a way he did not do as a child. This intellectual growth is accompanied by the push toward independence and self-identity that may lead the teenager not only to question our judgment but to choose noncompliance. Not only is he thinking for himself, he is deciding for himself. This often puts the teenager in conflict with the parent and stimulates anger within the parent.

The parent sees the teenager's behavior as defiant, rebellious, or irresponsible. The parent reasons, *This is not good for my son [daughter]. He is going to wreck his own life. This is not a pattern I can allow to continue.* Anger motivates a father or mother to take action. Unfortunately, if the parent does not realize that he or she is now dealing with a teenager rather than a child, the parent's action may in fact make the situation worse.

136

Why We Must Break Our Negative Anger Responses

When the teenager does not readily comply to the parent's request that he change his course of action, the parent often resorts to cold, harsh commands. "You do it or else," the parent loudly proclaims. Not wanting to be a child, the teenager chooses "or else," and the battle between parent and teenager rises to another level. Before the battle is over, parent and teen are hurling harsh critical words at each other like enemy soldiers throwing grenades. Both leave the battlefield wounded, feeling rejected and unloved. The situation has become much worse because of misguided anger. Verbal explosions and physical abuse on the part of parents never produce positive results.

In thirty years of marriage and family counseling, I have often wept as teenagers have recounted the painful words and destructive behavior of parents whose anger was out of control. What is even more tragic is the many young adults who were abused as teenagers and now find themselves treating their own children in the same manner their parents treated them. I shall never forget seventeen-year-old Eric who said, "Dr. Chapman, I used to think that my father loved me but now I know that he doesn't. All he thinks about is himself. If I do everything he wants, the way he wants it done, then he's OK. But how can I ever grow up if I don't have the right to think and make decisions on my own? I sometimes wish he would die or I would die. Either way, the pain would be over."

Patterns of misguided anger are often passed from generation to generation. These patterns must be broken. I cannot tell you how strongly I feel about this issue. As parents, we must come to grips with our own anger and learn how to handle it in a responsible, positive way. Otherwise, we will jeopardize all our good efforts at parenting. The teenager who is verbally or physically abused by an angry parent will no longer remember the acts of service, words of affirmation, quality time, gifts, and physical touch that were received in childhood. All they will remember are the cutting words of rebuke and condemnation and the screaming voice of their parent. They feel no love, only painful rejection.

If you recognize such misguided anger in your own life, I urge you to read this chapter carefully and take the hard steps required to bring healing in the parent-teen relationship.

Negative patterns from the past *can* be broken. We need not be slaves forever to misguided anger. Any parent can change destructive patterns into loving actions if they are willing.

BREAKING OUR DESTRUCTIVE PATTERNS

Let me suggest the following steps in breaking destructive patterns and establishing loving patterns of anger management.

1. Admit the truth.

First of all, we must admit the truth. We will not change directions until we admit we are going in the wrong direction. Admit it to yourself, admit it to God, and admit it to family members. "I have mismanaged my anger. I have often been out of control. I have said and done things that are wrong. My words were not kind, they were not loving. They were destructive and hurtful. And with the help of God, I want to change." Don't hesitate to bring God into the process. You need all the help you can get.

Write the above words on a sheet of paper. Modify them if you wish to express it in your own words. Then read it out loud to yourself and acknowledge the painful truth . . . "I have mismanaged my anger." Then admit it to God and confess your wrong behavior and ask His forgiveness.

Then one evening when the family is all together, tell them there is something you need to share. Pull out your paper and read it to the family. Tell them that you have admitted this to yourself, you've admitted it to God, and now you are admitting it to them. Tell them that you sincerely want to change. You might wish to say something like the following. "Over the next few weeks, I am going to be working on this. But if I lose my temper with any of you and start to yell and scream, you will help me if you will put your hands over your ears, walk out of the room, and if you like, take a walk around the block. I assure you that by the time you return, I will be in control and I will not resume the harsh words. I will ask you to forgive me and we'll go on from there. It may take me a little time but with

God's help, I'm going to change." Once you make this humbling speech, you are on the road to positive change.

2. Develop a strategy.

Now you are ready for step two: Develop an effective strategy for breaking destructive patterns. You have admitted to yourself that what you have done in the past is not acceptable. Now, how will you break those negative patterns? You have already initiated one strategy when you asked your spouse or children to walk out of the room if you begin to "lose it." Each time this happens in the future, you are reminded to confess your failure. There is something humiliating about confessing failure. The very act of confessing motivates you to change the behavior in the future. But what can you do to head off your anger before you explode?

Listen to the success of Rueul. During a marriage conference his wife and he attended in Spokane, he told me about his struggle with anger and acknowledged that he had often "exploded and said hurtful things" to his wife and children. I gave him some practical ideas on how to "stop the flow" of angry words and how he might channel his anger in a more positive manner. Two years later, I saw Rueul at another marriage seminar, this time in Seattle. He said, "Dr. Chapman, I don't know if you remember me, but my wife and I met you in Spokane and I talked with you about my anger. I just want to tell you that your suggestions really worked and they are still working."

"Tell me about it," I said. "Well, you know the idea about counting to 100 before you say anything? I've been doing that," he said. "When I get angry, I start counting and I start walking as you suggested. I've walked in the rain, I've walked in the snow, and I've walked in the sunshine, counting aloud. If people heard me, they would probably think I was insane. But for me, it's one of the most sane things I ever did. What I was doing before was really insane. I was destroying my wife and children. The walking and counting gives me time to cool down and take a more positive approach to my anger."

Rueul had found a strategy for breaking his destructive patterns of verbal abuse. He was substituting a new strategy for his old destructive patterns. There are other strategies besides counting to 100. One man told me, "When I get angry, I get on my bicycle and start riding. I ride until I've cooled down. Sometimes I ride several miles." One lady said, "When I get angry at my husband I simply tell him, 'Excuse me. I've got to go to the park.' I get into the car, drive to the park, take a walk or sit on the bench until I've had time to cool off. My husband agrees that this is much better than what I used to do."

Here are two other strategies couples used. Brenda told me, "My husband and I have agreed that when we get angry with each other, we will call a 'time out,' and one of us will walk out of the room. We have agreed that within five hours, we will come back and ask for an opportunity to discuss the issue. If we get heated again, we will call time out a second time. We have agreed it is better to call time out than to verbally destroy each other." Meanwhile, when Brenda became angry with a family member, the first thing she did was to go water her flowers. "The first summer I tried this, I almost drowned my petunias, but that's better than drowning my family with angry words."

All of these people have found a strategy for replacing their destructive behavior with an activity which allows them time to cool off.

3. Analyze your anger and look at your options.

The third step is to analyze your anger and look at your options. You may still feel angry after you have counted to 100[1]—or even 500—but now you are calm enough to begin to ask questions about your anger. *Why am I angry? What wrong has the other person committed? Am I judging their behavior without having all the facts? Do I really know their motive? Has my teen misbehaved or am I being overly sensitive? Are my expectations too high for the developmental level of my teen?* (Sometimes parents get angry with teens who are simply being teens.)

Once you have had time to think about the situation, then you can decide what action would be constructive. Among your many options, only two represent positive responses to anger. One is to release the anger, realizing that it is your problem, not their problem. Your problem may be due to any of the following: "I got up with a bad attitude this morning. . . . I've been under a lot of stress lately. . . . I didn't get much sleep last night. . . . My fuse is short. . . . I didn't get my way so I got angry."

Whatever the reason, recognize the anger is *your* problem and release it. You may say aloud or to yourself, "My anger reveals my selfishness. Therefore, I choose to release my anger realizing that it is distorted. The family member has done me no wrong; I have simply been irritated by his (her) behavior." Sometimes it is helpful to state your conclusions to God in the form of a prayer. "Dear God, I realize that my anger is not valid. I have been self-centered and overly demanding of my family. Forgive me for my wrong attitude. I release my anger to you. Help me to be loving toward my family members. Amen." You have made the conscious decision to release your anger and you have confessed what you believe to be your own failures.

On the other hand, your anger may be valid. The family member may have wronged you. You have the "right" to be angry. You have counted to 500, you have taken your walk, you have analyzed your anger, and you know that this is an issue which you must discuss with the family member. You cannot simply overlook it. A wrong has been committed; you have been hurt and the issue must be resolved. So the second positive response is to address the issue by talking with the family member. Before you initiate a conversation with your spouse or teen, however, it is helpful to think about how you will approach the situation.

In my book *The Other Side of Love,* a practical, tear-off card in the back of the book gives the following wording for approaching the other person: "I'm feeling angry right now but don't worry, I'm not going to attack you. But I do need your help. Is this a good time to talk?" My suggestion is that the card be posted on the refrigerator door and that whenever the adult is ready to talk with his spouse or family member, he take the card from the door, stand in front of the family member and read the message. This is a way of explaining that you are angry, telling yourself and the family member that you are not going to explode but acknowledging the need to process the issue. If it is not a good time to talk, then you set a time to talk.

4. Engage the family member in conversation.

Step four is actually *engaging the family member in conversation.* It is laying the matter before the person so it can be discussed. You can print the above warning on your own 3 by 5 card and place it on your refrigerator. Then be sensitive in choosing the time that you pick up the 3 by 5 card and read its message to your family member. If the person is in the middle of watching a TV program or a sports event, that is probably not the time to seek to initiate a conversation. If your spouse is busy fixing a meal or vacuuming, I suggest you wait. Try to choose a time when the two of you can be alone, not in the presence of other family members. This may mean waiting a few hours for the appropriate time and place. If you insist, "We are going to talk about this now," you are sabotaging the conversation before you ever start.

Once you find the time and place, let me suggest that you say something like the following. "I want to share my feelings with you because I value our relationship. I know that I may have misunderstood or misinterpreted the situation. But I want to tell you what I saw and how I felt. Then I would like for you to tell me your perspective. Perhaps I've missed something and I need your help in understanding it."

As you present your concerns, be as specific as possible. Talk about what you heard, what you saw, how you interpreted it, what your feelings are, and why you are upset. Limit your presentation to this one event. Don't go back and share similar events from the past. To do so is to overwhelm the other person with a sense of condemnation. They are likely to fight back for self-preservation, and the conversation can become an argument. Most of us can handle one incident, but we are overwhelmed when all of our past failures are paraded before us.

After you have shared your concerns about this particular infraction, then say to the family member, "I think you hear my concerns. Again, I realize that I may be missing something or I may have misinterpreted something. So please tell me your perception of the situation." Such a statement makes it easier for the other person to be open and honest with you. As he shares his perspective, please refrain from "butting in." If he makes one statement and you jump in to say "That's not right," you are creating a battle rather than working for a peace treaty. When you call a family member a liar, you stimulate strong negative emotions inside the person. Rather, listen carefully to what he or she is saying. Use reflective questions that will develop further understanding, such as "Are you saying . . . ?" or, "What I hear you saying is . . . "You are trying to get the individual to share further, and you are indicating an effort to understand his or her thoughts and feelings about the matter.

If indeed you disagree with the other person's perception, then it is fine to say, "It appears that we see this very differently. I guess that's because we are two different people. What can we learn from this that will make things better for the both of us in the future?" Such an approach will likely lead to a positive solution. If, however, you insist that your perception is the right perception and that your family member is wrong, you have won and she has lost, but no solution has been reached. The distance between you is as great as ever.

On the other hand, if you insist on looking for a solution, and learning something positive from the experience, you both come away as winners. Your anger is processed and the results are positive. It is this kind of positive anger management that sets a model for teaching your teenager to handle anger.

TEACHING YOUR TEEN TO HANDLE ANGER

Love and Anger: Two Key Relationship Skills

Obviously we cannot wait until we are perfect in our anger management skills before we begin teaching our teenagers. In fact, some parents do not realize that they have a problem with anger until they see their own behavior mirrored in their teenagers. When you see your teens yelling and screaming at you in anger, the logical question is "Where did they learn this?" Chances are they are following the model of one of their parents. It is the frightening thought that "my teenagers might turn out to be like me" that motivates many parents to begin to change their own patterns of anger management. Often we must learn *with* our teenagers how to handle anger in a constructive way.

Two of the most important relationship skills a teenager can learn are how to express love and how to process anger. The two are not unrelated. If the teenager feels loved, then he has a much better opportunity of learning to handle anger in a positive way. However, if the teenager's love tank is empty, the teenager will almost certainly handle anger poorly. Thus, the importance of parents learning the primary love language of their teenager and speaking it regularly.

Unfortunately, a full love tank does not mean that the teenager will automatically know how to handle his anger. Positive anger management is a relationship skill that must be learned. Parents who love their teenagers are usually in the best position to teach the teenagers these skills. So what are the important elements a parent must know to be successful in this educational task?

Your Teen's Anger: Implosive or Explosive?

First and fundamentally, the parent must start where the teenager is. By the time a child reaches the teenage years, she has already developed methods of responding to anger. As one mother said to me recently, "Dr. Chapman, how do you get a teenager to talk about her anger? When my fifteen-year-old daughter gets mad, she clams up. When I ask her 'What's wrong?' she refuses to talk about it. I don't know how I can ever help her if she won't talk about it." Another mother said, "I have the opposite problem. When my teenage daughter gets angry, everyone knows it. She goes ballistic. She screams and yells and sometimes jumps up and down like a two-year-old having a tantrum." These mothers have witnessed the two ends of the continuum. Most teenagers lean toward one of these destructive approaches to anger: implosion or explosion.

I use the word *implosion* for the silent teenager because when anger is held inside and goes unprocessed, it will eat away at the inner spirit of the teenager. Remember, anger is stimulated when the teenager perceives that the parent or someone else has wronged him. This sense of being wronged, if it is not processed with the parent or the individual who wronged the teenager, often leads to feelings of resentment, loneliness, isolation, and ultimately depression. Implosive anger may also lead to passive-aggressive behavior. The teenager is passive on the outside, refuses to deal with anger, but expresses the growing resentment by becoming involved in behaviors that are sure to hurt the person at whom they are angry, often the parent, or themselves. Passive-aggressive behavior may involve such dissimilar things as loss of interest in school or sports, drug use, or becoming sexually active, all of which are aggressive expressions of anger toward the parent. Sometimes after months of depression, these teenagers who have held anger inside often erupt with violent behavior.

On the other hand, numerous teenagers have *explosive* patterns of handling anger. When the parent does or says something that the teen perceives to be wrong, the teen responds with loud, harsh, sometimes cursing words that express their displeasure at what the parent has done or failed to do. Some teens also throw bottles, break pens, drive cars at breakneck speed, "accidentally" drop dishes, run lawnmowers over water hoses, and in other physically destructive ways exhibit their anger. If these destructive patterns are not changed, these are the teenagers who will in a few years verbally and physically abuse their spouses and children.

Not all teenagers go to the extremes that we have described in the preceding two paragraphs, but virtually all teenagers lean toward one of these two directions: implosion or explosion. Few teenagers have yet learned to manage their anger in a more mature and productive way which we described earlier in the chapter. For some parents, the task of teaching their teenagers proper anger management is a formidable task. The first step is in recognizing the patterns that presently exist in your teenager. You are not likely to lead them to patterns of mature anger management until you first identify where they are. Thus, I suggest to parents that you observe your teenager when he is angry and keep a record of how he processes his anger toward you or toward others. Two months of observation will show you where your teenager is in the development of positive anger management skills.

This is the first step in the parents becoming a positive change agent for the teenager. Three other steps will help parents help their teens learn to manage their anger, as we will see in the next chapter.

NOTE

1. Counting to 100, 500, or even 1,000 can be an effective means of restraining an immediate and uncontrolled anger response. For suggestions on how this can work, see Gary Chapman, *The Other Side of Love* (Chicago: Moody, 1999), 38.

chapter ten

LOVE AND ANGER:
HELP FOR OUR TEENS

Tom approached me after I had given a lecture on anger. I noticed the tears in his eyes as he said, "I have failed. I realized tonight for the first time that I have caused my daughter to withdraw in silence. Earlier when she would get angry with me, I would tell her how stupid she was. I would tell her she needed to grow up, that she shouldn't be so sensitive. I realize now that I pushed her away. For the past six months, she has shared almost nothing with me."

How do we help our teen when she has imploded with her anger—completely withdrawn and wants no communication with us? Once we recognize where our child is in her anger, whether holding it in (implosion) or spewing it out (explosion), we can help her. This chapter looks at the ongoing steps in helping your teen develop skills for positive anger management.

THE HARD WORK OF LISTENING

Once you have identified your child's faulty method for dealing with anger, you should take the next step in helping her to learn healthy skills in anger management. The second step is parents must do the *hard work* of listening to angry teenagers. I emphasize the words *hard work* because I can assure you this will not be easy.

We'll address the issue of the implosive (withdrawn) teenager shortly; in some ways that's the greater challenge. Let's begin with listening to the explosive teenager. This is the one with which I have the most personal parental experience. Our son was an *exploder.*

Listening to Fierce, Exploding Words

I am a marriage and family counselor. I have been trained to listen, but I assure you it was not an easy task to listen to the angry expressions coming from the mouth of my son. The "hard work " of listening may make it sound too easy. It was in reality a colossal task listening to my explosive teen. Yet I was convinced that the only way to have a positive influence on an angry teenager was to hear his concerns no matter how harshly they were delivered. The poem found at the end of this chapter, written by our son many years later, assured me that my listening was not in vain.

I still believe we must hear our teenagers' concerns no matter how harsh they sound. Why is listening to the teenager's expressions of anger so important? Because the anger cannot be processed unless the concerns that stimulated the anger are addressed. Parents cannot address these concerns until they have first heard them. Let's begin at the beginning. Why is the teenager angry? Because something happened that the teenager perceived to be unfair, stupid, or inhumane. Granted, the teenager's perception may be distorted, but in the teenager's mind, a wrong has been committed. (The teenager gets angry for the same reason the adult gets angry: a perceived wrong.) Thus when a teenager who is angry is expressing that anger verbally —even if the teen is yelling—the parents should be thankful. Because if they will listen, there is a good chance they will learn what is going on in the mind and spirit of the teenager. This information is essential if parents are to help the teenager process anger.

The parent must discover why the teenager is angry—what wrong the teenager perceives to have happened, what injustice the parent has perpetrated, in the teen's sight; indeed, what act of treason the parent has committed. If the parent does not discover this important information and resolve the matter with the teenager, the teenager's anger will be stored inside, and the explosive words will have been spoken in vain. If, on the other hand the parent hears the teenager's concerns and gets to the root issue, then the parent can have an intelligent response.

Losing Our Cool

The difficulty is that most of us as parents of teenagers respond negatively to our teen's explosive words before we ever hear their concerns. We get angry at the way our teenager is talking to us and often "lose our cool" by yelling at them. The parent says, "Shut up and go to your room. You are not going to talk to me like that." In so doing, the parent has stopped the flow of communication and eliminated the possibility of discovering the source of the teenager's anger. The household may get quiet, but anger is brewing inside both parent and teenager—anger that will not go away until it is processed further.

This is what I call "bottling" the teenager's anger. It is like putting a cap on the bottled-up anger inside the teenager. The teenager is now double angry. He is angry about his original concern but he is also angry about the way the parent treated him. The parent has compounded the problem rather than teaching the teenager how to handle anger positively.

The wise parent will focus on what the teen is saying, not the manner in which he is saying it. What is important at the moment is discovering the source of the teenager's anger. The teenager is the only one who can give you this information. If the teen is yelling at you, he is trying to tell you something. The wise parent will shift into the listening mode. I suggest that you reach for paper and pen and begin to record what you hear the teenager saying. This will help you direct your attention to the message being delivered rather than the manner in which it is delivered. Write down what you hear the teenager saying. What is it that the teen believes to be unfair? Don't defend yourself. This is not the time to fight; this is the time to listen. Negotiation or fighting may come later, but now we are gathering secret information which is absolutely necessary in order to reach a peace agreement with our teenagers.

MOVING TO ROUND TWO OF LISTENING

When the teenager finishes the initial explosion of angry words, share with the teen what you think you have heard him say and let him clarify. You might say, "What I think I hear you saying is that you are angry because I . . . Is that what you are saying?" Such a statement indicates to the teenager that you are listening and that you want to hear more. The teenager will inevitably oblige and give you more. It may be with the same intensity or the intensity may be somewhat reduced, but your teen will continue to share with you why he is so upset.

Continue to write what you are hearing. Refuse the temptation to defend yourself. Remind yourself that you are in Round two of listening.

When the teen subsides, again repeat what you think they are saying and give him another opportunity to make sure you are getting the full message. After the third round of listening, the teenager will sense that you have taken him seriously. The teenager will be shocked by the fact that you have taken notes and are intently giving them your attention. When the teenager senses that you have genuinely heard his concerns, then and only then are you ready to move to the third step. I cannot overemphasize the importance of listening intently to your teenager when he or she is angry.

DEALING WITH THE SILENT TEEN

What if your teen's anger is implosive rather than explosive? In some ways, the silent teenager is even more difficult to help. His refusal to share the things which concern him, the issues that stimulated his anger, renders the parent powerless. That is, the parent cannot respond to what is going on inside the teenager's mind until he or she has learned the teenager's thoughts and feelings. In some cases, this is why the teenager is using the silent treatment.

Silence and Power

When the parent is extremely controlling of the teenager's life, making all decisions for him, the teenager feels powerless. The teen is unable to develop independence and self-identity, and he believes silence is the only way to gain the upper hand with his parents. With silence, the teenager is in control, at least for the moment. He has something the parent wants and he refuses to give it.

When the parent panics and woefully moans to the other parent or other concerned adults that the teenager will not talk or when the parent verbally explodes and says loudly, "I can't help you if you don't tell me what's wrong," the teenager is winning the battle. That is precisely what the teen wants: to be out of your control. He is tired of your parental control; he wants to be independent. At the moment, silence is one way he can establish this independence.

Thus parents of silent teenagers need to ask the hard questions: Am I being overly controlling of my teen? Am I giving her enough freedom to think and make some decisions for herself? Am I allowing her to be a teenager or am I treating her as a child? For the overly controlling parent, the best approach is to communicate the following message: "I know that sometimes I get too involved in your life. I know that you are a teenager now and may not want to share all of your thoughts and feelings with me, and that's all right. But when you do want to talk, I want you to know that I am available. I am willing to listen when you want to talk." Then give the teen an expression of love, using the teenager's primary love language. Such a statement, accompanied by an expression of love, creates an atmosphere where the teen feels a sense of recognition. If the parent will maintain this position, I can almost guarantee you the teenager will begin to open up when he or she is angry with the parent.

Another reason why some teens choose silence when they are angry is that they have learned from experience when they share their anger with the parent, the parent will explode. These teens, tired of past explosions, choose to be silent rather than face the tirade of the parents' condemning words. The teens have felt embarrassed, shamed, condemned by the parents' words. They do not wish to go through that again. The easier approach is to clam up and refuse to share why they are angry.

The parents of such teenagers will never be able to drag the words out of their teens. Their efforts will be considered nagging and will push the teenager further into silence. What the parent must do is to confess their own past failures. Tearing down the wall of negative behavior is the first step in creating an atmosphere where the teenager will again share his/her anger.

A Time to Confess

That's what Tom decided to do. He went beyond his tears of regret to take some humbling yet healing action in front of his daughter, Tracy. After admitting to me, "I have failed," he told me his plan. "I'm going home tonight and confess my failures to her. Maybe she will give me another chance." He asked me to help him work out a confession statement so that he would not be guided totally by his emotions.

Here is the statement we came up with. Something like this could help any parent who is trying to end the silent treatment and is willing to confess his own responsibility.

"Tracy, have you got a few minutes that I could share something with you that is really important to me? If this is not a convenient time, I'd be willing to wait." Once Tracy gave permission, Tom would proceed. "I went to a meeting the other night where the speaker was discussing anger. And I realized that I have done you a disservice in the past. When you have come to me with your concerns, I have often been very insensitive and have cut you off. I remember specifically the times I told you that you were stupid and needed to grow up and not be so sensitive. I realize now that was very immature on my part. You were the mature one when you shared your concerns with me, and I'm sorry for the way I made you feel.

"I want you to know that when you are angry with me in the future, I want to be a listener. I will try to hear your concerns and respond in a positive way. I know sometimes you have gotten upset with me and I am certain that will happen in the future. If you'll tell me why you are upset, I will try to listen. I will try to respect your feelings and we can deal with the issue. OK?"

I told Tom that his daughter may not have any verbal response to his speech. I encouraged him not to pressure her to talk at that moment. But I asked him to give her an expression of love, using her primary love language. The step Tom took that night with his daughter was the first step in restoring the possibility of his daughter sharing her anger with him.

When teenagers realize that it is safe to share anger with their parents, they will do so. But when they feel threatened, intimidated, put down, shamed, or ill-treated, many teens will choose the route of silent withdrawal. The objective of the parent of a silent teenager is to create an emotional atmosphere where the teenager feels free to share anger. When the silent teenager begins to talk again, the parent must do the hard work of listening which we discussed above.

AFFIRMING THAT THEIR
ANGRY FEELINGS ARE VALID

Step three in teaching your teenagers a positive response to anger —after you've identified your teen's faulty method for dealing with anger and listened intently to the teen's expressions of anger—is to affirm the validity of the anger. I can hear some parents thinking, "Wait a minute. Often I don't believe my teen's anger is valid. I think they have misunderstood my actions. Sometimes they don't even have the facts straight. How can I affirm their anger when I don't agree with their perception?"

I'm glad you asked, because this is where many parents make a serious mistake. They confuse facts with feelings. The result is that parents get in arguments with teenagers about the facts, and the feelings get ignored. If the argument gets heated, it stimulates even more feelings which are also ignored.

Ignored feelings do not build positive relationships between parents and teenagers. That is why step three is so important. If you don't understand how to affirm the angry feelings of your teenager, you will never teach your teenager to handle anger positively. Get a cup of coffee or do whatever you have to do to be fully alert because what I am about to say is *extremely* important.

When you are angry, it is because you believe a wrong has been committed. Otherwise, you would not be angry. Granted, your perception of the situation may not be correct, but if I don't affirm your right to be angry, then you are not likely to be open to my presentation of the facts as I see them. It is my affirmation of your right to be angry that creates the emotional climate where you can hear my perception.

One of the best ways to be able to genuinely affirm another person's emotions is commonly called *empathy,* putting yourself in the shoes of the other person and trying to see the world through his eyes. For the parent, this means becoming a teenager for a moment, remembering the insecurities, the mood shifts, the desire for independence and self-identity, the importance of being accepted by peers, and the desperate need for love and understanding from parents. The parent who does not seek to have empathy with his teen will have difficulty affirming the teenager's feelings of anger.

Curtis demonstrated the power of empathy when he said to me, "it's amazing what happened when I tried empathy. My daughter was angry with me because I had taken her driving privileges away for a week. She was yelling at me about how unfair it was and how embarrassed she was going to be to tell her friends that she couldn't drive them to school this week because her father had impounded her car. In the past, I would have argued with her and told her that she should be glad that I took it away for only one week. I would have told her that her friends could get another ride and that she deserved to feel embarrassed. This would have created more anger in her. She would have yelled nasty things at me. I would have said a few more words to her, then walked out of the room and left her crying. That's happened more times than I want to admit. But having listened to your lecture on empathy, I put myself in her shoes and remembered how hard it was to lose driving privileges for a week.

"I didn't have a car when I was her age but I remember the time my father took my driver's license for two weeks and wouldn't let me drive the family car. I remembered how embarrassed I felt. It's amazing when I tried to see the world through her eyes, I could understand her emotions," Curtis continued. "So I said to her, 'Sweetheart, I understand why you are angry with me. And I can understand how it will be embarrassing to you not to be able to drive your friends to school. If I were a teenager, and I was once, I would be angry and embarrassed also. But let me tell you where I am as a parent.

"'We agreed that if you got a speeding ticket, you would lose your driving privileges for a week the first time. And if it happened the second time within a year, you would lose your license for two weeks. Now, you knew the rules; we all agreed on the consequences. If I didn't hold you to the consequences, I would be a poor parent because the reality of life is that when we break the rules, we have to suffer the consequences. I love you so much and that is why I have to enforce the rules even though I am very sympathetic with what you are feeling right now.'

"I gave her a hug and walked out of the room," Curtis said with tears in his eyes. "But for the first time, I felt I had handled my daughter's anger in a positive way."

Such an empathetic statement by a parent does not remove the teenager's feelings of embarrassment, but it does take the edge off of the teenager's anger. When the parent identifies with the teenager's anger and affirms it as being OK rather than arguing with the teenager, the teen's anger subsides because she has been treated with dignity and not ridicule. It will be apparent that step two, listening to the teenager, is a prerequisite to step three, affirming the teenager's anger. Parents cannot honestly empathize with the teen's anger if they have not heard the teen's perception of the situation.

Marie's teenage daughter was angry with her because she would not buy her another outfit that she "needed." It was the third such "needed purchase" her daughter had requested in as many weeks; Mom had already bought the first two. But not this time; the budget simply would not allow it, Marie explained. When her daughter poured forth her angry words, accusing her mother of not loving her, instead of following her normal pattern of retaliation, Marie listened to her daughter. She took her notepad and wrote down the key concerns her daughter expressed. Then, rather than arguing with these concerns, she said to Nicole, "I think I understand and I can see why you could be so angry with me. If I were in your position, I would probably be angry with my mother also." Such an empathetic statement would not have been possible if Marie had not first listened to Nicole's concerns. Listening creates the possibility of empathy.

EXPLAINING YOUR PERSPECTIVE AND SEEKING RESOLUTION

When the teenager has been thoroughly heard and then receives an empathetic statement regarding his anger and other feelings, you can more readily take the final step in processing anger: Explain your perspective and seek resolution.

Now and only now is the parent ready to share his or her perspective with the teenager. If the parent does this before following the first three steps, the results may be an extended argument with the teenager that will typically end with harsh, cutting words that the parent will later regret. If you have listened carefully, and affirmed the teenager's anger, then the teenager will listen to your perspective. Your teen may not agree with you, but he will hear you and the issue can be resolved.

In Marie's situation, having expressed understanding and affirmation of Nicole's feelings, Marie said, "If I had unlimited resources I would buy you the outfit. But I don't. The fact is that in the last two weeks, I bought you two outfits which you also wanted. There are always limits to what we can buy and we have reached our limit." Nicole may not be happy with her decision. She may still choose to be angry, but in her heart, the teenager knows that her mother is right. Because her mother has listened to her carefully and affirmed her feelings, the teenager will not be sitting around with bitterness toward her mother. However, suppose that when Nicole asked for the outfit Marie would have exploded with, "I'm not getting you another outfit. I've bought you two outfits in the last two weeks; that's enough. You think you have to have everything. I can't believe how self-centered you are. Don't you know the rest of the family needs clothes also?" Nicole would have felt rejected by such a response, and almost certainly she would have held bitterness in her heart toward her mother.

When Your Teen Is Right (It does happen.)

Sometimes when parents have listened to the teenager's concerns, they realize that the teenager is right. Mary Beth said, "I will never forget the day my daughter Christy got angry with me because I went into her room and cleaned up her desk. She told me in no uncertain words that she was angry with me, that I had violated her space, that I had no right to go into her room and mess with the things on her desk, that I had thrown away some things that were very important to her, and that if I ever did that again, she would leave home. That's when I realized how deeply I had hurt her and how strongly she felt about the matter. I could have argued that I had the right to go into her room and do anything that I wanted to do. I could have argued that if she had straightened up her own desk, I wouldn't have to do it for her. But instead I listened to her.

"I think that was the day that I realized for the first time that my seventeen-year-old daughter was becoming a young adult, that I could not treat her as a child any longer. So I said to her, 'I am sorry. I realize now that what I did was wrong. At the time I was just trying to get the desk clean but I understand what you are saying and I realize that I had no right to throw away some of your things. In fact, I had no right to clean your desk. If you will forgive me, I promise I will not do that again.' I think that was the day I started relating to my daughter as a young emerging adult."

Because parents are not perfect, we often make mistakes, which in turn stimulate anger in our teenagers. If we will listen to the teenager and be honest, we will recognize our wrong behavior. Confession and requesting forgiveness always form the most positive approach when we realize we have wronged our teenager. Most teens will forgive if parents make a sincere apology.

On the other hand, often the parent will have a totally different perspective from that of the teenager. This perspective needs to be shared openly and freely in a kind but firm manner. John listened carefully as his son Jacob poured out his anger toward his father. Jacob was angry that his father would not loan him the money to pay for his car insurance. When Jacob turned sixteen, John had bought him a car with the understanding that Jacob would pay for gas, oil, and insurance. That was a year and one-half ago. The insurance payment was due every six months. Jacob made the first two payments without any problem, but now he was short on cash and felt that his father should loan him the money so that he could continue to drive the car. Jacob knew that his father had plenty of money; it would not be a problem for him to make the loan.

John listened to Jacob carefully, making notes as Jacob talked. Then John responded. "So you think that I should make the loan because I have plenty of money and it wouldn't hurt me to do so?"

"That's right," Jacob said. "It's a little thing for you; it's a big thing for me. And if you don't loan me the money, I can't drive the car for at least two weeks."

John listened again as Jacob explained his thoughts. Then John said, "I can understand why you would want me to do this. I know it will be very inconvenient for you not to drive your car for two weeks. But let me tell you where I'm coming from. As a parent, my responsibility is to help you understand how to manage money. We agreed at the very beginning that you would pay the gas, oil, and insurance. You have known for six months that the insurance payment was coming due. Instead of saving the money, you spent it. That was your choice. That's fine. I'm not complaining about how you spent the money. But since you made that choice, you don't have enough money to pay the insurance.

"I think I would be doing you a disservice to bail you out," Jacob's father continued. "I think this is a strong lesson for you on learning to handle money. During the next two weeks, I am willing to loan you my car when I can, I will drive you places when I cannot loan it to you. But I'm not going to loan you the money for your insurance. I think I would be failing you as a parent if I did that. Do you understand what I'm saying?"

Jacob dropped his head and mumbled, "I guess so." Jacob wasn't happy but he understood what his father was saying. He was willing to accept it because his father had listened carefully, affirmed his concerns, and expressed understanding.

Our goal is always to help our teenagers work through their anger to the point of resolution. Unresolved anger in the heart and mind of the teenager is one of the worst things that can happen. Unresolved anger breeds feelings of bitterness and resentment. The teenager feels rejected and unloved. The teen's unresolved anger makes it almost impossible to receive expressions of love from the parent. Many parents are frustrated by the teenager's refusal to accept parental love so they try harder, only to be further rebuffed. If the parent is going to successfully communicate love to the teenager, the parent must seek to deal with the teenager's unresolved anger. If the teenager's anger has been stored over a period of time, the parent will have to create a climate where the teenager is free to share the issues about which he is angry.

Acknowledging past failures may be a part of creating this environment. For instance, you might say, "I realize that in the past, I have not always listened to you when you were angry with me. Sometimes I have said very hurtful and critical things which I deeply regret. I know that I have not been a perfect parent, and I would very much like to deal with my failures. If you would be willing, I would like for us to have a conversation sometime in which you can honestly share with me where I have hurt you. I know that such a conversation may be painful for you and for me, but I want you to know that I am willing to listen."

Statements like these open the door to the possibility of the teenager revealing stored anger and giving the parent a chance to process the issues. If the teenager does not eventually respond to such parental overtures, perhaps professional counseling will be required. If the teenager is not willing to go for counseling, the parents can show their own sincerity by going for counseling themselves. Eventually the teen may be willing to join them in the counseling process.

Teaching your teenager to accept anger and process it in a positive way is one of the greatest contributions you will ever make to the emotional, social, and spiritual life of your teenager. The teen learns to process anger by experience. We start where the teenager is and help our son or daughter process anger even if it involves listening to the teen's initial screams. Later, we can teach better methods of communicating anger. But we must never allow the teen's language to keep us from listening to the teen's message.

The poem on the next page was written to me when my son was in his twenties. It's one reason why I am a believer in the healing power of listening to teenage anger.

DAD

You listened way past dark.
This is what you gave to me.
You had ears to hear
the exploding symphony of my youth—
Knife words, scissor syllables slicing thin air.
The others left.
You stayed
and listened.

When I blew holes in the ceiling—shotgun screams
rapid firing flames
ripping angels' wings open,
you waited,
mended the wings,
and we continued somehow.
To the next day
The next meal
The next bomb.

And when they all ran for cover
　　　For shelter
　　　For protection
you stayed out on the battlefield
exposed to fire from all sides.
You risked your life
When you had me.
You risked your life listening
Way past dark.

Derek Chapman
December, 1993

chapter eleven

LOVE AND INDEPENDENCE

Matt and Lori had requested a consultation with their family physician at which they poured out their concerns about their thirteen-year-old son, Sean. "His personality has changed," began Matt. "He is so unpredictable." "He has never been rebellious," added Lori, "but now he questions almost everything we say. And his language has changed. Half the time we don't know what he's really saying. A couple of weeks ago, he cursed me. Sean has never cursed."

"We're afraid that Sean has some neurological problem," Matt said. "Like maybe a brain tumor," Lori added. "We wondered if you would examine him and let us know what you think."

Their doctor agreed, and two weeks later Sean came in for an examination. After a thorough physical exam, including a CAT scan, the physician informed Matt and Lori that Sean was a perfectly normal teenager. There were no neurological problems. What they were experiencing were actually signs of normal adolescent development. Matt and Lori were both relieved and confused. Relieved that there was no physical problem but confused as to how they should respond to this frightening stage of Sean's development. They knew they could not ignore his behavior.

Matt and Lori were experiencing the normal trauma of parents whose children suddenly become teenagers. The apple cart seems to have turned upside down. What worked before suddenly no longer works and the child they thought they knew so well has suddenly become a stranger.

We have been talking about the teenager's emerging independence and desire for self-identity. But in this chapter, we want to focus on the changes that typically occur during this period of the teen's development. When parents know the ways that their teen's independence and quest for self-identity manifest themselves, they can learn better ways to affirm their teens and show love. And, yes, they will be able to more effectively speak their teen's love language.

TWO PERIODS OF CONFLICT

Do you know the two periods in which parents often have heightened conflict with their children? Researchers say the first occurs during what is typically called the "terrible twos," the second around the time of puberty. These two periods are tied together by one common thread: independence. During those terrible twos, the child is struggling to demonstrate physical independence from the parents. Little legs take them places their parents cannot see, and little hands do things that greatly frustrate parents. What parent does not have stories about trees painted on wallpaper with mother's lipstick, powder dumped on the bedroom carpet, drawers opened and rummaged, and on and on.

Jump from that toddler year to the onset of puberty, the second stage of heightened parent-child conflict. These conflicts still revolve around independence. Of course, the teenager is at a greatly advanced stage of life, so the messes he makes and the rules he breaks are of much greater consequence as is the intensity of the parent-teen conflict. In other words, parents can expect an increase in confrontations when their teen reaches early adolescence. According to experts Steinberg and Levine, the good news is "confrontations between parent and child usually peak in the eighth or ninth grade, then decline."[1]

At both of these frustrating stages of the child's development, it is helpful if the parent knows what to expect and has some strategy for responding in a positive manner. Our concern here, of course, is with the second stage, during the early teen years.

THE NEED FOR INDEPENDENCE . . . AND LOVE

First, let's look at some of the common behavioral patterns you can expect. The teenager's need to be independent will be expressed on many fronts. Along with this need for independence, the teenager continues to need parental love. Often, however, the parent interprets the teenager's move toward independence as an indication that he no longer wants parental affection. This is a serious mistake.

Our goal is to encourage the teenager's independence while at the same time meeting the teen's need for love. The behavioral characteristics which accompany the teen's search for independence normally cluster around the following areas.

THE DESIRE FOR PERSONAL SPACE

The teenager wants to be a part of the family but at the same time wants to be independent from the family. This often expresses itself in the need for personal physical space. Teenagers may not want to be seen in public with their parents. This is especially true if they think they will run into their friends. The reason is not that they don't want to be with you, but rather that they want to look older and more independent. "Drop me off in the parking lot and I will meet you at the car in two hours." These are the words of a teenager who does not want to be seen in the shopping mall with the parent.

The mother who thought she was going shopping with her teenager may be greatly upset by the teenager's attitude. But if she understands the teenager's need to be independent, Mom will respect this request and express love to the teenager, using the teen's primary love language as they leave the car. The teen will feel both loved and independent. The parent who expresses hurt or anger at the teenager's request will probably precipitate a verbal battle with the teenager, and the teenager will walk away feeling both controlled and unloved.

Allowing the teen to sit with friends rather than family at the theater or church, if accompanied by an expression of love, is a way of both affirming independence and meeting the teen's need for love. Occasionally allowing the teenager to remain at home or to eat dinner with a friend while the rest of the family goes to a restaurant serves the same purpose.

Their Own Room

Teenagers often request their own room. They may have been content to sleep in a room with a younger sibling for the first twelve years of their lives, but be assured that in the teenage years if there is any possible way, teenagers will seek their own space. They are willing to move to the attic or the basement; they will even choose the end of a hallway underneath the stairs—anywhere to have their own place. Parents often find these requests frustrating. What the teenager is asking doesn't seem reasonable to the parent. Why would they want to sleep in a damp basement when they have a perfectly nice room with a younger sibling? The answer lies in the need to be independent.

I suggest that if at all possible, parents seek to comply with the teen's request. Once the space is provided, the teen will want to decorate it in keeping with her own taste. (This is when the parent will be glad that the teenager's space is in the basement!) The teenager is sure to choose colors, forms, and fabrics that you would not have chosen. The reason again is independence.

Providing private space and the freedom to decorate it as the teen desires, if accompanied by meaningful expressions of love by the parent, will foster the teen's independence and keep the teenager's emotional love tank full. However if the granting of private space and the freedom to decorate it as one chooses comes on the heels of weeks of arguments about the stupidity of doing so, the teenager loses self-esteem, and an emotional wall is erected between the teenager and the parent even when the parent finally acquiesces to the teen's request.

Their Own Car

Teenagers will want their own wheels. In our affluent Western culture, most teenagers will want to have their own car as soon as they are able to obtain a driver's license. Again the push is for independence. "If I have my own car, I can drive myself to school, to swim meets, to church activities, and to the mall. It will save you all kinds of time." (Most parents find this appealing.) Few things infuse teenagers with a greater sense of independence and power than driving off in their own car. In the next chapter, we will revisit the car issue as it relates to the whole matter of teenage responsibility that goes with freedom. We will discuss the matter of who pays for the car and what are responsible expectations for the teenage driver. At the moment, however, we are talking about fostering the teenager's need to be independent while at the same time communicating love.

Assuming the parent is financially able and the teenager is reasonably responsible, this is an area where the parent can express trust and confidence in the teenager while at the same time fostering independence. Remember, gift giving is one of the five love languages. Even if it is not your teenager's primary love language, make much of the gift you are giving when you make it possible for the teenager to have a car. If the teenager can drive away feeling loved, trusted, and independent, the parent has helped him take another step toward adulthood.

THE DESIRE FOR EMOTIONAL SPACE

Teenagers need emotional space. In the earlier years, your child may have told you everything—what happened at school, the dream they had last night, how difficult her homework is, etc., but in the teenage years, you may feel shut out. When you ask the teen what happened at school, she may respond, "Nothing," or "Same old stuff." When you ask your teenage daughter about one of her friends, she may accuse you of prying. This doesn't mean that she is covering up misbehavior. One way teenagers establish emotional independence is by keeping their thoughts and feelings to themselves. Parents should respect this desire on the part of teenagers. After all, do you share all of your thoughts and feelings with your teenager? I hope not.

A part of what it means to be an adult is that we choose when and what to share with others. Your teenager is in the process of becoming an adult. "I know that sometimes you don't want to share your thoughts and feelings with me. I understand and that's fine. But if you do want to talk, I want you to know I'm always available." Those are the words of a wise parent who has learned the value of giving the teenager emotional space.

Another way in which teenagers express their need for emotional space is to withdraw from expressions of love they formerly received. Don't be surprised when your teenage daughter rejects your efforts to help her do something. For years, your acts of service were taken as an expression of love. Now she wants to do it for herself, and she may do it in a way very different from the way you have done it. Sometimes it is not because the teenager does not need your help, it is because she does not want to be reminded that she needs your help. She wants to be independent. Rather than pressing the issue, the wise parent will back off and say, "If you need my help, let me know." Such words spoken along with a meaningful expression of love leave the teenage daughter or son feeling independent, loved, and creates an atmosphere where your growing child may indeed request your help.

Your thirteen-year-old daughter may pull herself away from your hugs not because she does not want physical touch, but because this is what you did when she was a child. She is now on the way to adulthood and doesn't want to be treated as a child. The wise parent will find new ways of expressing physical touch that the teenager will welcome.

When you give your teen instructions on how to respond to a relative who is to visit tomorrow, be prepared for him to do exactly the opposite of what you have requested. Such requests often seem childish and phony to the teenager. When you give the teenager words of affirmation, make sure your words are sincere. If the teenager senses that you are trying to manipulate his own feelings by giving kind words, he will reject your words as insincere.

Behind all of this is our teenagers' desire for emotional space. They want to be loved but they don't want to be smothered as if they're children. This is where learning new dialects of the love languages becomes so important in communicating love to your teenager.

THE DESIRE FOR SOCIAL INDEPENDENCE

Choosing Friends over Family

Not only does the teenager want physical and emotional space, the teenager also desires social independence from parents. This desire for social independence is expressed in numerous venues. *Teenagers often choose friends over family.* The family has always done things as a family. Now the teenager doesn't want to go with the family. You have planned a picnic for Saturday afternoon. On Thursday evening, you tell the children your plans, and the teenager says, "Count me out."

"What do you mean, 'Count you out?'" you reply as a dad. "You are part of the family."

"I know, but I have plans already," the teen responds. "I'm going somewhere with my friends."

"Then tell them there's been a change in plans," Dad says. "This is a family outing and it is important that you be there."

"But I don't want to be there," the teenager says. This is the first round of what will become a major battle if the parent doesn't quickly realize that he is dealing with a teenager, not a child.

Parents can coerce children into going on family outings. Once the child is there, she will likely have a good time. But if parents try the same tactics with a teenager, they will be picnicking with a reluctant traveler all afternoon and evening. The teenager will not snap back and enjoy the outing. She will exert her independence against your coercion.

In my opinion, it is a far better approach to allow the teenager not to go, especially since you announced it at such a late date. I don't mean that the teenager should never go with the family. On events where you think the teenager's presence is extremely important, then you should expect the teenager to attend. But these occasions should be announced well in advance; this gives your teenager not only chronological time but also emotional time to prepare for the event. Parents should also explain why they feel it is important for the teenager to attend the event. If teenagers feel that their schedule and interest have been considered, they will likely join the family with a positive attitude. On the other hand, teenagers need to do some things apart from the family in order to establish social independence.

The parent who realizes the value of the teen's independence will foster it by agreeing to allow the teenager to do social events apart from the family and will accompany that affirmation with expressions of love rather than argument. The parent who argues with the teenager and later reluctantly gives in has neither fostered independence nor expressed love. The teenager's desire to be with friends is not a rejection of parents; it is evidence that his social horizons are widening beyond the family.

Upon reflection, most parents realize this is exactly what they had hoped would happen. What parents would want to keep their teenager socially bound to them forever? It is the teenage years when social independence is emerging. Wise parents help children build a positive foundation for later social experiences beyond the family.

Playing Their Own Kind of Music

Another area in which the desire for social independence will be expressed is in music. *Teenagers will choose their own music.* Nothing is more central to teenage culture than music. I would not be so foolish as to suggest the type of music to which your teenager will listen. If I told you what is popular today, I can assure you something else will have supplanted it by the time you read this chapter. What I can tell you is that the music your teenager will choose will be different from the music you enjoy. How can I be so certain of this? The answer is found in one word: independence. Your teenager wants to be different from you.

One way in which teens express independence is in the music they choose. If you have exposed your children to what you consider to be good music throughout their childhood, have no fear. That music will continue to influence your teenager throughout life. Music has a way of touching the heart and soul of man. The influence of good music never fades but at the moment, your child is going through the teenage phase of life. This is a time for establishing independence. Be assured their choice of music will be affected by this emerging independence.

In the preteen and early teen years, parents need to establish clear guidelines as to what is acceptable and not acceptable in musical lyrics. For example, lyrics which depict murder, brutality, and perverted sexual experiences as normal behavior should not be considered appropriate music for teens. The teen needs to know that the purchase of such music will result in parental confiscation and destruction with no financial refunds. With these boundaries in place, I think parents may allow the teen freedom of choice, knowing that the teen will explore various musical styles. Most music CDs and tapes now have ratings that indicate the nature of content (such as language, sexual or violent themes); this is a good place to help your teen start his evaluation (and to set reasonable rules).

The parent who criticizes the teen's choice of music will be indirectly criticizing their teen. If such criticism continues, the teenager will feel unloved by the parent. However, if the parent affirms the teen's freedom of choice and continues to express love in the teenager's primary love language, the teenager's sense of independence is fostered and the teenager's need for love is met. I encourage you to read the lyrics of your teenager's music. (I say *read* because you will probably not be able to understand the words if you listen.) Find out what you can about the artist and musicians who write and sing the music your teenager chooses. Point out things you like about the lyrics and positive things about those who perform. Listen as your teenager chooses to share his own impressions.

If you will take this positive approach to their music, occasionally you can say, "You know, it troubles me a bit that in this song that is otherwise rather positive, there is this line that seems to be so destructive. What do you think about that?" Since your teenager knows that you have not been critical of their music, in fact you have made many positive comments; he will be inclined to hear your criticism and perhaps even agree with you. Even if he disagrees, you have planted a seed of question in his mind. If one of your teenager's music idols is arrested for drug use, overdoses, or divorces his/her spouse, be sympathetic, not judgmental. Express pain and concern for the person and sadness over the situation. You are empathizing with your teenager's emotions and the teen will feel affirmed. Remember the teenager is already thinking logically; he will draw his own conclusions. You don't need to preach a sermon. If the teenager feels your emotional support, he will feel loved.

Speaking a Different Language and Wearing Different Clothes

Teenagers will speak a different language. When your child becomes a teenager, she will learn a new language. It is called "teenalise." Please don't try to learn it. The whole purpose is to have a language that parents do not understand. Why is this so important? The answer is social independence. The teen is putting distance between herself and the parent, and language is one means of doing this. If you try to understand the teen's language, you will defeat the whole purpose. Wise parents simply accept the teen's new language as an evidence that the teenager is growing up. It is perfectly legitimate periodically for the parent to say, "Would you like to explain that to me in English?" However, if the teen's response is negative, the parent should not press the issue.

Teens understand each other's language but adults are not supposed to comprehend. The teen is connecting with those of his own age. He is establishing social relationships outside the family and "teenalise" is the language his new family speaks. If the parent chooses to make fun of the teenager's new language by saying such things as "Would you please explain that word to me. I don't think it is in my dictionary," the teen will feel rejection rather than love. The wise parent allows the teen this new expression of social independence and continues to love the teenager.

Teenagers have a different dress code. I can't tell you what your teenager will be wearing; I can tell you it will be different from what you are wearing. This new wardrobe will be accompanied by hairstyles and colors you have never seen before. Their accessories will include colors of nail polish you find outlandish, and their jewelry may be worn in places you have never imagined. If the parent gets "bent out of shape" about all of this and accuses the teenager of being rowdy or pagan, the teenager will withdraw. If the parent is highly controlling and demands that the teenager return to normalcy, the teenager may do so in the presence of the parent (that is, dressing as he did at age eleven), but he will do it with great resentment. And when the parent is not around, the teenager will revert to being a teen.

It is helpful if parents will see the role of dress in the broader social arena. Dress is primarily dictated by culture. If you doubt this, then ask yourself, "Why do I wear the style of clothing I wear?" Chances are it is because people in your social circle wear similar clothing. Look at the people who work with you, live in your community, attend your church, and otherwise interact with you in social settings. Chances are, all of you dress similarly. Teenagers are following the same principle. They are simply identifying with teenager culture.

Just as adult fashions come and go and come again, so do teenage fashions. Last week I observed in the teen culture of Seattle the same short, flat top, peroxide-bleached hair that was popular in the 1950s. Two weeks earlier, my wife had commented that the teenagers were wearing "pedal pushers" again, only now they call them "Capri pants." Whatever the current fad of teen dress, it serves the same purpose for each generation. The teen is establishing a social identity independent from that of parents.

I recently attended a wedding at which one of the groomsmen wore an earring. At the reception an older gentleman called me aside and said quietly, "Dr. Chapman, can you explain to me the meaning of that?" as he pointed to the young man with the earring. I said, "Let me put it this way. It's very similar to green hair." "Oh," he said, as though he understood. I'm not at all sure he did, but that's fine with the teenager. Parents who accept the teen's need for social independence and see the teen's dress styles in this context can be honest about their own preferences but allow the teen the freedom to be a teenager; knowing that when the teenager gets to be an adult, he will be wearing clothing similar to that of other adults with whom he identifies. Parents who create a world war over the teen's clothing are fighting a useless battle which turns a normal developmental phenomenon into a divisive issue between parent and teenager. Such battles do not change our teenagers' ideas, and offer no positive rewards for parents.

Wise parents share their opinions if they must but back off and give the teenager freedom to develop social independence. Meanwhile, they continue to fill the teenager's tank by speaking his/her primary love language and sprinkling in the other four languages when possible.

THE DESIRE FOR
INTELLECTUAL INDEPENDENCE

Earlier we discussed the teenager's developing intellectual skills. The teen is coming to think more abstractly, logically, and globally.

The teen is testing his own beliefs. He is looking at things that earlier he accepted without question, and now he is applying the test of reason and logic. This often means that he questions his parents' beliefs as well as those of his teachers and other significant adults in his life. These questions tend to cluster around three significant areas: values, moral beliefs, and religious beliefs.

Values

The teen is sure to question his parents' values. What is important in life? The teen looks at what his parents have said and what his parents have done with their own lives. He often sees discrepancies between the parents' stated values and the parents' demonstrated values. The father who asserts that the most important thing in life is family relationships but who in fact is so absorbed in his vocation that he has little time for family can know that his teen will see this inconsistency. The mother who says that faithfulness in marriage is important but who ends up having an affair with a man at work will most certainly be seen as hypocritical by her teenage daughter. "But you said . . ." is often a part of the teenager's barrage of words at the parent whose actions do not match his or her stated values.

Even if parents are true to their values, the teenager will sooner or later question those values. The teen must answer for himself what is important in life. *My parents have said that getting a college degree is the most important thing for my future. But I'm not sure that is correct. Some of the smartest people I know did not go to college and some of the most wealthy people in the world did not attend college. How can I be sure that college is best for me?* Thus reasons the teenager.

Parents who wish to be an influential part of their teenagers' reasoning process must shift from monologue to dialogue, from preaching to conversation, from dogmatism to exploration, from control to influence. Teenagers need and want their parents' input into these important areas of life, but they will not receive it if the parent treats them as a child. In childhood, the parents told the child what was right and the child was expected to believe it. That is no longer true when the child becomes a teenager. The teenager wants to know why; what is the evidence?

If parents are willing to enter the world of dialogue, to think critically about their own values, to share reasons and yet be open to the teen's opinions, the teenager will receive the parental input and thus be influenced by the parents' values. However, if the parents maintain the stance "It's true because I said it's true," they will have lost all influence on the teenager's choice of values. "I've always thought this was important and here's the reason why—. Does that make sense to you? How do you feel about it?" This is the approach of the parents who want to be a part of influencing their teenager's values. Numerous conversations, each picking up where the last left off but none judgmental nor dogmatic—this is the process of parent-teen interaction that allows the teen intellectual independence and at the same time gives the teen the benefit of the parents' thoughts.

When such open dialogue is accompanied by meaningful expressions of love, the parent is both fostering intellectual independence and meeting the teenager's need for emotional love. The parent who says, "I respect your right to choose your own values. You have seen my life. You know my strengths and my weaknesses. I believe that you are highly intelligent and in my heart, I know you will make wise decisions," is speaking the love language words of affirmation while encouraging the teenager's intellectual independence.

Moral Beliefs

While values answer the question "What is important?" morals answer the question "What is right?" Man by nature is a moral creature. Beliefs about what is right and what is wrong permeate all human cultures. I believe that is because man is made in the image of a personal, moral God, so that image is reflected in man. Whatever one's belief about the origin of morals, the cultural reality is that all people hold moral beliefs. Your teenagers will question not only your values but your morals. Again, they will examine not only your words but your actions.

If you declare it is right to obey civil law, the teenager wants to know why you are breaking the speed limit. If you say it is right to tell the truth, then your teenager asks, "Why did you lie to the person on the other end of the telephone and tell them that Dad was not at home?" If you say it is right to be kind to others, the teenager will ask why you treated the store clerk in an abusive manner. If you say that racism is wrong, then the teenager wants to know why at the shopping mall you walk briskly down the hall and avoid eye contact whenever you see a person of another ethnic group approaching.

All of this can be extremely annoying to parents who have learned to live with their own inconsistencies. Annoying or not, our teenagers will be persistent in pointing out our moral inconsistencies.

Beyond this, our teenagers will question our moral beliefs as well as our practices. They will ask themselves—and us—the hard questions: If murder is wrong, then is abortion murder? If violence that ends in the destruction of human life is wrong, then why are we entertained by Hollywood's versions of violence? If sexual monogamy is the ideal, why have thousands of adults chosen serial sexual partners? Is right and wrong to be determined by the consensus of society? Or is there a natural, moral law that transcends society's opinions? These are the deep issues with which our teens wrestle, issues with which their parents once wrestled.

Many parents find it troubling that their teenagers revive these old unsettled moral issues. However, if as parents we refuse to talk about our teens' moral concerns, they are left to the influence of peers and other adults who are willing to discuss these issues. If we are not willing to admit our inconsistencies between belief and practice, our teens will cease to respect our opinions.

We do not have to be morally perfect to influence our teenagers but we do need to be morally authentic. "I realize that I've not always lived up to my own beliefs in this area, but I still believe that this is right and that what I have done is wrong." Such statements, made by sincere parents, restore the respect of teenagers in the parents' authenticity. Parents who get defensive about their own moral beliefs when teenagers ask probing questions will again drive the teenager elsewhere to seek input on moral issues. Parents who welcome the teenagers' moral questions, who are willing to talk about their own beliefs and practices, who are open to listen to opposing viewpoints, and to give their teenagers reasons for their own moral beliefs—those parents are able to keep the road to dialogue open and thus positively influence their teens' moral decisions.

After such discussions about moral issues, be sure to give affirmations of your emotional love. This will keep your teenagers' love tanks full and create an atmosphere where your teen feels free to come back for additional dialogue.

Religious Beliefs

Whereas values answer the question "What is important?" and morals "What is right?" religion seeks to answer the question "What is true?" Religious belief systems are man's effort to discover the truth about the material and nonmaterial universe. How do we explain our own existence and the existence of the universe? Beyond the material world, is there a spiritual reality? Why is belief in spirit beings pan-human—that is, why has mankind throughout history in all cultures had a belief in a spirit world? Is this evidence that such a world exists? And if so, what is the nature of that world? Is there a God? And is the world His creation? If so, is God knowable?

These are the questions teenagers are asking, questions which have sometimes lain dormant for years in the hearts and minds of their parents. They are questions which perhaps were never adequately answered by the parents themselves.

Whatever your religious beliefs or disbeliefs, at some point your teenagers will wrestle with these issues. These are the questions humans have always asked, and teenagers are human. Man is incurably religious. The French physicist, Blaise Pascal, once said, "There is a God-shaped vacuum in every heart."[2] Saint Augustine said, "Thou hast made us for Thyself, and the heart of man is restless until it finds its rest in Thee."[3]

Your teenager is restless. She will question your religious beliefs. She will examine the manner in which you apply your beliefs to your daily life. Again, if she discovers inconsistencies, she may well confront you with these. If you become defensive and refuse to talk about religious issues, then your teenager will turn to peers and other adults. But your teenager will not cease to ask religious questions.

Your teenager also may explore other religious beliefs and may even reject aspects of your own religion. Most parents find this extremely upsetting. In reality, it is a necessary step for your teenager in developing his own religious beliefs. Actually, parents should be more concerned if the teenager simply adopts the parents' religion without serious thought. This indicates that to the teenager and perhaps to the parent, religion is simply a cultural facade, serving social purposes rather than addressing the deeper questions of life's meanings.

When the teenager announces that he will no longer go to Mass, the synagogue, Sunday school, or the mosque, he is calling attention to himself as a person independent of his parents. And he is expressing a desire for intellectual independence. It will be comforting for parents to know that research has shown that "while teenage rejections of religion may be dramatic, they are seldom permanent."[4]

AN EXPLORATION IN PROCESS

It is difficult for most parents to react calmly when their teenager talks about rejecting their religion, but parental overreactions may close the door for dialogue. Remember, the teenager is establishing his independence not only in the other areas that we have discussed, but also in the intellectual area, which includes moral values and religious beliefs. This is simply a part of the teenager's broader process of questioning and exploration. It is more an expression of intellectual independence than it is a rejection of religion. If parents keep this in mind, they are less likely to be overly judgmental of the teenager's religious thoughts at the moment.

A better approach is to listen to the teenager's thoughts. Let them express freely why they find this religious belief to be interesting or satisfying. Share your own thoughts on the subject but in a nonjudgmental manner. Tell your teenager you are glad to see she is thinking about these issues. When you get really bold, ask for her opinions about how well you have lived by your own religious beliefs. You may discover why the teenager is looking in another direction.

This is not a time for dogmatism, although you may hold your religious beliefs very deeply. This is a time for encouraging exploration. If you are deeply convinced of the validity of your own religious beliefs, that indeed what you believe fits closely with what is real about the world, then you should have a measure of confidence that your exploring teenager, if sincere, will eventually end up with beliefs similar to your own. If, on the other hand, your religious beliefs are not held deeply and you are not at all certain about whether they fit with ultimate reality, then perhaps you should be encouraged that your teenager is on such a search. Perhaps he or she will discover what you have not.

The fact is, your teenager is going to explore religious thoughts. The questions is, "Do you want to be a part of that exploration and do you want to love your teenager in the process?" If the answer is yes, then you must again shift from monologue to dialogue and create an atmosphere for open, honest discussion about religious issues. You must give your teenager the right to think thoughts differently from your own. You must be willing both to share evidence and listen to opposing evidence. You must acknowledge that your teenager is in process and you must allow time for the processing of religious beliefs.

If you do this, all the while filling the teenager's emotional love tank, the teenager will feel loved and will develop intellectual independence. The teenager will develop the religious beliefs by which he will live and you have been a positive influence during the search.

OUR TEENS' NEED TO DECIDE FOR THEMSELVES

It will be obvious that in all of these areas—values, morals, and religion—our teenagers will be making decisions. Underlying most of the conflicts between parents and teens is the basic question about the teenagers' right to make independent decisions. If the parent recognizes this right to independent thought and recognizes that the teenager's decisions are in process and is willing to invest the time and create the atmosphere for meaningful dialogue in a loving setting, the teenager will continue to be "plugged in" to parental influence.

If, however, parents draw lines in the sand, make dogmatic proclamations about what teenagers are going to believe and do, the parents will create adversarial relationships with their teens. Thousands of parents have walked this road and have experienced estrangement from their teenagers. Teenagers have turned to peer groups—sometimes very destructive peer groups—and other adults—sometimes evil adults who were willing to give the teenager acceptance and a surface love for favors, pleasures, and self-gratification.

Remember, teenagers will exert their independence. It's part of becoming adults. Wise parents recognize this as a developmental stage through which teenagers must pass and seek to cooperate rather than hinder their teenagers' development. Loving the teenager through this volatile process is extremely important. If you can foster your teenager's independence in the ways suggested in this chapter while keeping his love tank full, the teen will grow up to be a responsible adult, finding his place in society and making his contribution to the world.

Parents who fail at this critical stage may well be estranged from their teenagers for years and see their teenagers struggle with finding their place in the world. Creating an atmosphere where their teenagers can develop social, intellectual, and emotional independence is one of the parents' greatest gifts to teenagers.

At this juncture I know some of you are asking, "But what about boundaries? What about responsibility?" I'm glad you are asking the question. It reveals that you understand the implications about what I've said in this chapter. And it brings us to chapter 12, where I wish to discuss these very issues. In fact, I request that chapters 11 and 12 be read and studied together. They are two wheels on the same chariot: independence and responsibility.

NOTES

1. Lawrence Steinberg and Ann Levine, *You and Your Adolescent* (New York: Harper & Row, 1990), 150.

2. George Sweeting, *Who Said That?* (Chicago: Moody, 1995), 302.

3. Ibid., 370.

4. Lawrence Kutner, *Making Sense of Your Teenager* (New York: William Morrow, 1997), 44.

chapter twelve

LOVE AND RESPONSIBILITY

Michael's father purchased an old clunker that Michael and he worked on several weekends. When Michael got his driver's permit, his father taught him some of the finer points of driving. First, they tried afternoons; later Michael got experience driving at night. One weekend he and his father went camping with Michael driving to the campsite. All was fine until Michael finally got his driver's license.

Hey, I'm free! Michael told himself. *Dad doesn't have to go along.* He began to dream of driving wherever, whenever, and however he pleased. Michael didn't understand when his father insisted that there would be rules on when, where, and how he would drive the car.

What Michael was about to learn is that freedom and responsibility are opposite sides of the same coin—one never exists without the other. This is always true in the adult world, and the teenager also must learn this reality. Adults are allowed the freedom of living in a house as long as they take the responsibility of paying the monthly mortgage payments. The electric company allows freedom to burn lights as long as the customer takes the responsibility of paying the monthly bill. All of life is organized around the principles of freedom and responsibility. The two never stray far from one another. Of course, the teenager does not know this reality. It is a part of parenting to help the teenager make this discovery.

As the loving parent encourages teenage independence, so parental love means teaching the teen to be responsible for his own behavior. Independence without responsibility is the road to low self-esteem, meaningless activity, and eventually boredom and depression. We do not gain a sense of self-worth from being independent. Our worth comes from being responsible. Independence and responsibility pave the road to mature adulthood. The teenager who learns to be responsible for his own actions while developing his independence and self-identity will have good self-esteem, accomplish worthwhile objectives, and will make a meaningful contribution to the world around him. Teenagers who do not learn responsibility will be troubled teenagers and eventually troublesome adults.

THE ROLE OF LAWS (BOUNDARIES)

Responsibility requires boundaries. All human societies have boundaries, typically called laws. Without social boundaries, society would self-destruct. If everyone simply did what was right in his own eyes, the results would be chaotic. When the majority of people abide by the laws; that is, they are responsible citizens, the society thrives. When a significant number of individuals choose to walk their own way and live irresponsibly, the society suffers the negative consequences. Our own Western society is experiencing the results of irresponsible living on the part of many teenagers and adults. This is evidenced in the number of murders, rapes, thefts, and other violent crimes committed daily. Not only does the individual suffer for his/her irresponsible behavior, but the society at large also suffers.

In the family setting, parents are responsible for establishing rules, or boundaries, and seeing that the teenager lives responsibly within these boundaries. The idea that teenagers will rebel if parents establish boundaries is untrue. In fact, research indicates that "the majority of adolescents feel that their parents are reasonable and patient with them most of the time. More than half admit 'when my parents are strict, I feel that they are right, even when I get angry.'"[1]

Lawrence Steinberg, professor of psychology at Temple University, observed, "What causes adolescents to rebel is not the assertion of authority but the arbitrary use of power, with little explanation of the rules, and no involvement in decision making."[2] The problem is not parental authority; the problem is parents who express their authority in a dictatorial, unloving manner. When your child was younger, you could make arbitrary rules and your child would seldom question your right to do so, though they may have disobeyed your rules. However, teenagers will question whether your rules are right. They will question whether your rules were made for the benefit of the teen or simply to satisfy your own whims. "Do it because I said so," simply doesn't work with teenagers. If you continue such a dictatorial approach, you can be assured your teenager will rebel.

FORMING RULES WITH YOUR TEENS

Because the teenager is developing independence, he/she needs to be a part of forming rules and setting consequences. Wise parents will bring their teenagers into the circle of decision making, letting them express their ideas on what are fair and worthy rules. Parents should share reasons for their own ideas and demonstrate why they think the rule is good for the teenager. Those who do so will create an atmosphere that fosters the teenager's independence while at the same time teaches the teenager that there is no freedom without responsibility.

In such open "family forums," parents and teens can meet, while parents still are the authorities. They have the final word, but the parents will be wiser when they know the teenager's thoughts and feelings about the matter. And if the teenager has had a voice in making the rule, he is more likely to believe the rule is fair and less likely to rebel. Studies show "that young people whose parents are willing to engage in discussion with them are more affectionate and respectful, and more likely to say they want to be like their parents, than are young people whose parents insist on always being right."[3]

Parents are not only responsible for establishing the boundaries but also for enforcing the consequences when these rules are violated. Again, if teens have participated in deciding what the consequences will be, they are more likely to believe that they are fair and less likely to rebel when the parents enforce the consequences. As parents, we must remember that our goal in raising teenagers is not to win an argument but to teach our teenagers to be responsible while they are becoming independent. The principle is "If you can accept the responsibility, then you can have the freedom. If you cannot accept the responsibility, then you are not ready for freedom." When our teenagers understand that the two always go together, they will have learned a major lesson which will serve them well not only in adolescence but also in adulthood.

THE IMPORTANCE OF LOVE

If this process of teenage independence and responsibility is to move smoothly, parents must lubricate the process with the oil of love. When teenagers feel loved by the parents—when they deeply sense that the parents have their well-being in mind, that rules are made and enforced for the benefit of the teenager alone—then independence and responsibility are more likely to emerge. Keep your teen's love tank full, and his rebellion is likely to be only sporadic and temporary. On the other hand, if your teen does not feel loved—if he views your rules as arbitrary and self-serving, and he senses that you are more concerned about your own reputation and success than in the teenager's well-being—he will almost certainly rebel against rules and you as the rules enforcer.

Remember, efforts to control teens by coercion will almost certainly fail. Coercion cannot accomplish what love was designed to create, namely feelings of positive regard toward parents. Love is indeed the most powerful weapon for good in the world. Parents who remember this and make conscious efforts to continue to communicate emotional love to the teenager will be doing the first and most important step in teaching them responsibility while fostering independence.

Steinberg, a recognized expert on adolescents, said, "When parents back off, because they think the adolescent doesn't want or need their affection anymore, teenagers feel abandoned. Trite as it may sound, love is the most important thing you can give your adolescent."[4] It is giving the teenager emotional love that creates a climate where we can both cooperate with their emerging independence and at the same time insist on responsible behavior. Having said this, we are ready to examine the process of establishing and enforcing rules for teenagers.

A SPECIAL FAMILY FORUM

It should be obvious by now that whatever rules were established when your teenager was a child cannot be arbitrarily carried into the teenage years. The teenager is at a different stage in life; this calls for rethinking and reforming the rules. Parents who simply try to "slide" into the teenager years without reflection, conversation, or attention to family rules will soon see their teenager rebelling. Parents who are proactive will call for a family forum, acknowledging to the teen an awareness that he/she is now a teenager and that this calls for rethinking our family rules to allow more freedom and more responsibility.

The parent who acknowledges this reality before it dawns upon the teenager will have the respect and the attention of the teen. Teenagers are interested in more freedom and more responsibility. This is one family forum they will gladly attend.

Some tips on having this family forum and a sample introduction for explaining the purpose to your teen are included in appendix 2. Being proactive by calling such a family forum before the teenager starts to complain about the childish rules he must live by is a strategy of great wisdom. The teenager who is caught off-guard by his parents announcing his emerging independence and responsibility is far more likely to be a friendly participant in such a family forum than the teenager who has insisted for six months that such a forum be called.

SOME RULES ABOUT RULES

However, if your teenager is fifteen and you have never had such a forum, it is never too late to shock your teenager by taking the initiative to reexamine the rules. Let me suggest three guidelines for making rules and three guidelines for setting consequences during such a forum.

1: Rules should be as few as possible.

Sixteen pages of family rules will not only take a long time to write, but they will likely be ignored. This is one area of life where less is better. Too many rules overwhelm the teenager, will not be remembered, will create a nightmare for parents to enforce, and will make life much too rigid. Teenagers need some room for spontaneity and lightheartedness. Too many rules make the teenager paranoid and fearful.

What are the really important issues? Typically the answer to this question will cluster around avoiding those things which are physically, emotionally, or socially detrimental to the teenager's well-being and encouraging those things that will foster the teenager's accomplishment of worthy goals. Responsible living is saying no to those things that destroy and yes to those things that build.

Rules should point the way toward this objective. Later in this chapter, we will look at several areas of teenage responsibility and seek to apply this principle. The objective of rules is not to regulate every moment of the teenager's life. It is to provide important boundaries within which the teenager can make choices. Remember, God only came up with ten rules—they're called the Ten Commandments.[5] And Jesus summarized these in two.[6] Since you are not as wise as God, you will probably have a few more than ten. I can assure you that your teenager will try to be more like Jesus.

2. Rules should be as clear as possible.

Ambiguous rules make for confusion for both the teenager and the parent. "Come home at a reasonable hour" is sure to be interpreted differently by teenager and parent. "Be inside the house at 10:30 P.M." is clear. The teenager may break the rule but there is no confusion about what the rule means. "Don't ever drive more than three miles above the posted speed limit." Anyone intelligent enough to drive will have no difficulty in understanding this rule.

When the rule is clearly delineated, a teenager is aware when the rule is broken. He may try to cover his mistake. He may even argue that it didn't happen. He may rationalize as to why it happened. But the teenager knows that the rule was broken. However, if the rule is ambiguous, the teenager is certain to argue about the parent's judgment that the rule was broken. Unclear rules set the stage for argument. Teenagers will certainly enter the stage and give a wonderful performance. Clear rules deter such theatrics.

3. Rules should be as fair as possible.

I say "as possible" because none of us is perfect in our understanding of what is fair. You and your teen may well disagree on the fairness of a rule. By means of open dialogue, seeking to understand each other's viewpoint, you and your teenager can arrive at a consensus on what is fair. Don't give in when you are convinced that your rule is in the best interest of the teenager, but be willing to bend when you feel that doing so will not be detrimental to the teen's well-being.

To the teenager, fairness is very important. As we discussed earlier, the teenager is wrestling with values, morals, logic, and reason. If a teenager's sense of fairness is violated, the teenager will experience anger. If the parent cuts off discussion and arbitrarily decrees the rule, and refuses to deal with the teenager's anger, the teenager will feel rejected and will later resent the parent.

Every effort should be made to hear the teenager's concern about fairness in forming rules. If the teenager agrees that the rule is fair, he is not likely to rebel when the parent enforces the rule. Which brings us to the matter of consequences.

RULES ABOUT CONSEQUENCES

Rules without consequences are less than worthless; they are confusing. Teenagers will not respect parents who do not seek to lovingly but firmly enforce the rules by letting the teenager suffer the consequences when rules are broken. Suffering consequences is an important reality in adult life. If I do not pay the mortgage payment, next month I will pay additional finance charges. If in three months I haven't made the mortgage payments, I will be evicted. If I break the speed limit and am issued a traffic ticket, I must not only pay the fine but my insurance premiums may also increase. Consequences can be tough but they foster responsible living. A flashing blue light seen in the dark causes drivers to take their foot off the accelerator. The fear of paying the consequences is a motivator to follow the rules.

Here are three guidelines for formulating and enforcing consequences.

1. Consequences should be determined before a violation.

Most social laws incorporate this concept. The amount of additional fees I will pay when I miss the mortgage payment is already determined before I miss the payment. The bank or lending agent does not arbitrarily decide "a late fee" after I have violated my payment contract. In most states and cities, the fine for a traffic violation is determined before the violation occurs. If we are preparing our teenagers to live in the adult world, wouldn't it be logical to apply this principle while they are teenagers?

I am amazed at the number of parents I meet across the country to whom this thought has never occurred. They wait until the teenager violates the rule; then, often in anger, they pronounce the consequences. The nature of the consequence is often determined by the emotional state of the parent at the moment. The chances of the teenager agreeing that the consequences are fair are almost nil. On the other hand, if parents are in a good mood, there may be no consequences at all. The teenager is obviously confused by this arbitrary method of determining consequences.

I suggest that the consequences for violations should be determined at the time the rules are formulated—and that the teenager should be a part of the process. If the teenager is going to be a part of formulating the rules, why should she not be a part of determining the consequences? We have already observed that teenagers have a keen concern with fairness. Letting them be a part of setting the consequences is helping them develop their moral judgment. Often teenagers will be harder on themselves than the parent will be. You may think that one week without driving privileges would be a fair consequences for violating a given rule. The teenager may suggest two weeks. The important thing is to agree on a consequence that the teenager believes to be fair.

The value of agreeing upon predetermined consequences is that when the violation occurs, the parent and the teenager already know what is going to happen. The parent is not as likely to overreact in the heat of anger, and the teenager is far more likely to accept the consequence as being fair since he had a part in determining the consequences. If it was determined beforehand that the football is not to be thrown inside the house and that the first violation will result in the football being impounded in the trunk of the car for two days, while the second infraction within the same month impounds the ball for an entire week, then the parent is not as likely to rant and rave about the teenager throwing the football inside the house. She will simply intercept the football and put it in the trunk. The teenager may be momentarily upset, but he will likely acknowledge that the consequences were justified.

Parents save themselves a lot of grief when consequences are determined before a violation occurs. It is a win-win situation. Parents are less frustrated and teenagers have a greater sense that fairness has reigned. Another step has been taken in reaching the goal of teenage responsibility.

2. Consequences should be administered with love.

Parents must not be gleeful in administering consequences. Suffering the consequences of wrongdoing is painful in the adult world and in the world of the teenager. What adult would not resent the police officer who laughs as he writes you a ticket for a traffic violation? Teenagers will experience the same resentment when parents seem to take pleasure in administering the consequences of the teenager's wrongdoing. Neither should the parents be harsh and cold in administering consequences. "I told you so. If you had listened to me, you wouldn't be in this mess." Such a statement may alleviate some of the parents' frustration, but it will not have a positive effect upon the teenager.

Our teenagers need to sense that we love them in spite of the fact they have violated the rule. Our teenagers need sympathy and understanding, but they do not need us parents to capitulate and alleviate the consequences.

"I know that it will be very difficult for you not to be able to drive the car this week. I wish I didn't have to take your keys. But you know the rule and you know the consequences. Because I love you, I don't have any other option. I must let you experience the pain of having broken the rule." Such understanding and empathy with the teenager helps the teen to accept the consequences as being fair and loving. The teenager, though upset, will not resent the parent who administers the consequences in such a kind, caring manner.

It is also appropriate after such a confrontation to speak the teenager's primary love language as a final gesture of love. For example, if the teen's love language is physical touch, a pat on the back or a hug will speak volumes as you walk away with the keys. If acts of service is the teen's love language, then fixing her favorite dessert will fill up her love tank in spite of the pain she is feeling at having lost the car. If words of affirmation is the teen's love language, then verbally affirming the teenager before and after you administer the consequences will assure her of your love and will make the consequences bearable. This is another occasion when understanding the primary love language of your teenager is exceedingly important. To speak one of the other languages is certainly appropriate but will not be nearly as effective emotionally as speaking the teen's primary love language.

3. Consequences should be administered consistently.

Consequences should not be administered at the whim of the parent. By nature, all of us are influenced by our emotions. If parents are feeling good and are in a positive mood, they are often inclined to simply overlook the teenager's infraction of rules. In contrast, when the parents are in a bad mood or overly stressed and perhaps angry with someone at the office, they often come down hard on the teenager when a family rule is violated. Such inconsistency will create anger, resentment, and confusion in the heart of the teenager. The teenager's sense of fairness is violated. He will feel angry, and an argument and aggressive behavior will probably soon follow.

Parents who determine the consequences before the violation, allow the teenager to be a part of determining the consequences, and who administer the consequences in love are more likely to be consistent. The ideal is to kindly, firmly administer the consequences consistently in love. Parents who do this will be cooperating with the teenager's need to learn responsibility. The teenager, though not always happy, will be a willing participant in the process.

ESTABLISHING AREAS OF RESPONSIBILITY

Without trying to be comprehensive, let's look at some of the areas of family life that will require rules and consequences in order to teach your teenager responsibility and at the same time foster independence. Formulate your rules and consequences in response to these two questions: (1) What are the important issues in helping my teenager develop into a mature adult? (2) What dangers need to be avoided and what responsibilities need to be learned? Yes, some rules will be prohibitions, designed to keep the teenager from words or behavior that will be physically or emotionally destructive to himself or others. But other rules will be designed to help your teenager practice positive behaviors that will enhance his own maturity and enrich the lives of those around him.

Here, then, are some of the more common areas where parents and teenagers will need to formulate rules and consequences.

1. Household Opportunities

I say *opportunities* rather than *duties* because it sounds more positive. In reality, both elements exist. In a healthy family, every member has certain duties which must be performed to keep life flowing in a positive manner. However, such duties also represent opportunities for service. In recent years, our society has lost some of its emphasis on the value of altruistic service. However, it is still true that those who are most honored among us are those who have an attitude of service. The self-centered, self-serving person may be financially successful but is seldom held in high esteem.

If teenagers are to learn to serve beyond the family, they must first learn to serve the family. Teenagers need real household responsibilities that enhance the lives of other family members. These will differ in every household but may involve such things as supervising a younger sibling, helping to cook dinner, washing the family car, taking care of the family pet, mowing the grass, trimming shrubs, planting flowers, vacuuming floors, cleaning commodes, dusting, and washing clothes. These responsibilities may shift from time to time so that the teenager has an opportunity to learn skills in various areas of household maintenance.

It's important that the teenager sees himself as a part of a family and understands that in a family everyone has responsibility. As a teenager, he is acquiring more and more abilities. This means not only more freedom to do things away from the home but more responsibilities at home. The teenager certainly will have more responsibilities than his eight-year-old sibling. With these responsibilities come the freedom to stay up later, to spend some time away from the family, etc. In my opinion, such freedoms should always be tied with appropriate responsibilities. If the teenager demonstrates that he is mature enough to take responsibilities seriously, then he is also mature enough to have greater freedoms.

In the family forum where rules are made and consequences determined, this principle should be clearly understood. In this framework, parents are not then inclined to force a teenager to perform household duties. Rather the teenager has an opportunity to demonstrate maturity by shouldering responsibilities gladly and thus gain more freedom. If the teenager chooses not to perform assigned family responsibilities, then the consequences are determined in terms of loss of freedoms. For example, if the driving teenager is assigned the responsibility of washing the family car by noon on Saturday and the predetermined consequence is that failure to do so means that he will lose driving privileges for two days, wise parents will not stay on the teenager's back to wash the car. It's a choice—he chooses to shoulder responsibility and have the accompanying freedom or he chooses to be less mature and lose those freedoms. I can assure you that the teenager will seldom lose such freedoms and parents will not waste time and energy fretting over whether the teenager washes the car.

The principle is simple: If the teenager performs his responsibility, he feels good about himself as a mature young person and reaps the benefit of greater independence. Let's assume that a younger teenager is assigned the responsibility for putting dishes in the dishwasher and washing pots and pans after the evening meal and having the task completed within one hour after everyone leaves the table. The predetermined consequence of failure to keep this responsibility is missing the next family meal, and not being able to order in pizza or go out with friends while the family eats that meal. With this understanding, the parent will not be tempted to scream at the teenager when he leaves the table and starts talking on the telephone. The teen knows the rules. All the parents need to do is to make sure that the teenager suffers the consequences if the rule is violated. I can tell you that most teenagers will miss only one meal.

You may hear them say to their friend on the phone, "I've got to go now. My life depends on it. Call you later." The teenager is learning responsibility and freedom. Freedom to eat is correlated with the responsibility of work. Incidentally, there is biblical precedence for such a rule. Paul, the Christian apostle to the Gentile world, said, "if a man will not work, he shall not eat."[7] This applies also to teenagers.

2. Schoolwork

What are the important issues regarding the teenager's education? This is the question you and your teenager will answer together. Most parents will feel that graduation from high school is nonnegotiable. In Western culture, the teenager without a high school diploma will be seriously hampered in living a satisfying adult life. If the parent agrees, then this is stated as nonnegotiable. You then ask, "What are the rules that will help the teenager accomplish this objective?" Generally this would involve regular attendance at school and the successful completion of assignments. Typically, both of these are graded on the teenager's report card which parents receive periodically. Rules could be very simple: attendance at school daily unless sick at home or in the hospital, successful completion of all assignments at school and all homework assignments. If the attendance rule is broken, the consequences might be that for every day missed at school, the teenager will spend Saturday reading a book and making a verbal report to the parent on what was read. They will not be allowed to leave the house for the normal hours they would have been at school. Most teenagers will lose only one Saturday.

Performance of schoolwork is a little more difficult to judge but is normally reflected in grades and/or a visit with the teacher. When the parent discovers that the homework assignments are not being completed and/or the teenager's performance at school is less than satisfactory, the consequence could be that the assignments will be completed on Saturday or Sunday afternoon even though the teacher indicates that they will not improve the grade. The parent will closely supervise the completion of these "not for credit" assignments. Such rules and consequences free the parent from daily harassing the teenager about completing his homework. The teenager chooses to be responsible and have the freedom of Saturday and

Sunday afternoon for more pleasurable activities or the teenager loses that freedom because he was irresponsible.

3. Use of Automobiles

The opportunity for a teenager to drive a car is a privilege, not a right. Teenagers are not entitled to have their own car or to drive the family car whenever they wish. Driving is a freedom that is earned by responsible behavior. This reality should be clearly understood by the teenager long before he is old enough to get a drivers license. Again, teenagers need to understand the relationship between freedom and responsibility. The fact is most parents want their teenagers to have the freedom of driving a car, but many parents fail to connect this freedom to drive with responsibility. Consequently, teenagers see driving as an inalienable right.

What are the key issues in a teenager driving a car? The parent and teen probably will agree on some of the following: the teenager's physical safety, the safety of other drivers and passengers, and obedience to all traffic laws. These are fundamental concerns. Other parents and teens may agree on certain rules regarding the teenager helping to finance this privilege by buying gas out of his allowance or earnings. Others will want rules about securing permission from parents on when the car may be driven and when the teenager must return. From these concerns, specific rules will be formed along with appropriate consequences.

The following are suggestive. *Rule:* Obey all traffic laws. *Consequences:* If the teenager receives a ticket for any traffic violation, he will lose driving privileges for one week and will pay for the ticket out of his allowance or earnings. If a second violation occurs within three months, he will lose driving privileges for two weeks and make appropriate payment. *Rule:* Never allow a friend to drive your car. *Consequence if violated:* lose driving privileges for two weeks. Other rules may address such issues as curfews, payment of car expenses, regular vacuuming of the car and auto maintenance.

4. Money Management

Money hassles are common between parents and teenagers. Many times this is because parents have not established clear rules and clear consequences. What are the major concerns regarding money and teenagers? The first reality is obvious: money is limited. Few families have unlimited resources, which means the teenager cannot have all that he or she may desire. A second major concern is that the teenager learn basic principles of money management. One simple fundamental principle is "When money is gone, purchases cease until more money is obtained." The violation of this principle on the part of many adults has been the source of deep financial problems. That is why in my opinion, teenagers should never be given a credit card. Credit cards encourage spending beyond one's income, and such spending is an extremely poor practice to teach teenagers.

Fundamentally, a teenager cannot learn to manage money until he has some money to manage. This has led many parents to the decision that the teenager should be given a regular allowance rather than coming to the parent every two days asking for another $20 to buy this or that. The parent who doles out $10 here and $20 there to meet the teen's specific request of the day does not teach the teenager to manage money. A far better approach in my opinion is for parents and teens to agree on a weekly or monthly allowance. With the allowance, there needs to be a clear understanding of what areas of expenditure the teenager is responsible for. This may include: clothing, food, music, gas, etc. For example, parents may give the teenager $100 a month (or $25 a week) out of which the teenager will buy all of their meals away from home unless they are accompanied by a family member, all of the gas for their car if they are of driving age, and all of their clothes except what the parents agree to buy. (This should be clearly delineated such as: "We will buy all of your underclothing, all of your socks or hose, three pair of shoes per year, and one coat per year. Everything else will be your responsibility." Parents may choose to buy additional clothing items at Christmas or birthdays.) Such an arrangement gives the teenager the ability to learn to manage money.

Parents need to be as realistic as possible in setting the amount they will give the teenager. Once the amount is set, it should not be changed simply because the teenager complains, "It's just not enough." If the teenager wants more than he can purchase with the allowance, then the teenager must secure a means of earning money outside the family. If they are not old enough to work in a fast-food restaurant, they can mow lawns, baby-sit, deliver papers, and numerous other jobs available to younger teens. In this arrangement, the teen is not only learning how to manage money, he is learning the value of money by choosing to work to secure additional funds. However, if the parents break down and give the teenager additional funds when the teenager complains, the parent is sabotaging the teen's learning of financial responsibility. In affluent America, thousands of parents have undermined their teenager's fiscal well-being by freely supplying money at the teenager's request.

Be sure you communicate to the teenager that you are giving her an allowance because you love her and you want her to learn to handle money responsibly. You are not giving it to the teen because of her household duties. That is a totally separate matter of responsibility. I suggest that the teenager not be allowed to earn additional funds from parents. It confuses the issue of normal expected household responsibilities. Far better to let them earn the money outside the family. I also believe that loaning the teenager money is a mistake. It is teaching the teenager to purchase beyond one's income. This is teaching the teenagers the wrong lesson.

5. Dating

The subject of dating creates trauma in the hearts of many parents. Some parents remember their own dating experience and don't want their teenagers to do what they did. Some parents hear and shutter at statistics like the following compiled by the National Commission on Adolescent Sexual Health in 1994–95: "By the time they are 20 years old, more than 3/4 of adolescents have had sexual intercourse. Every year one million teenage girls become pregnant; more than 1/2 million have a child; and 3 million teenagers acquire a sexually transmitted disease."[8] Such statistics encourage some parents to vow never to let their teenagers date. "If I can keep them away from the opposite sex until they are twenty, maybe they will be mature enough to handle it" these parents reason. Also, there is much confusion on what constitutes a date. If a date is considered one boy and one girl going out for a hamburger and later spending three hours in the backseat of a car stimulating each other sexually, then one may question whether teenagers should date at all. But if dating is a group of teenagers, male and female, going out for a hamburger and later attending a ballgame or going to a dance, then dating can be a positive experience in building the teenager's self-esteem and developing relationship skills necessary for mature adult romantic relationships.

I won't indicate when your son or daughter should begin dating, though Steinberg warns that girls who begin dating in early adolescence risk being caught up in "a misty, romantic feeling" and will typically date older boys who are "likely to overpower [the teenage girls] psychologically as well as physically."[9] Steinberg also indicates that early dating also affects the girl's relationships with other girls her age. Because she is dating an older boy, she tends to associate with older girls. This may gain her temporary acceptance with the older crowd but will alienate her from girls her own age. As a result, she loses the valuable experience of intimate friendships with girls her age. After thirty years of marriage and family counseling, I am convinced that early adolescence is the time for the teenager to develop same-sex friendships, gradually followed by group activities involving girls and boys, and moving in later adolescence to one-on-one dating. As teenagers mature, they feel more comfortable with the opposite sex and are more confident about themselves and are better able to handle dates and potential romance. To short-circuit this process of social and emotional development by encouraging one-on-one dating in early adolescence is a serious mistake.

If you happen to concur with my opinion, then the time to paint this picture in the mind of your child is when they are nine, ten, and eleven. Then they enter the teenage years with no pressure for early dating, expecting rather to spend more time away from family and with friends of the same sex under the supervision of the friend's parents or under your own supervision. They will anticipate group activities with members of the opposite sex and feel little pressure to pair off until later adolescence.

Obviously, I am picturing the ideal and this does not account for the teenager's varying personality, insecurities, peer pressures, and other factors which may push the teenager to seek emotional solace in a romantic relationship in the early teenage years. This is another reason why emotional love from parents is so important to the young teenager. This is especially true of the opposite-sex parent. If the teenage girl feels loved by her father, she is less likely to seek emotional love from an older teenager. The teenage boy who feels loved by his mother is less likely to exploit a younger girl for his own emotional or physical pleasure.

So you are having your family conference with your thirteen-year-old teenager, seeking to formulate rules and consequences for his or her dating behavior. What are the central issues? I would suggest that concern for your teenager's physical and emotional health would be at the top of the list. Second and perhaps equal in importance is the healthy development of emotional and social maturity that will equip your teenager for a romantic relationship when the time comes. The objective is not to stifle the teenager's relationships with members of the opposite sex, but rather to foster wholesome relationships that help the teenager build a foundation for the more mature adult relationships that are to follow.

What rules might foster such healthy social maturation? *Rule:* Same sex friendships with teenagers of their own age will be encouraged in early adolescence. But for your teenager to spend the night with such a friend, you must first have met the teenager and talked with their parents. (This safeguards your teenager getting involved with someone whose values and lifestyle might be detrimental to your teenager.) Any such overnight visit must be done when parents are in the home. *Consequences for violation:* No such overnight visits for three months, and no allowance for one week. *Rule:* The teenager is free to attend group activities involving boys and girls so long as there is adult supervision and the parent approves of the activities. Parents reserve the right to say "no" to any activity they feel would be detrimental to the teenager's well-being. *Consequences for violation:* No such group activities for one month, and no allowance for one week.

When the teenage daughter is fifteen or the son is sixteen, you will discuss the possibility of one-on-one dating. During this year, the parent reserves the right to determine if, when, and whom the teenager dates. When the girl is sixteen and the boy seventeen, the parent agrees to trust them with the decision of who they date. But all dating must be done on Friday or Saturday nights. *Rule:* The parent reserves the right to request the teenager to abstain from a dating relationship where the partner is involved in drugs or alcohol or is known to be sexually active with other dating partners. *Consequences of violation:* If the teenager refuses to break off such a destructive relationship, the parent withdraws driving privileges for one month and all allowances are frozen for one month. At the end of the month if the teenager has not complied, restrictions will be extended for another month. At this stage, the teenager must know that to make unwise decisions is to suffer the consequences. They cannot have their freedom of driving and allowances if they are irresponsible in their relationships.

Please understand that these rules and consequences are only suggestive. Each parent and teenager must work out what they believe to be fair and workable. Obviously the earlier these rules and consequences are formed, the more likely the teenager is to see them as fair and for his/her benefit.

Alcohol and Drugs

More and more teenagers are taking more and more drugs at earlier and earlier ages. The results are obvious—more teenage alcoholics and drug addicts. Nothing destroys independence faster than alcohol and drug addiction. What can a parent do to guarantee that their teenage son or daughter will not get involved with drugs and alcohol? The answer—nothing. Parents cannot follow teenagers twenty-four hours a day and make sure they do not ingest alcohol and drugs. There are, however, things a parent can do to make drug use less likely.

First and most powerful is to model abstinence. Teenagers who watch parents take a drink every night to unwind are far more likely to use and abuse alcohol. Teenagers who watch parents misuse prescription drugs are much more likely to become drug users. I cannot overstate the power of parental model at this point. Once the model is in place, however, there are other things that parents can do to make their teenagers less likely to be involved in drug use.

Let's come back to our paradigm of rules and consequences.

What are the major concerns surrounding alcohol and drug abuse? Usually the key issue is fear of the teenager becoming alcoholic or drug addicted. This is certainly a legitimate fear. A second concern may be that the teenager will be riding with a drunken driver and be hurt or killed in an automobile accident. A third concern is that the teenager might associate with other teenagers who abuse drugs and alcohol and in that mind-altered state commit violent crimes. All of these are very real and legitimate concerns.

What rules might address these concerns? In the family forum, parents should certainly express their desire that the teenager abstain from drug and alcohol use. Parents should explain that this is not because of some ill-founded, illogical, religious or personal belief but is based on the facts that have been clearly researched. Knowing that the teenager will someday be an adult and can make his own decisions about drug and alcohol use, it is perfectly legitimate for parents to insist that while the teenager is at home, the rule is no alcohol and no drugs.

Consequences for violation should be stringent. It should be pointed out to the teenager that most drugs are illegal and are in violation of state and federal laws. If the teenager is found in possession of illegal drugs, he may suffer not only parental consequences but judicial consequences. One parent suggested that the first offense would remove driving privileges for one month. The second offense, three months. The third offense, the car which had been purchased by the parent would be sold and never replaced by the parent. If the parents lovingly and firmly administer the first two consequences, chances are the car will never have to be sold. If, however, they let the first two slide, you can be certain that the teenager will proceed further in his substance abuse.

As you explore these and other areas of teaching your teenager responsible behavior, you will want to periodically reevaluate rules and consequences, giving the teenager more freedom and more responsibility as he gets older but never separating the two. All rules and consequences should have the best interest of the teenager in mind and should be formed after much thought with due consideration to the teenager's thoughts and feelings but under the canopy of loving, parental authority. The loving parent cares enough to do the hard work of forming rules and enforcing consequences.

NOTES

1. Lawrence Steinberg and Ann Levine, *You and Your Adolescent* (New York: Harper & Row, 1990), 16.

2. Ibid.

3. Ibid., 16–17.

4. Ibid., 16.

5. See Exodus 20.

6. The two commandments Jesus said were the greatest were to love God with a whole heart and to love your neighbor as you love yourself; see Mark 12:30–31.

7. 2 Thessalonians 3:10.

8. Lawrence Kutner, *Making Sense of Your Teenager* (New York: William Morrow, 1997), 141.

9. Steinberg and Levine, *You and Your Adolescent,* 187.

chapter thirteen

LOVING WHEN YOUR TEEN FAILS

Daniel was a big man with thick brown hair and a well-trimmed beard. He had all the trappings of success and was highly respected in the community. However, in my office, his tears now were watering the roots of his beard.

"I can't believe it, Dr. Chapman. It all seems like a bad dream. I wish I could wake up and it would all have been just a nightmare. But I know it is not a dream; it's reality. And I don't know what to do. I want to do the right thing, but in my state of mind I don't know if I am capable of doing the right thing. A part of me wants to strangle him and ask, 'How could you do this to us?' Another part of me wants to take him into my arms and hold him forever. My wife is so upset she couldn't even come with me today. He's coming home tomorrow and we don't know how to respond."

Daniel's tears, anger, frustration, and confusion all focused on his nineteen-year-old son who had called home from college the night before and informed them that he had gotten a girl pregnant and that she refused to have an abortion. He told them that he knew this news would hurt them and that he knew that what he had done was wrong. But he needed help and he didn't know where else to turn. Daniel and his wife Micki had spent a sleepless night trying to console each other but there was no consolation. Their son had failed and there were no easy answers.

Only those parents who have received similar phone calls can fully empathize with Daniel and Micki. The pain seems unbearable. Emotions rush through their bodies like the waters of Niagara. Hurt, anger, pity, sorrow, and deep love—the kind of love that brings more hurt, anger, pity and sorrow—slosh through their minds like socks in a washer. They hope against hope that when the sun rises tomorrow it will all be a colossal hoax, but in their hearts the parents know that they must face the reality of broken dreams.

TEENS WILL FAIL

As I recall Daniel and Micki's pain, I am reminded of what child psychologist John Rosemond said, "Good parenting is doing the *right* thing when a child does the *wrong* thing."[1]

That's what this chapter is about: the right response to our teens' wrong choices. The fact is we cannot keep our children from failing; we cannot keep our teenagers from failing. Our best efforts at loving and parenting them do not guarantee their success. Teenagers are persons, and persons are free to make choices, good or bad. When teenagers make poor choices, parents suffer. This is the nature of parenting. Because we are related, when the teenager fails, the shock waves are felt by the rest of the family. No one feels the trauma more deeply than the parents of the teenager.

Not all teenage failures are of the same magnitude. As with physical earthquakes, there are minor tremors and there are 7.5 quakes. Obviously the aftermath of one is not the same as the other. Alex missed three consecutive free throws—any one of which would have sealed victory for his team—as his friends and family watched. Alex failed, but his failure was a small tremor compared to the failure of Daniel and Micki's son, unless of course the scout from the major university was in the stands that night. Which brings me to another observation.

KINDS OF FAILURES

Failure to Meet Our Expectations

Not only are there different levels of failure, there are different kinds of failure. Alex illustrates failure to perform up to one's ability or the expectations of parents. These kinds of failure occur all the time in the field of sports, the arts, schoolwork, debate team, etc. Some of these performance failures occur because parents or teenagers have accepted unrealistic expectations. If the goal is unrealistic, then failure is inevitable. Parents should understand from the outset that not every player can win the gold medal. If parents are only satisfied with perfection, they will be dissatisfied with their teenager. Performance goals, if not attainable, will create discouragement.

In competitive events, parents may need to help the teenager reframe the results. Coming in second place in the playoff tournament is not failure. If there are thirty teams in the league, it means your team is better than twenty-eight. Coming in last place in the marathon means that you are a better runner than the 100,000 people who didn't enter the race. If your teenage daughter was playing clarinet in the marching band that placed 10th among 100 high schools in competition, her band ranked in the 90th percentile! That's cause to celebrate, not to bemoan the band's "poor showing."

Of course, everyone would like to win whatever the competition. However, the fact that there can only be one winner does not mean that everyone else is a loser. In our highly competitive "winning is everything" culture, teenagers are often set up to fail by well-meaning adults, sometimes parents.

Another reason some teenagers experience performance failures is that they have been pushed into areas of performance in which they have little or no interest or aptitude. Because of the parent's interest in athletics, the teenager is pushed into the athletic arena when the child really wanted to play in the band. The teenager could have been an excellent trumpet player; instead, she is "sitting on the bench," feeling like a failure in the athletic world. Pushing teenagers into areas where they have no interest is setting them up to fail.

I once knew a father who pushed his son to become a medical doctor. His son struggled through organic chemistry and physics in college and after two emotional breakdowns finally made it through medical school. On the day of his graduation, he presented his M. D. sheepskin to his father and refused to go for his residency. The last I heard, he was working at McDonald's trying to decide what he wanted to do with his life. Certainly parents may expose the teenager to their own areas of interest, but they must not seek to manipulate the teenager into following their own desires when they do not coincide with the teenager's interests and abilities. Parents who recognize this tendency in themselves should rent and view the film, *Dead Poet's Society.* This story of a young high school student who could not please his father will leave you weeping but wiser.

Moral Failures

A second category of teenage failure is far more devastating to both the teen and the parent. It's what I am calling *moral failures.* These failures occur when the teenager violates the moral code by which the family has lived through the years. From earliest childhood, parents communicate their moral values to their children. It is hoped by most parents that in the teenage years, though the teens may test these moral values, they will come to adopt them as their own. Obviously, this does not always happen.

Teenagers violate moral codes in two ways. Some make the conscious choice to reject the family's moral values and establish their own. Others, while accepting the family's value system, in practice violate its precepts. Either of these creates pain for the parents and usually for the teenager. Parents truly grieve when their son or daughter makes a moral decision that the parents know is wrong. They know that consequences are in store for the teen. And the teen usually senses that the parents feel let down, or at least sense the pain of or even estrangement from his parents.

The consequences for moral failures can often be devastating to parents. Most parents have secretly asked themselves the question "What would I do if my teenage daughter called and said 'I'm pregnant'? Or if my son called and gave me the message his girlfriend is pregnant [the same message that Daniel and Micki received]? What would I do if I learned that my teenager was using or pushing drugs? What would I do if my teenager informed me that he/she had AIDS or some other sexually transmitted disease? What would I do if I received a call from the police department saying that my teen had been arrested for theft or assault?"

In truth, those are questions that thousands of parents will be forced to answer during their child's teenage years.

BRINGING REDEMPTION TO
YOUR TEEN'S MORAL FAILURES

In the remaining pages of this chapter, I want to suggest some practical ideas that have helped other parents process teenage moral failure in a redemptive manner. When we use our teen's failure to show compassion and restoration, we are acting as good parents, "doing the right thing when [our] child does the wrong thing," as Rosemond says.

1. Don't blame yourself.

Before you help your teenage son or daughter, deal with your own response. The first response of many parents when their teen fails is to ask, "What did we do wrong?" It is a logical question, particularly in a society that has placed so much emphasis in recent years on the value of proper parenting. However, in many self-help books and parenting seminars we have overestimated the power of positive parenting and failed to reckon with the teenager's freedom of choice. The fact is teenagers can and will make choices both in the home and outside the home. These choices always have consequences. Poor choices produce detrimental results, whereas wise choices bring positive fruit.

Parents cannot be in the physical presence of their teenagers twenty-four hours a day and control their behavior. You did this when your daughter was three, but you cannot do it when she is thirteen. As frightening as it may seem, your teen must be given freedom to make decisions.

Choices expand during the teenage years. This is a necessary and usually healthy process, but it does increase the risk of teenage failure. Parents who blame themselves are doing their teenager a disservice. The bottom line is the teenager made a poor decision and is now suffering the results. If the parent takes the blame, it removes the guilt from the teenager. The teenager is more than happy to find someone else who will take the blame for his present woes. When he is able to roll his guilt on your shoulders, the teen is less likely to learn from the failure and more likely to repeat it in the future.

Parents who are most prone to take the blame for their teen's moral failures are parents who realize that they did a poor job of parenting in the earlier years. They have been reading books, attending seminars, and coming to understand that they violated some of the basic concepts of good parenting. I do not wish to convey the idea that parents are not responsible to be good parents. What I am saying is that you are responsible for your own failure, not the failures of the teenager. If you recognize specific failures in your past parenting patterns, confess these to God and the teenager. Seek forgiveness from both but don't accept responsibility for your teenager's poor choices.

2. Don't preach to the teenager.

Usually the teenager is already feeling guilty. Teens know when their behavior hurts parents. They are aware when they violate the moral codes they have been taught. Preaching is unnecessary. To Daniel, the tearful father we met at the beginning of this chapter, I said, "When your son comes home from college tomorrow, don't let your first words be words of condemnation. Don't say, 'Why did you do this? You know this violates everything we've taught you through the years. How could you do this to us? Don't you know you are tearing our hearts apart? You have ruined everything. I can't believe you could be so stupid.'"

"I understand that you may have all of these thoughts and feelings," I continued, "but your son does not need to hear such condemnation. He is already having those thoughts and asking himself those questions. If you make these statements and ask these questions, he may become defensive and stop wrestling with the questions himself."

A teenager who has failed needs to wrestle with his own guilt, but he does not need further condemnation.

3. Don't try to fix it.

The natural response of many parents is to try to minimize what has happened. To jump into a "damage control" mode and try to protect the teenager is, in my opinion, an extremely unwise move. If you seek to remove the natural consequences of the teen's failure, you are working against your teen's maturity. Teens learn some of life's deepest lessons through experiencing the consequences of failure. When these consequences are removed by parents, the teenager gets another message. The message is one that fosters irresponsibility. "I can do wrong and someone else will take care of the consequences." Such a conclusion makes it difficult for the teenager to learn responsibility.

I know it is difficult to watch our teenagers suffer the consequences of their decisions, but to remove the consequences is to remove one of life's greatest teachers. I remember the parent who said to me, "The most difficult thing I have ever done in my life was to walk out of jail and leave my son behind bars. I knew I could get him out on bail but I knew that if I did, he would be selling drugs again that night. For his own good, I chose to let him suffer the consequences of his own wrongdoing. In retrospect, it was one of the best decisions I ever made on his behalf."

Thus far, we have focused on the negatives: Don't blame yourself, don't preach to the teenager, don't try to fix it. Now let's turn to the positive side.

4. Give your teenager unconditional love.

First, demonstrate unconditional love to your teen. This does not contradict what we have just said. Allowing the teenager to experience the consequences of his own failure is itself an act of love. In so doing, you are looking out for the well-being of the teenager, which is the essence of love. However, what I am focusing on in this section is meeting the teen's emotional need for love. This is where the five love languages are exceedingly important. If you know your teenager's love language, this is the time to speak that primary language loudly, while giving the other four love languages as often as possible.

207

The teen's moral failure creates feelings of guilt. These emotions push the teenager away from you. As Adam and Eve tried to hide in the garden from the presence of God, so your teenager may try to hide from you. The teen may fear your condemnation. God's response to Adam and Eve is a good model for parents. Indeed, He let them suffer the consequences of their wrongdoing but, at the same time, He gave them a gift. They were trying to hide themselves with fig leaves. He gave them leather coats. The wise parent will give love to the teenager no matter what the failure.

Daniel and Micki told me later that when their son arrived home from college, they met him at the door with outstretched arms. They each gave him a long tearful embrace and said, "We love you." Then they sat down and listened as their son confessed his wrongdoing and asked their forgiveness. Unconditional love creates the climate for open dialogue. The teenager needs to know that no matter what he has done, someone is there who still believes in him, who still believes that he is valuable, and who is willing to forgive. When the teenager senses emotional love from parents, he is more likely to face the failure head on, accepting the consequences as deserved, and try to learn something positive from the experience.

5. Listen to the teenager with empathy.

We said earlier that this is not the time for preaching. It is a time for empathetic listening. Empathy means to enter into the feelings of another. Parents need to put themselves into the shoes of the teenager and try to understand what led to the failure as well as what the teenager is feeling at the moment. If the teenager senses that parents are trying to understand and identify with her feelings, the teenager is encouraged to continue talking. On the other hand if the teenager senses that parents are listening with a judgmental attitude, ready to condemn her actions, the conversation will be short-lived and the teenager will walk away feeling unloved and rejected.

Empathetic listening is enhanced by asking reflective questions such as "Are you saying that this is what you were feeling at the time? Are you saying that you felt that we would not understand? Is this what you are saying?" Such reflective questions give the teenager a chance to clarify thoughts and emotions and the parents an opportunity to understand. Empathetic listening leads to understanding, which creates the platform for being able to truly help the teenager.

6. Give the teenager support.

Once you have listened and have come to understand the thoughts and feelings of the teenager, you are now in a position to give emotional support. Let the teen know that while you do not agree with what he has done and that you cannot remove all the consequences, you want him to know that you are with him and will stand by his side as he walks through the process of dealing with the consequences of this failure.

After Daniel and Micki had listened to their son's story and had shared their tears of regret, Daniel said to his son, "I want you to know that Mom and I are with you. Obviously we are not happy about what has happened. We don't know all the results that must be faced. But we will walk with you through the process. We hope that you will do the responsible thing by the young lady and the baby and we will do all we can to support you. This does not mean that we will take care of the financial expenses. That is something we believe to be your responsibility. But we will encourage you, pray for you, and do everything we can to help you become a stronger person on the other side of this."

Those are statements of emotional support. The teenager needs to know that even though he has failed, he is not alone in life. Someone cares enough to join him in his pain and difficulty.

7. Give guidance to the teenager.

Give your teenager guidance. By guidance, I do not mean manipulation. Parents who tend to have controlling personalities often want to control the teenager's behavior after a moral failure. When the parent decides what ought to be done and tries to convince the teenager to do it, this is manipulation, not guidance. Guidance is helping the teenager think through the situation and make wise choices in responding to the consequences of the moral failure.

Parents must take seriously the feelings, thoughts, and desires of the teenager. These must not be swept away as being insignificant. Because the teenager has had a moral failure does not mean that the parents must now make the decisions for the teenager. The teenager cannot become a responsible adult without having freedom to grapple with his situation and make decisions regarding where he goes from here.

One way in which parents may give guidance to a teenager is by helping the teen follow his own thoughts to their logical conclusion. For example, Daniel and Micki's son said, "One of the thoughts I had is simply to leave the state, move to California and try to start my life over again." Micki was wise not to follow her desire to say, "That is a stupid idea. That won't solve anything." Rather she asked, "If you could find enough money to get to California, what kind of work would you pursue?" After her son shared his ideas on the subject, she said, "Would you see yourself sending money to take care of the child's expenses?" to which her son responded, "Certainly. I'm going to do the responsible thing."

"Perhaps you could contact our car insurance agent and get him to check out the insurance rates in California," Micki then suggested. "I think he also has a relative who lives out there who may give you some idea of what it would cost you to rent an apartment." With these and several other questions, Micki was helping her son think about the implications of his idea of moving to California.

Parents who learn how to give this kind of guidance will continue to influence their teenager's decisions in a positive direction. However, parents who make quick judgments and dogmatic statements about their teenager's ideas will stop the flow of communication and drive the teenager to someone else for guidance. The teen may even make a foolish decision as a defensive reaction to the parents' "know it all" attitude.

This kind of guidance is difficult for many parents to give. It is easier to tell our teenagers what we think and to make dogmatic statements about the validity or absurdity of their ideas. This does not help a teenager develop his own decision-making skills. The teenager does not need commands; he needs guidance.

Another way of giving guidance is to share your ideas as possibilities. "One possible approach might be . . . " is far more helpful than "What I think you ought to do is . . . " Remember, in spite of moral failure, the teenager still wants to develop independence and self-identity. Parents must not forget this major motif of the teenage years in trying to help their teenager learn from failure. You may well see possibilities that your teenager does not see. Your teenager could profit from your insights if you share them as possibilities, not as "oughts."

If this approach seems difficult for you, perhaps you can write out your ideas as you would normally express them. Then go back and modify them to be stated as possibilities rather than oughts. For example, some of Daniel's original thoughts were, "I think you ought to drop out of school for at least this semester and get a job so you can save some money to help with the expenses associated with the birth of the child. You will need some counseling. We can help you with that. Then next fall, you can go back to college part time. Maybe she will decide to let the child be adopted and your ongoing expenses may cease at that point." On and on Daniel thought about what he would say to his son. Normally this is the way Daniel would have expressed his thoughts—be straightforward and tell his son what he should do. In so doing, Daniel would be taking far too much responsibility.

However, if Daniel takes these same ideas and expresses them as "possibilities" rather than "oughts," he will create a much healthier climate. Daniel might say, "One possibility would be for you to drop out of school for a semester so that you could get a job and make some money to pay for the baby's expenses. You may also find it helpful to get some personal counseling. If you like, Mom and I would be willing to pay for that. Then next summer after the baby is born, you can see if the mother decides to allow the child to be adopted. This may create a totally different situation. Of course, there are other possibilities. Think about it and if you like, we can talk about it again later."

In terms of words, the change in these two presentations is very slight. But in terms of enhancing personal growth and responsibility, the latter is light years ahead of the former. Daniel's son is far more likely to be influenced if Daniel chooses to use the second approach. Guidance, though much more difficult than commands, is by far the more effective way to help a teenager learn to make responsible decisions.

If after all of your dialogue, you see a teenager about to make what you think to be a detrimental decision, one that simply will make the situation worse rather than better, you can continue to give guidance if you share it as advice rather than commands. The issue is to recognize the teenager's autonomy as a person and that ultimately, he will make his own decisions.

In such a situation, a parent might say, "Brad, I certainly want this to be your decision because you are the one who will have to live with the consequences. But I want to share with you my fears if you make that decision." You share your fears and then say, "Those are the things that make me feel it might be better to take another approach." Then you share your own ideas. You have not removed the responsibility of decision making from the shoulder of your teenager nor have you blatantly demanded that your teen do what you want, but you have given the teen the benefit of your thoughts and feelings stated in a way that he is more likely to receive.

If in the end, the teenager makes the decision that you believe to be unwise then you allow him to suffer the natural outcomes of that decision. If those outcomes turn out to be negative and the teenager fails again, you repeat the process discussed above, remembering that you cannot control the life of your teenager. Being a responsible parent is helping your teenager learn from his own mistakes.

TEENAGE FAILURE
THROUGH DRUGS AND ALCOHOL

Since drugs and alcohol abuse are such a major problem in our society, I feel compelled to say a word to parents about helping teenagers who fail in this area. But first a word about prevention. The best thing parents can do is to be proactive in the early teenage years in regards to tobacco, alcohol, and drugs, applying the principles we have discussed in this chapter and in chapter 12 about letting the teenager experience the consequences of his choices.

In a family forum, Jack and Sarah explain to their thirteen-year-old that now that he is a teenager, they know he may be pressured by his friends to smoke, to drink, and to use drugs. "Since you are now a teenager, we believe you are old enough to be an informed citizen on these matters. Therefore, one of the things we are going to do as a family is to attend the informational classes at the local hospital on the detrimental effects of smoking cigarettes." Jack added that "Mom and I want you to know the facts before your friends try to pressure you to smoke."

Most teenagers will respond positively to such an opportunity and, having seen pictures of diseased lungs, will choose not to smoke. As a wise parent, you can take a similar approach both to alcohol and drugs, whether it is attending a class that is available in your community or reading and discussing the detrimental effects of alcohol and drugs through books or booklets you receive through your church or the mental health department of your local government or books you find in the library. Giving your teenager information about the detrimental effects of alcohol and drugs is information that can lead the teenager to make wise decisions before he is pressured by his peers to drink or use drugs.

After giving your younger teenager such foundational information, you may periodically clip articles from the newspaper about young people who are killed by drunken drivers. You may want to take your teenager for a visit to the local rescue mission and let her sit through a meal and a service with the men or women whose lives have been wrecked by alcohol and drugs. In so doing, you are giving your younger teenager a picture of the other side of drug and alcohol use that she will never see on television.

You may also talk with your teenager about the way advertisers seek to exploit people by showing her only one side of drinking and drug use. If your teenager can begin to see that advertisers are seeking to exploit her and other young people, she is likely to respond negatively to the lure of TV advertisements and the pressure of peers. This proactive approach is in my opinion one of the best things parents can do for younger teenagers.

However, if you did not have such a family forum when your daughter or son was thirteen and you find out that your fifteen-year-old is already smoking cigarettes, rather than ignoring it, hoping it will go away, or searching the teenager's drawers and throwing away the cigarettes hoping they will not return, it is far better to confront the teenager with the knowledge you have received and say to your teen, "I think you know that it is my sincere desire that you not smoke. My reason for that is that smoking is so extremely detrimental to health. However, I know that I cannot make that decision for you. I can keep you from smoking in the house, but I cannot control your behavior when you are away. If you are going to smoke, I want it to be an informed decision. Therefore, I am going to ask you to attend the informational classes held at the local hospital on what happens when people smoke. I know that I cannot make you attend these classes but because I care so much about you, I am going to strongly urge you to attend." If the teenager attends, he can then make an informed decision. Most teenagers will choose not to smoke when they know the facts.

However, if the teenager refuses to attend the classes, the parents can do two things. First, they can make certain the teenager does not smoke in the house—feel free to mention the dangers to other family members of secondhand smoke in the house. Second, until the teenager attends the class, the parent can withhold allowances and privileges as a leverage to encourage the teenager's compliance. Again, you are not making the teenager do anything; you are simply demonstrating that freedom and responsibility always go together. They no longer have the freedom of receiving an allowance until they attend the class.

Perhaps the substance is not tobacco but alcohol or drugs. Alcohol and drug abuse not only can impair and eventually destroy the life of the user, but either one will harm the lives of all those around the user. If your teenager is an addict, you need professional help. I strongly suggest two steps. One, discover and begin attending a local Al-Anon meeting. Al-Anon is a national group designed to help parents who have teenagers (or other family members) who are hooked on alcohol or drugs.[2] Second, go for personal counseling. Find a counselor who has expertise in helping parents make wise decisions about how to relate to their teenager who is addicted. Parents cannot handle this alone. They need the wisdom of those who are experienced in working with addicted teens. There are programs that can help. These programs are worth exploring, but you need the wisdom of a professional to help you make wise decisions in the process. If the parents of an addict do not get help themselves, they are not likely to be able to help their teenager.

THE POWER OF LOVE

Many parents can join Daniel and Micki in saying, "The darkest night of our lives was the beginning of a deeper and more meaningful relationship with our teenager." Love is the key for turning tragedy into triumph. Parents who will love enough not to blame themselves, not to preach, not to try to fix it, who will listen with empathy, give support and guidance—all in the spirit of unconditional love—will likely see their teenager take giant steps toward maturity as they walk through the consequences of teenage failure.

What I have tried to say in this chapter is that the teenager who fails does not need parents who walk behind, kicking him or condemning her for a personal failure. Nor does the teen need parents who will walk ahead, pulling him, trying to get him to conform to the parents' wishes. What the teenager needs is parents who will walk alongside, speaking the teen's love language with a sincere desire to learn with the teenager how to take responsible steps after failure. Parents who do this will indeed be successful parents. John Rosemond was right: "Good parenting is doing the *right* thing when a child does the *wrong* thing."

NOTES

1. John Rosemond, *Teen-Proofing: A Revolutionary Approach to Fostering Responsible Decision Making in Your Teenager* (Kansas City: Andrews McNeal Publishing, 1998), 170.

2. To find a local chapter of Al-Anon, check the Yellow Pages of your telephone directory or call the national headquarters at 1-800-344-2666.

chapter fourteen

LOVE LANGUAGES IN THE SINGLE PARENT FAMILY

Amanda's world is not easy. It hasn't been easy for a long time. She's a single-parent mom with two teenagers, Marc, age fifteen, and Julie, age thirteen. She has raised them alone since her husband left when Marc was ten.

She has felt the trauma of a difficult divorce and has worked through her own sense of rejection. Soon she took charge of her life. With the help of her parents, Amanda finished her nurse's training and since then has worked at the local hospital. Without working full-time, she would not have made it because her husband's child support payments were inadequate and often sporadic.

In spite of all that she has accomplished, Amanda lives with an underlying sense of guilt. Because of her job, she was not able to spend as much time with the children as she would have liked. She was not always able to attend their after-school activities. Julie was only eight when her father left; now she's a developing adolescent, and Amanda still can't spend as much time with her and her brother as she would like. She feels that Julie and Marc are growing up, slipping through her fingers, and she wonders if they are ready for what lies ahead. One day she tells herself, *I did the best I could*. The next day she says, *I'm not sure I did enough*. Lately Marc has been talking back and is often critical of his mom. Julie wants to start dating and Amanda thinks she is too young.

In my office, Amanda said, "I'm not sure I am up to this. I think I've done fairly well up until now, but I don't know if I can endure the teenage years."

I was hearing from Amanda what I have heard from hundreds of single parents through the years. "Will someone please help me? I'm not sure I can do this by myself."

Fortunately, there is help for parents like Amanda. Most communities provide single-parent support groups, sponsored by churches and other civic groups. Most libraries have numerous volumes directed to single parents. Some of the national organizations have web sites offering helpful information over the Internet. At the end of this chapter, you will find a list of some of these resources. I will not seek to duplicate the information that is available through other resources. The focus of this chapter is to help the single parent effectively meet his or her teenager's emotional need for love.

COMMON CHALLENGES

Receiving Love from One Parent

Of course, each single parent household is unique. However, there are some common threads which run through single adult families that often make this a more difficult task than when both parents are present. Most obvious is the reality that only one parent is the custodial parent. Though joint custody where the child theoretically spends an equal time with each parent sometimes works in early childhood, it seldom is workable with teenagers. By far the most common arrangement is that the mother will be the custodial parent while the father sees the teenager either regularly or sporadically, and in fewer cases, never. Thus in the day-to-day experience of life where the teenager needs to feel loved, there is only one parental lover. Ideally, the teenager needs a mother and a father who are expressing love on a daily basis. In a single parent family, this is simply impossible. Almost never does the non-custodial parent have daily contact with the teenager. This is a reality which the custodial parent must accept. That is one reason why the content of this book is so important for single parents.

If you are the only parent giving love on a daily basis, it is extremely important for you to discover and speak your teen's primary love language. Otherwise, you may be loving your teenager by acts of service when they are craving words of affirmation. As one single mom said, "I can't believe the difference in my daughter. I attended a workshop where they were discussing the five love languages and how to discover your teenager's primary language. It became obvious to me that my daughter's love language was quality time. I had been giving her words of affirmation and wondering why she was responding so negatively. When I started giving her quality time, most of which was taking her with me as I ran errands but focusing on her, it is amazing how her attitude changed. Within two weeks, she was a different person, and the whole climate in our house greatly improved."

Erupting Emotions

Another common factor in single parent homes is that the feelings buried in childhood often erupt in the teenage years. The emotions of hurt, anger, and rejection which were seldom expressed in childhood may give rise to low self-esteem, feelings of inadequacy, and depression or critical words and abusive behavior. What is interesting is that these emotions and the resulting behavior are seldom expressed in the presence of the non-custodial parent. This may be because the teenager believes the parent would not understand or perhaps would not care, or it may be that the teen does not want to disturb the positive aspects of the relationship with the non-custodial parent. It is the custodial parent who bears the brunt of the teenager's formerly dormant emotions.

This is extremely hard on most custodial parents. Often such parents feel unappreciated and experience anger toward the teenager. The parent who has worked hard to care for the child feels that she is mistreated by the teen.

Please know that you are not alone in having such feelings. Such emotions are common for single parents when their children become teenagers. Remember, your teen's strong emotions are in keeping with his or her developing desire for independence and self-identity. As an emerging adult whose intellectual, spiritual, and moral values are being formed, your teen is forced to grapple with what appear to be the inequities of life. This process can be positive. If the teenager is to enter adulthood with some level of maturity, these hurts from the past must be surfaced and processed. However, this may be painful for both teenager and parent.

THE PROPER RESPONSES

Focus on the Teen's Emotions

The important issue for the custodial parent is to focus on the teenager's emotions, not the teenager's behavior. This is exactly the opposite of what we typically do. Listen to Roberta as she describes her frustration with her fifteen-year-old son, Samuel. "He seems so down on himself. No matter how much I praise him, he expresses feelings of inadequacy. He seems depressed much of the time. I try to be happy and upbeat. I try to focus on the positive things about our lives, but he continues to mope around the house. Nothing I do seems to make any difference."

Roberta is trying to change Samuel's behavior and ignore his underlying feelings. Instead, she must realize that behind her teenager's behavior that's based upon his depression and low self-esteem are deeper feelings of hurt, anger, and rejection. These are the emotions that need to be discussed. If she continues to focus her attention on trying to talk the teen into a more positive self-esteem and more positive actions, telling Samuel how smart and capable he is, her efforts will produce minimal results. However, if she can create an atmosphere where Samuel can talk about his childhood and particularly the emotions centering around the divorce, death, or abandonment of the father, she will begin to see a change in his attitude toward himself.

I'm not suggesting this is an easy process. It is not something that happens in one conversation. These hurtful emotions from the past and the thoughts and memories surrounding them must be expressed by the teenager again and again while the custodial parent listens sympathetically. The surfacing and sharing of these hurts is necessary if the teenager is to find emotional healing.

Madison complained of a different problem. "My sixteen-year-old has gone ballistic," she said. "The other night, she actually cursed me. I could not believe my ears. Several times she has thrown things, sometimes at me but usually at the wall. This behavior is totally uncharacteristic." As I later talked with Madison's daughter, I discovered that she had recently started dating. The prospects of having a romantic relationship with a male had surfaced all of the dormant emotions that she had toward her father. Since her father had abandoned her, she feared the abandonment of her boyfriend. The anger she had held under wraps was now erupting. She was angry with her mother, whom she still somewhat blamed for the divorce. She was angry with her father for walking away, and even more angry that he had shown so little interest in her since he left. This angry behavior was actually a positive indicator that she was now beginning to deal with the hurts of the past.

When Madison understood this, she was able to focus on helping her daughter talk about these buried emotions rather than condemning her daughter's negative behavior. The behavior will eventually subside if the inner pain can be processed through talking and sympathetic listening.

Listen and Tell the Teen the Truth

In processing the teenager's hurts of the heart, the custodial parent must not only do the hard work of listening but must also tell the truth. When the teen's father left, you gave simple explanations that seemed to satisfy the child at the time. You thought the issues were settled. Now the teenager is bringing all of it to the surface again, only now the teenager will ask much more specific questions. She wants to know what went on before the divorce; she wants to know what the marriage was like in the earlier years. She will ask, "If my father is so bad, then why did you marry him?" If the mother died, the teenager will again ask questions about the nature of the illness or accident. "Tell me again, what was Mother like? What did she say about me?" These are typical questions of the teenager—hard, painful, probing questions, but questions that deserve answers.

Whatever you do, don't make excuses for your own behavior or for the behavior of your ex-spouse. Tell the truth. If your teenagers find out later that you lied about the details, they will lose respect for you. Perhaps you felt that when they were children, they could not handle the truth. But now they are teenagers, and their emotional healing demands that they know the truth.

Marjorie, the mother of a fourteen-year-old, said, "The hardest thing I ever did was to answer the questions of my teenage daughter. I know I should have told her earlier, but it never seemed to be the right time. Now she was asking the hard questions, and I had to choose whether I would lie or tell the truth. It was the most painful night of my life when I told her that I was never married to her father, that I met him at a beach party, had sex with him, and never saw him again. Before that, I had always told her that he left when she was young. At first, my daughter was angry. She said I should have told her earlier, but the thing that hurt me most was when she said, 'So you really didn't want me. I was an accident.'

"I listened to her angry words and I told her I understood how she could feel that way but I hoped my actions since that night had demonstrated to her that I loved her from the very beginning. We had many talks in the weeks following that night. We've cried, laughed, and hugged each other. I've never felt closer to my daughter than now and I think she loves me in a more mature way than ever before. I always knew the day would come when I would have to tell her the truth. I had hoped I would have the courage. I'm glad I did." The old adage is true: the truth hurts. But it is also true that the truth heals.

Knowing and speaking your teenager's primary love language can be an extremely helpful part of this truth-telling experience. A touch, a word of affirmation, a gift, an act of service, or quality time will help create the climate where the painful process of healing the past can take place. Marjorie's daughter later said to me, "It was Momma's hugs that brought me through. I have never felt so hurt in my whole life as when Momma told me the truth. I wanted to run, I wanted to scream, I wanted to kill myself. But when Momma hugged me, it felt like a blanket of love." Her primary love language was physical touch and it spoke deeply to her hurting heart. Marjorie also spoke the other love languages. She gave her much quality time and long discussions. She verbally affirmed her love on numerous occasions. There were special gifts and acts of service—all of which played a role in her daughter's healing. But physical touch was the blanket of love.

Respect the Teen's Unrealistic Desires

One other challenge for the single parent should be mentioned, along with the parent's proper response. The teenager in a single-parent family will experience many unrealistic desires. You may hear your teenage son say, "I wish Daddy would come to my games." But you know the reality is his daddy lives a thousand miles away, has a new wife and two children. He is not coming to your son's games. Your sixteen-year-old daughter may say, "Daddy is going to buy me a car," but you know that her father is deeply in debt and could not buy her a car even if he wanted to. These impossible dreams are a part of the teenager's imagination. It is a subconscious attempt to have the kind of family the teenager desires.

The natural response of many custodial parents is to blast these dreams with grenades of reality. In my opinion, this is a serious mistake. Far better to affirm the teen's desires and let reality dawn a day at a time. "You wish that your father would buy you a new car. That's a good thought. I wish he would too." "You wish that your father could come to your games. I wish he could too. That would really be nice." If you have these kind of positive responses to your teenager's unrealistic desires, you are affirming the teen as a person. If you feel compelled to blast his ideas and say something negative about your ex-spouse, you are encouraging the teenager to keep his desires to himself. In accepting and affirming these desires, you will encourage the flow of communication. Often the teenager already knows that these are impossible dreams, but dreaming is a part of his coping with the less-than-ideal realities.

If you have contact with your former spouse, you can share some of the teenager's desires. This should never be done in a demanding way but simply as a matter of sharing information. "I thought you'd like to know that several times Seth has said, 'I wish Daddy could come to my games.' I know that's probably impossible, but if it ever would work out, it would mean a lot to him. If not, maybe you could ask about his games when you call him." This is good information for the non-custodial parent. "Stephanie has said several times that you are going to buy her a car when she turns sixteen. I'm not asking you to do it, but I thought you'd like to know what she's been saying." On the other hand, sharing the teen's desires with the non-custodial parent is sometimes best done by the teenager, especially if the parents are in an adversarial relationship. To say to the teenager, "Maybe you should share that with your father," might be the encouragement the teenager needs.

For some parents who are pessimistic by nature, it will be extremely difficult to do what I have just suggested. By nature, they see the glass half empty and they spill this pessimism on their teenager. If this happens to be a part of your personality, I urge you to go for personal counseling and seek to turn your own spirit in a more optimistic direction. Dreams, even impossible dreams, are a part of what makes life bearable on the dark days, and who knows what is impossible. Even the Scriptures say, "Where there is no vision, the people perish."[1]

If the teen's desires are unrealistic, that will eventually become obvious. But as the teen shares desires, he is sharing information that the parent otherwise would not know. Often many of these desires are in keeping with the teenager's primary love language. Chances are the teen who is wishing that his father would come to his games has the primary love language of quality time while the teenager who is asking for a car may be exhibiting the language of gifts. Certainly a teenager may have desires that fall outside his or her primary love language, but if you catalog the desires, you will find that the majority fall within the parameters of the teen's primary love language.

FOR NON-CUSTODIAL PARENTS

Now let me share some words with non-custodial parents. I hope you do not feel that I have been unfair to you in the earlier portion of this chapter. The fact is, you can play a significantly important role in the life of your teenager. Your teenager needs you. Many non-custodial parents acknowledge that they need help in knowing how to parent their teenagers. Some non-custodial parents see the teenager on a regular basis such as every other weekend or one weekend a month. Others live hundreds of miles from their teenagers and visits are sporadic interlaced with phone calls and E-mails. How do you make the most of what you have? Let me deal with a couple of pitfalls and then share some positive ideas.

Avoid the Pitfalls

One common pitfall is what is sometimes called the "Disneyland Daddy" syndrome. This is where the time with your teenager is spent in taking your teen to ball games, video shops, movies, and other amusement centers. Your attention is focused on activities rather than the teenager himself. Because of the limited amount of time these parents have with their teenagers, they tend to plan each meeting in advance and try to have fun with their teenager. The teenager and parent come to the end of the visit exhausted. Don't misunderstand me. There is nothing wrong with having fun with your teenager and most teenagers enjoy activities. But let's face it, life is not always fun and games. Your teenager needs to see you in more normal settings. Since you are excluded from the everyday routines of your teenager during the week, you may have little idea of what is going on in the mind and heart of your teenager. This requires open dialogue in a relaxed and sometimes not so relaxed atmosphere. The parent cannot meet the emotional needs of the teenager until he first discovers those needs.

It is not uncommon that fathers and teenagers have different views about the visitation relationship. Research indicates that the father often thinks he has fulfilled his responsibility, whereas the teenager feels something is missing. The father thinks he has been loving, but the teenager feels rejected. One study indicated that whereas most fathers thought they had fulfilled their obligations, three out of four teenagers had the impression that they did not mean very much to their fathers. "They thought that their fathers were physically but not emotionally present."[2] It seems apparent that the Disneyland Daddy syndrome is not the most positive approach for parenting your teenager.

Another pitfall is taking advantage of your teenager. One fifteen-year-old girl tells of arriving at her father's house for the weekend and being told that he had to leave because of an appointment and asked her to baby-sit two younger half brothers until he and his wife returned. He and his wife returned the following evening well after midnight. Obviously, this teenager did not find her visit to be very satisfying. When her next regularly scheduled visitation rolled around, she refused to visit her father.

I am not implying that the teenager cannot do work during the visit. In fact, involving your teen in the normal flow of your life can be a very positive experience. Simple things like going to the grocery store or bank together can be meaningful to your teenager. But the teen knows when she is being taking advantage of, when your interests center on yourself rather than the teenager, and the teen will quickly resent such behavior.

The third pitfall is to assume that your teenager is emotionally stable if he is not talking about problems. Teens are often reluctant to share their emotional struggles with the non-custodial parent. There are many reasons for this. Some fear that if they are honest about their feelings, their fathers will reject them even further and that visits will cease. Some who remember their father's violent outbursts from younger years fear the wrath of fathers if they share their honest thoughts and feelings. Others fail to share because they don't want to "rock the boat." Better to have a calm surface relationship than to get into an argument and make things worse, they may think. The bottom line is that silence does not indicate health.

Most teenagers whose parents live apart have the kind of feelings and thoughts discussed earlier in this chapter. They desperately need to share those thoughts and emotions with you. The wise parent will create an atmosphere where this can be done without fear of retaliation. In most cases, the parent will need to take the initiative by saying something like, "I know that my not living with your mother has probably caused a lot of hurt and struggle in your life. If you'd like to talk about it, I want you to know that I am willing to listen. If I continue to do things or fail to do things that disappoint or hurt you, I hope you will tell me. I want to be a better father, and I'm open to your suggestions." Your teenager may not immediately respond to such an invitation, but if he becomes convinced that you are sincere, sooner or later you will hear his struggles.

Deal with Any Personal Issues

If you are a non-custodial parent and have little contact with your teenager because of your own personal problems—emotional struggles, financial problems, drug addiction, etc.—let me encourage you to take steps to deal with your problems. After more than thirty years of marriage and family counseling, I can predict that the day will come when you will regret your lack of involvement in your teenager's life. You can avoid those regrets by taking positive action now to face your problems head on and get the help you need.

Find a counselor, minister, or trusted friend and be honest about your own needs. Let someone guide you in finding the necessary help in turning your life in a more positive direction. When you begin to take these steps, your teenager will begin to respect you and you are one step closer to a meaningful relationship with your teenager.

Be Involved and Speak Your Teen's Love Language

On the other hand, if you are having regular contact with your teenager, let me encourage you to make the most of your visits, phone calls, E-mails, or letters. Share with the teenager what is going on in your life, both your successes and failures. Be honest and real with your teenager. The teenager is looking for authenticity. Take time to ask questions that will probe your teenager's thoughts, feelings, and desires. You need not have all the answers. In fact, it's better if you don't have all the answers. The teenager needs to learn to think for himself. Seek to get in touch with the teenager's emotions. Don't limit your time to surface talk. Ask your ex-spouse for ideas that might enhance your contacts with the teenager.

In addition, don't criticize the custodial parent when you are with your teenager. If the teenager is critical about the other parent, listen to what the teen is saying. Then ask his advice on how you might help. Be sympathetic with the teenager's criticisms, but don't join in by adding your own.

Above all, learn how to speak the five love languages. Discover your teenager's primary love language and speak it often. Your greatest contribution to the well-being of your teenager is to let her know that you care about her well-being, and you love her. Don't assume that she feels your love. Many parents are speaking their own love language and assuming that the teenager feels loved. Thousands of teenagers do not. There is no substitute for speaking the primary love language of your teenager.

Whatever your relationship has been through the years with your teenager, it is never too late to make it better. An honest confession about past failures and requesting the teenager's forgiveness could be the first step on a long road of renewing a warm, loving relationship between you and your teenager. The journey may be painful for both of you, but I can assure you it is a journey worth taking.

IMPORTANT GUIDELINES

As we conclude this chapter, let me offer to both custodial and non-custodial parents several important guidelines for showing love to your teenagers.

1. *Listen to your teenager.* You cannot adequately raise teenagers without listening to what they are saying. Parents who ignore the statements of teenagers will almost certainly fail to meet the teens' emotional needs, nor will parents be able to guide them in a positive direction. Guidance starts where the teenager is. Without listening, the parent will be unable to take the first step. In listening to the teenager, you are speaking quality time; you are giving your teen undivided attention. You are communicating that the teen is a person worth knowing and you are giving a portion of your life to the teenager.

2. *Teach your teenager to handle anger in a positive way.* This may mean working on your own patterns of anger management. Most single parents have had their own share of anger. Some of them have learned to handle it constructively; others are holding it inside, while still others are exploding with angry words and behavior. Your teenager is not likely to be open to your help until they see you taking steps to manage your own anger. If you or your teenager need improvement in this key element of personal relationships, I encourage you to read again chapters 9 and 10 on love and anger.

228

3. *Kindly but firmly keep the boundaries in place.* The teenager needs the security of knowing that parents care enough to say no to those things they believe to be detrimental to the teenager. If the two of you can talk about boundaries and have the same list of rules and consequences, so much the better. This communicates to the teenager that both parents care equally about his well-being.

4. *Above all else, give your teenager unconditional love.* Good or bad, right or wrong, the teenager needs to feel that someone cares, someone genuinely loves him. The persons he would most like to love him are his parents. If each of you will join in the common goal of keeping your teen's love tank full, you will be creating the best possible atmosphere in which to raise your teenager.

5. *Consider joining a single-parent study group.* These are available in most communities, often sponsored by civic groups, churches, and colleges. Such groups typically form a two-way street. Someone will have walked your road and have practical ideas for you. Others have recently entered the world of single parenting, and you will be able to encourage them. Such groups can be very helpful in the difficult task of being a successful single parent.

6. *Enlist the help of extended family, friends, and churches.* If your extended family lives nearby and you think they would be a positive influence on your teenager, don't hesitate to ask for their help. A grandfather, uncle, or older cousin can often supply much of what an absent father has failed to do. Grandmothers have been lifesavers for many troubled teenagers. If family members do not live nearby or you believe they would be a negative influence on your teenager, then look for friends who can help you.

Along with civic groups and colleges, I have mentioned considering churches as a single-parent resource. Churches can be not only the source of spiritual encouragement but a place for building wholesome friendships. Many churches provide weekly classes for single adults while providing exciting activities for teenagers. Make it a family thing and when you get home, discuss what you've learned.

In the context of the church and family, many single parents have found individuals who have played significantly positive roles in the development of their teenagers. You need not walk alone; there are people in your community who care. Keep searching until you find them.

Sooner or later your teenager will reach adulthood. They will be immeasurably blessed if they can honestly say, "I know my Mother loved me. I know my Father loved me." It is my sincere hope that this chapter will help you toward one day hearing that blessing.

NOTES

1. Proverbs 29:18, King James Version.
2. Shmuel Shulman and Inge Seiffge-Krenke, *Fathers and Adolescents* (New York: Routledge, 1997), 97.

Resources for Single Parents

Adlrich, Sandra P. *From One Single Mother to Another: Advice and Encouragement from Someone Who's Been There.* Ventura, Calif.: Regal, 1991.

Burkett, Larry. rev. ed. *The Financial Guide for the Single Parent.* Chicago: Moody, 1997.

Coleman, William L. *What Children Need to Know When Parents Get Divorced: A Book to Read with Children Going Through the Trauma of Divorce.* Minneapolis: Bethany House, 1998.

Dobson, James. *For the Teen: Preparing for Adolescence.* Ventura, Calif.: Regal Books, 1989.

Hart, Archibald D. *Helping Children Survive Divorce: What to Expect; How to Help.* Dallas: Word, 1996.

Hunter, Lynda. *A Comprehensive Guide to Parenting On Your Own.* Grand Rapids: Zondervan, 1997.

Kniskern, Joseph Warren. *When the Vow Breaks: A Survival and Recovery Guide for Christians Facing Divorce.* Nashville: Broadman and Holman, 1993.

Richmond, Gary. *Successful Single Parenting: Bringing Out the Best in Your Kids.* Eugene, Ore.: Harvest House, 1990.

chapter fifteen

LOVE LANGUAGES IN THE BLENDED FAMILY

One July week a few years ago, I served as the counselor at a youth camp in the beautiful Blue Ridge Mountains of North Carolina. Michael had asked for an appointment, and I invited him to hike to the lookout tower while we talked. (I've found that teenagers talk more freely while walking.) We had been on the trail about fifteen minutes, making small talk, when I asked about Michael's family. He said, "That's what I wanted to talk with you about. I don't like having a stepfather.

"Before Mom married Rod, things were great," Michael continued. "Mom and I got along well. I felt like she respected me. Now I feel like I am a child again. She and Rod have come up with all these stupid rules. I know it was Rod's idea because Mom is not strict like that. But now Mom is siding with Rod and they are making my life miserable. I wish I could go live with my dad."

What Michael said to me that day has been heard numerous times in counselor's offices across this country. Most teenagers find life in the blended family extremely difficult. In Michael's case, he had made an adjustment to one arrangement years ago, and now he was upset by an all-new family arrangement. He had learned to cope with living with his mother and younger sister after his father left them six years ago. He had worked through the trauma of feeling rejected by his father. He and his mom had many long conversations in the months after his father left. Michael knew about his mother's sacrifice and about her role; she had worked hard in order to meet the needs of the family. "Mom had depended upon me to look after my sister in the afternoon after school until she got home," he said with both pride and confidence. "I also helped out with the laundry, and she counted on me to keep the car clean. Mom was treating me like an adult."

Now that Rod had entered the family, all of that had changed. Rod wanted to wash the car with Michael and he was telling Michael things about how to wash the car that Michael already knew. "Does he think I'm stupid?" Michael asked.

As I listened to Michael, I was relatively sure that his stepfather was sincere and was trying to bond with Michael by doing things together. But I also knew that if Michael's stepdad didn't wake up to the reality that Michael was a teenager whose independence was being threatened, that he would eventually find himself rejected by Michael. I also knew that while Michael's mother was presently siding with her new husband, it was only a matter of time that her concern for Michael would cause conflicts between her and Rod. Research has discovered that the number one cause for divorce in second marriages is conflicts over child rearing,[1] and the divorce rate in second marriages is substantially higher than in first marriages.

The blended family is established in a very different way from the original biological family. For the original family, the couple had a period of time together before the child came. The child entered the world as an infant, and the couple learned the skills of parenting over time. The blended family, on the other hand, seldom gives the couple an extended period to be alone. The children are immediately a part of the family. Often, the children are now teenagers who are developing their own independence and self-identity. All the normal struggles in this process are intensified for the teenager who wakes up to find himself a part of a blended family.

THE TEEN'S PERCEPTIONS
AND THE PARENT'S FEARS

Often the teenager perceives that his own developmental process is being thwarted for the sake of his parents' happiness. If this resentment is not processed, it will soon become bitterness, and the bitterness will lead to rebellion. Meanwhile, parents often enter a second marriage with three overwhelming fears: fear of losing their teenager's love, fear of rebellion, and fear of ruining their teenager's lives. One mother said, "I have ruined my daughter's life, first by my divorce and then by remarrying. How could I have been so stupid?" These fears often lead the biological parent to forget the basic concepts of discipline and anger management which we have discussed earlier in this book. The parent placates the teenager and ends up ostracizing the new spouse.

Numerous other challenges may face the blended family: fighting between stepchildren, sexual abuse between stepteenagers or between the teenager and the new spouse, conflicts between biological parent and the stepparent over what is appropriate family guidelines, conflicts between the blended family and the other family over what is best for the teenager. On and on the list of potential challenges extends.

It is not my purpose to paint a bleak picture. It is my purpose to be realistic and to offer hope. I believe that understanding the five love languages and applying them in the blended family will do much to create a climate where blended families can succeed. Since the basic emotional need for all of us is the need to feel loved and since love is the oil which greases the wheels of family relationships, then if we can learn to effectively communicate love, we can create a healthy environment for the blended family. In a loving atmosphere conflicts can be resolved, the teenager can continue a healthy process toward independence, and parents can enjoy a growing marital relationship. However, when the emotional need for love is not met, then the family often shifts into an adversarial mode. Much heat is generated but little understanding results.

Let me encourage you to take seriously the concepts we have shared in the earlier chapters of this book. Practice speaking the love languages to each other, talk about various dialects you might use in expressing love to the teenager, determine the teen's primary love language as well as your own. Read a book on the dynamics of blended family relationships. (See the resources listed at the end of this chapter). Realize that teenagers will not always be open to your expressions of love. Don't take it personally. Try a different approach the next day. Learn from your mistakes. Now, let's look at some of the common challenges of loving teenagers in a blended family.

FEELINGS OF REJECTION AND JEALOUSY

Often the teenager will be slow in responding to the love of a stepparent. There are many reasons for this. First, the teen may fear rejection by the stepparent. As the stepparent, you may have difficulty understanding why the teenager draws away. After all, you have decided to love the teenager; you have made honest efforts at reaching out and expressing love. What you must understand is that the teenager has already suffered the trauma of parental rejection as he watched his parents go through the divorce. Perhaps this happened when he was a child, but the trauma is a painful memory for the teenager, one he does not want to see repeated. He doesn't want to go through new hurts.

Second, the teenager may also be jealous of the stepparent's relationship with his biological parent. He could see you as a threat to his relationship with that parent. Since you came along, he may be receiving less attention from the biological parent. The teen may also be jealous of the affection you show toward your biological children. Another common struggle for teenagers in blended families is the feeling of being disloyal to his mother if he responds to the love of his stepmother or disloyal to his father if he responds to the love of his stepfather.

An additional reason teenagers may not easily respond to the love of a stepparent is that they see the stepparent as a threat to their independence. This is something of what Michael, whom we met at the beginning of this chapter, was feeling toward his stepfather Rod.

DEALING WITH THE TEEN'S FEELINGS

Listen Carefully, Affirm, and Show Compassion

What can a stepparent do to overcome some of these barriers? The first step is to give the teenager freedom to be who he is. The emotions and fears which we have just discussed are real to the teenager even if they are not expressed. Don't try to talk the teenager out of his thoughts and feelings. If the teen chooses to talk, listen carefully and affirm his emotions. "That makes a lot of sense. I can understand how you would feel that way." These are statements of affirmation.

In contrast, lofty proclamations will ring empty with the teenager. "You don't have to worry about me. I'm never going to leave. And I'm certainly not going to take your mother away from you." The teenager will respond far more to your actions than to your promises.

Like any adolescent, the teenager growing up in the blended family will express rebellion in his or her search for self-identity and independence. Always understand that in a blended family as well, hurt, grief, and depression often underlie the teen's rebellious behavior. If you judge the behavior without reflection upon the emotions, you will misjudge the teenager. Remember that, and you will show compassion and mercy.

Respect the Teen's Biological Parent

Second, don't try to take the place of the biological parent of the same sex as yourself. Encourage the teenager to love and relate to their biological parent whenever that is possible. Don't verbally deprecate the biological parent in front of the teenager.

DEALING WITH YOUR
OWN THOUGHTS AND FEELINGS

Recognize Your Various Feelings and Fears

Next, be honest with yourself about your own thoughts and feelings. If your marriage is shaky, you too may be pulling back from the teenager because of your fear of another divorce. You don't want to get close to the teenager because you don't want to hurt him again. You may also feel guilty because you do not have a close relationship with your own biological children. It may seem unfair to build a close relationship with stepchildren when there is so much distance between you and your own children. And there is also the possibility that you may withdraw from the teenager because you are jealous of the time and attention he gets from your spouse. There is also a bit of selfishness in all of us. It is difficult to get outside our own wants, wishes, and desires. Self-centeredness, however, will ultimately destroy any relationship.

How do you deal with these thoughts and emotions which can be barriers to building a love relationship with your stepteenager? I suggest that you begin by talking to yourself. Admit the thoughts and emotions. They will not go away by trying to ignore them. But be sure to tell yourself the truth. Selfishness leads to isolation and loneliness. The happiest people in the world are those who give, not those who grab.

Love Your Children and Your Stepchildren

Remind yourself that love is like a river: you can withdraw enough to water a flower here, a tree there, a garden down the stream and the river will still be flowing tomorrow. You can love your wife, your biological children, and your stepchildren and have love left over for others. Your spouse can love her biological children and you and still have love left over for your biological children.

The reality is you cannot love your spouse and fail to love her/his children. The parental relationship will not allow the two to be separated. Remember, you always reap what you sow. Love, and eventually you will be loved. Give, and it will be given to you. Success in the blended family is not found in "getting rid of the children." It is found in loving the children toward maturity.

Patience is a necessity for stepparents who are committed to loving stepchildren. Teenagers, unlike younger children, do not just sit there and soak in the love you offer. The teen has his own thoughts, past experiences, and behavior patterns. Research has shown that it typically takes a minimum of eighteen months to two years for the teenager and stepparent to form a loving relationship.[2]

How do you know when the teenager is bonding with you? The signs include the following. The teenager will begin to show spontaneous affection and willingness to receive your love. He will initiate conversations and activities with you. He will express awareness of your needs and will ask your opinion. When this happens, you are reaping the sweet fruit of unconditional love. Building a strong loving relationship with your stepteenager is one of the best things you can do for your marriage. All parents love their biological children. When they see a spouse making consistent efforts to relate positively to their teen, their love for the spouse is enhanced.

DISCIPLINE IN THE BLENDED FAMILY

Discipline typically becomes a major area of struggle for blended families. Most biological parents do not agree on all the details surrounding the discipline of children. In a blended family, the differences are magnified because one of you is the biological parent and the other a stepparent and because each of you had a history in another family before you became a part of a blended family.

The purpose of discipline is to help our teenagers grow into mature, responsible adults. The process may be more difficult in the blended family than in the original family, but it is not impossible. Let me encourage the two of you to read again the material in chapter 12 on love and responsibility. This will help you get the basic concepts of discipline clearly in mind.

About Changes in Family Rules and Discipline

The teenager knows that things are going to be different now that the stepparent has arrived. Some things will have to change. For example, if the stepparent also brings teenagers to the marriage, there may have to be new guidelines about how the teen dresses and undresses in the house. Don't try to be a lone ranger in determining what these guidelines will be. As parents, you have the final word, but teenagers need to be a part of the process in deciding the rules and the consequences when rules are broken. It is highly possible that you and your spouse will have major disagreements over what the rules or consequences should be. My rule of thumb is that in the first year of the blended family, the stepparent should defer to the biological parent's wishes. As emotional relationships are enhanced, these can be revisited in the future if the stepparent feels the guidelines are not adequate.

Minimal changes make for maximum acceptance in the early stages of the blended family. If you establish the family forum early with the understanding that any family member can call a forum anytime he or she feels that something about family life needs to be changed, you will establish a vehicle for processing emotions and ideas. If in these forums you take seriously the thoughts and feelings of the teenager as well as younger children while maintaining the right to have the final word, you will create an atmosphere in which family conflicts can be resolved.

Obviously if members of the family feel loved by each other, it will be much easier to create such a climate. Thus speaking each other's primary love language remains vital to healthy relationships among family members.

About Enforcement and Consistency

When consequences must be enforced, during the first year of the blended family it's better for the biological parent to be the enforcing parent. Later when there has been more bonding between stepparent and teenager, either parent can enforce the consequences, especially if the consequences have been determined beforehand and are clearly understood by all. Speaking the teenager's love language before and after enforcing the consequences enhances the likelihood that the teenager will receive the consequences as fair.

Consistency in enforcing consequences is extremely important, particularly in a blended family. In Scott and Marcia's blended family, the rule was that bicycles were to be placed in the garage before 8 P.M. The consequence for failing to do so was losing the privilege of riding the bicycle the next day. Everyone agreed that this was a fair rule and in the summer when the days were longer, the time was extended to 9 P.M. The rule was tested three weeks later when Marcia's thirteen-year-old, Erica, left her bicycle in the neighbor's yard. At 9:10 P.M., the neighbor's son knocked on the door with Erica's bicycle in tow.

Marcia thanked the neighbor's son, put the bicycle in the garage, and calmly informed Erica of what had happened, reminding her that she could not ride the bicycle the next day.

The next afternoon, Erica came to her mother, wearing her most winsome smile and said, "I have a favor to ask. I know I left my bike out last night but this afternoon, all the girls in the neighborhood are riding over to the park. Mom, if you will let me go, I won't ride my bicycle for the next two days. Two days for one. That's fair, isn't it, Mom?"

Marcia wanted to say yes. It would be much easier and Erica's offer did sound fair, but Marcia knew that if she complied, it would give Erica the wrong message. So she said, "I'm sorry, Erica. But you know the rule and you know the consequences. You don't get to ride the bicycle the *next* day after you leave it out."

Seeing that her winsome smile and pleasant approach wasn't going to work, Marcia switched to the whining mode. "Oh, Mom. Please, Mom. It's fair, it's fair. Two days for one. Two days for one. It's fair, Mom."

"I'm sorry," Marcia said, "but you know the rule."

Then Erica turned on the pressure. "How could you do this to me? All the girls are going. I don't like all of these new rules. It wasn't this way before Scott came. You used to be understanding and kind. Now you are all hung up on enforcing the rules. It's not fair. I don't like living in this house."

Marcia wanted to strike back and to tell Erica to leave Scott out of this, that it had nothing to do with him, but wisely she kept those thoughts to herself and said, "Sweetheart, I know you want to go riding with the girls. I wish I could say yes, but that's simply not the way life is. When we do wrong, we have to suffer the consequences. Sometimes those consequences are very painful. I understand how you could be upset. And I understand that sometimes you wish Scott weren't here, that maybe you think I might give in if Scott weren't here. I hope that's not true. I loved you before Scott and I love you now. I'm enforcing the rule because I know it's best for you."

"Don't give me that *best for you stuff*," Erica muttered as she walked out of the room. Marcia breathed a sigh of relief and secretly asked herself, *Am I doing the right thing?* In her mind, she knew she was right, but in her heart she wondered. Erica sulked and stayed in her room the rest of the afternoon and evening, and the next morning silently left for school. However, that afternoon she was back to her normal cheerful self and never mentioned it again. (This happened four and one-half years ago and Marcia reports that Erica has never left her bicycle out of the garage again.) Teenagers learn responsibility when consequences are enforced.

About five weeks later, Scott's fifteen-year old-son, Matt, also left his bicycle out past the appointed hour. Scott discovered it when he came home from a meeting that evening. He put the bicycle in the garage and informed Matt that he would not be able to ride his bicycle the next day. "OK," Matt said. "I understand. I just forgot." Imagine Marcia's consternation when the next afternoon she heard Scott say to Matt, "How about taking your bicycle and going to the store and getting some bread? I need to mow the grass."

Marcia softly said, "Scott, I thought Matt wasn't supposed to ride his bicycle today" to which Scott flippantly responded, "We need some bread and I need to mow the grass. He's helping me. It's OK."

Matt rode off to the store but Marcia went inside, feeling betrayed. *I can't believe he did that,* she said to herself. *When Erica finds out, I will never hear the end of it.* (It will be obvious to the astute reader that Marcia needs to count to 100 and take a walk around the block. When she returns, I hope that Scott is ready to hear her read the 3 by 5 card hanging on the refrigerator. "I'm feeling angry right now but don't worry, I'm not going to attack you. But I do need your help. Is this a good time to talk?" See chapter 9.)

Scott has violated one of the cardinal principles of good parental discipline: consistency. Unless he confesses his wrongdoing to Marcia and Erica, the emotional barrier he has erected by his actions will impede his efforts to build a loving relationship with his wife and stepdaughter. Matt is also the loser because of his father's inconsistency. Few things are more important in the blended family than the parents being committed to consistency in enforcing the consequences.

OTHER AREAS OF CONFLICT

Attitudes and Behaviors of the Other Parent

Another common area of challenge to the blended family is relating to the teenager's other family, i. e., the other biological parent, whether remarried or single. Often parents have unresolved feelings from the previous marriage. One or both parents may still harbor anger, bitterness, or hatred for the ex-spouse. Some also still have feelings of love for the former spouse which can be troublesome to the new partner.

In addition, behavior patterns which led to the divorce may still persist and be troublesome. For example, the workaholic husband who never came home when he promised may now be late in picking up the teenager for the visitation weekend. This may irritate the teenager's mother just as it did when she was married to his father. The whining, "pick at the details" mother may still irritate the ex-husband as he tries to work out the logistics of spending time with his teenager. Many of these conflicts center around "the visitation" because this is the arena in which the ex-spouses most often have contact.

Furthermore, the biological parents will blame each other for any emotional or behavioral problems which the teenager may exhibit. Sometimes the other biological parent may make negative comments about you and your spouse to the teenager. These comments are repeated to you by the teenager, typically when he is angry. Sixteen-year-old Kyle spouted out to his mother, "Dad said that he couldn't buy me a car because he had to spend all of his money paying for everything over here." Seventeen-year-old Lisa was in a fray with her stepmother when she said, "Mother said that you are just a slut because you took my father away from us. I'll never forgive you for that."

Different Sets of Values

Sometimes the values of the other household are vastly different from your own. This may be one of the factors which led to the divorce. The greatest struggle between families is often in the area of moral values. The presence of pornographic literature, the use of strong profanities, or the use of alcohol and drugs may no longer exist at home, but they remain when the teenager visits his non-custodial parent. The types of movies, videos, or television programs the teen can watch during such visitations may differ from yours; so may the religious beliefs—all of these may become sources of conflict. However, unless these activities are illegal, the custodial parent cannot regulate what takes place when the teenager is with the other parent.

This is where your own positive program of love and discipline is so important. If the teenager is learning from you that every choice has consequences, if you are giving the teenager choices and making sure he suffers the consequences when he makes poor choices, the teen is more likely to carry this truth with him when he visits the other family. He may be exposed to thoughts and behaviors that you would prefer he not hear or see, but he is more likely to make wise decisions because of the solid love and discipline he has experienced with you.

Keeping the teenager's love tank full is also a deterrent to wrong-doing. The teenager is naturally drawn to the parent from whom she feels genuine love. If the teenager knows you have her best interest in mind and feels deeply loved by you, she is less likely to be pulled into negative behaviors by the other parent. For one thing, she doesn't want to hurt you and second, she knows that the other parent is not looking out for her well-being or that parent would not expose her to such destructive practices.

In responding to these conflicts with the other family, never fight fire with fire. Do not seek to combat a former spouse's negative behavior by "giving them a dose of their own medicine." Kindly but firmly respond to their behavior in what seems to be an appropriate manner. Do not let their behavior intimidate you and do not seek to intimidate them. The objective is not to defeat your ex-spouse (or the other biological parent you cannot truly replace). The objective is to keep your own marriage growing and to work toward helping your teenager develop into a responsible young adult. Open communication between you and your spouse and teenager about the difficulties you are experiencing with the other family and discussing possible ways to handle the conflict can be a learning experience for your teenager.

A RECIPE FOR A STRONG BLENDED FAMILY

In summary, let me emphasize four basic ingredients that lead to a healthy blended family. You can enhance the power of these four ingredients by teaching the family to speak each other's primary love language.

First and foremost, there is unconditional love. Parents must take the lead in unconditionally loving each other and unconditionally loving all the children in the family. The message your teenager and younger children need to hear is: "We love you no matter what." Do not say or imply by your actions, "We love you if you will be kind to each other; we love you if you do what we say; we love you if you will love us." Anything less than unconditional love is not true love at all. Love is a choice. It is choosing to look out for the other person's interests. It is seeking to meet their needs. Every teenager needs to know that there is someone who cares deeply about him, who believes that he is important, and who believes that with hard work, he can make life better not only for himself but for others.

Giving the teen *gifts, affectionate touches, acts of service, quality time,* and *words of affirmation* are the five fundamental ways of expressing unconditional love. Your teenager needs to hear you speak all five languages, but he/she needs heavy doses of their primary love language.

Second is fairness. Please remember that *fairness* is not *sameness.* Each of your children is different, even if they are your biological children. Sometimes in efforts to be fair, parents treat each child alike. In fact, this is very unfair. Because children are different, what makes one child feel loved will not necessarily make another feel loved. If one teenager's love language is gifts and the other quality time and you give each of them a gift of equal value, one received far more than the other emotionally. Fairness means seeking equally to meet the unique needs of each child or teenager.

Third is attentiveness. Express interest in your teenager's world, going to activities where adults are permitted, showing interest in her school and social life, listening to her ideas, desires, and feelings; in short, get into her world and stay there. Research shows that most teenagers want more time with their parents, not less.[3]

Fourth is discipline. Teenagers desperately need boundaries. Parents who take the attitude "You are a teenager. Do what you want to do" are setting the teenager up for failure. Life without boundaries soon becomes a meaningless life. Parents who love will set boundaries to protect the teenager from danger and to guide the teenager toward responsible self-control.

When parents in the blended family commit themselves to these fundamentals, they can beat the odds and create healthy family relationships.

NOTES

1. Tom and Adrienne Frydenger, *The Blended Family* (Old Tappan, N. J.: Revell, 1984), 19.

2. Shmuel Shulman and Inge Seiffge-Krenke, *Fathers and Adolescents* (New York: Routledge, 1997), 123; Frydenger, *The Blended Family,* 120.

3. Lawrence Steinberg and Ann Levine, *You and Your Adolescent* (New York: Harper & Row, 1990), 13.

Resources for the Blended Family

Dunn, Dick. *New Faces in the Frame: A Guide to Marriage and Parenting in the Blended Family.* Nashville: LifeWay, 1994.

Eckler, James D. *Step-By-Step Parenting: A Guide to Successful Living with a Blended Family.* Cincinnati: Betterway Books, 1993.

Frydenger, Tom & Adrienne. *The Blended Family.* Old Tappan, N.J.: Revell, 1984.

Marsolini, Maxine. *Blended Families.* Chicago: Moody, 2000.

EPILOGUE

Two winds are blowing across the horizon of contemporary teenage culture. One carries the heartfelt cries of thousands of teenagers yearning for community, structure, guidelines, and purpose. The second is the swirling wind of confusion that threatens the first and noble wind.

For many teenagers, the world does not make sense and life hardly seems worth the effort. These teens, caught in that swirling, confusing wind, often spend much of their lives in depression, and sometimes end it all in acts of self-destruction, often taking others down with them.

I deeply believe that the most important influence on the teenager's mood and choices is parental love. Without a sense of parental love, teenagers are more prone to being swept along by the wind of confusion. However fast or slow the wind, the direction will not be in their own best interests or the interests of society. In contrast, teenagers who genuinely feel loved by their parents are far more likely to respond to the deep longings for community, to welcome structure, to respond positively to guidelines, and to find purpose and meaning in life. Nothing holds more potential for positively changing Western culture than parental love.

My purpose in writing this book has been to give practical help to sincere parents who genuinely want their teenagers to feel loved. It has been my observation after thirty years of marriage and family counseling that most parents love their teenagers. But it has also been my observation that thousands of these teenagers do not *feel* loved by their parents. Sincerity is not enough. If we are to effectively communicate love to a teenager, we must learn the teen's primary love language and speak it regularly. We must also learn the dialects, within the primary love language, which speak most deeply to the soul of the teenager. When we are doing this effectively, we can sprinkle in the other four love languages and they will enhance our efforts. However, if we do not speak the primary love language of the teenager, our efforts to speak the other four love languages will not fill the love tank of our teenager.

I have tried to be honest in communicating that effectively loving a teenager is not as easy as it may seem, and certainly not as easy as loving them when they were children. Our teenagers in many ways are "moving targets." Not only are they actively involved in pursuing many interests, they also experience radical mood swings. Both of these make it difficult for parents to know which language or dialect to speak on a given day. The whole process of loving teenagers is also compounded by the teen's emerging independence and developing self-identity. As parents we cannot minimize these factors if we wish to effectively communicate love to our teenagers.

Although I have written primarily to parents, it is my desire that grandparents, school teachers, church youth leaders, and other adults who care about teenagers will become more effective lovers of teens by reading and practicing the principles found in this book. Teenagers need to feel the love not only of parents, but also the love of other significant adults in their lives. Every adult encounter leaves the teenager feeling loved or unloved. When the teenager feels loved by the adult, the teenager is open to instruction and influence by that adult. When a teenager does not feel loved, the words of adults will fall on deaf ears. The teenager desperately needs the wisdom of older, more mature adults. But without love, the transfer of wisdom will be ineffective.

It will be obvious to the astute reader that this is not a book to be read and laid aside. Rather, its principles should be practiced daily. As surely as the body of the teenager needs food daily, so the soul of the teenager craves love. I wish I could place this book into the hands of all parents of teenagers and say, "I wrote this for you. I know that you love your teenager. But I'm not certain that your teenager feels your love. Don't assume that all is well. Learn the primary love language of your teenager and speak it regularly. It is not easy. I know. I've been there. But it's worth the effort. Your teenager will be the bene-factor, and so will you."

Nothing is more important to future generations than effectively loving the teenagers of this generation.

appendix one

HOW TEENAGERS GOT THEIR NAME

Before there were teenagers, there were teenagers . . . but they did not go by that name. Not until the early 1940s were adolescents known as much more than growing kids; but social and industrial changes, propelled by a world war, would change all that. The "teenager" would appear, a distinct culture in a distinct age group—no longer boys and girls, but not men or women, either. They were in transition, moving toward adulthood, testing and changing in their search for identity and independence. Here's how teenagers got their name.

A decade before World War II, most children aged thirteen through nineteen had worked for a living on farms, in factories, or at home—whatever their families required of them. They helped their parents provide for the younger children in the family. They had little choice in the matter and continued in this working mode until they themselves were married.[1] They were simply a part of their family of origin and did what was expected of them until they were old enough to marry. There was no separate teenage culture through which they passed from childhood to adulthood. There were no teenage movies, music, or fashions because there were no teenagers.

The Great Depression of the 1930s changed all of that. With the collapse of the economy, jobs evaporated. The few jobs that were available went to fathers, and these adolescent workers were left standing idle. Feeling that they were a drain on their families, thousands of them took to the road in search of work. They took freight trains to distant cities or walked to the neighboring villages, but most of them were disappointed. Sleeping in public parks or back alleys, often begging for food, these young people posed a major social problem. As sociologist Grace Palladino wrote, "Adolescent runaways or transient youth, as they were called, forced adult society to focus on teenage problems."[2]

This social dilemma led to President Franklin Roosevelt's National Youth Administration (NYA), designed to provide training and job opportunities for America's disillusioned youth. This in turn led to a national emphasis on the public high school. Until this time, attending high school was not even an option for most American youth. For example, in 1900 only 6 percent of the nation's seventeen-year-olds earned diplomas from high school. In contrast by 1939, close to 75 percent of fourteen- to seventeen-year-olds were high school students.[3] The idea was that high school would provide a vocational training program in a disciplined, wholesome environment. In this setting, youth would discover their talents, develop goals, establish good work habits, and, upon graduation, become productive citizens.

This movement of vast numbers of young people from the workforce (or the unemployment lines) to public high schools created the social setting for developing a separate "teenage culture." As Palladino noted, "At the very same time that educators and NYA counselors were focusing on teenage futures, adolescents themselves were discovering a much more immediate, exciting world—a world of radio music, dancing, and fun. As the economy began to recover in the late 1930s (largely due to the outbreak of war in Europe), high school students were developing a public identity that had nothing to do with family life or adult responsibilities."[4]

This was the first teenage generation where a majority went to high school. By 1938 they were making a name for themselves as "bobby soxers" who lived to dance to the swinging beat of big band music. Although they were not "teenagers" yet in their own or anyone else's mind, the concept of a separate, teenage generation was beginning to gain ground. High school students discovered a beat and a language that was all their own.

These high school students who gained national fame in the 1930s as bobby soxers established the paradigm that later was characterized by the term *teenagers*. They developed a new cultural lifestyle featuring unique fashions, music, dance, and fads. Their saddle oxford shoes, gored skirts, and Angora sweaters became the new symbol of high school life. "They riled their parents with a maddening language that only their friends understood. Worse yet, they spent time and money organizing fan clubs and lined the streets for hours on end whenever a band came to town, just to catch a glimpse of their favorite swing musicians."[5]

Advertisers for the retail market began to see potential in these carefree high school students whose main concern in life was to have a good time and dance. They dubbed the term "teeners," later "teensters," and in 1941, "teenagers."[6] Like bobby soxers, teenagers were identified with the high school student's world of dating, driving, dancing, music, and fun. *Life* magazine offered this picture of the teenager. "They live in a jolly world of gangs, games . . . movies . . . and music. . . . They speak a curious lingo . . . adore chocolate milkshakes . . . wear moccasins everywhere . . . and drive like bats out of hell."[7]

Clearly teens were developing their own culture. Interestingly, then, as now, parents, educators, and church leaders often decried what they considered to be the downward drift of teenage culture. Dr. Leslie Hohman, columnist for *Ladies Home Journal,* argued that adolescence would never focus on "real achievement" if everything in their teenage years was "glossed over and made too exciting." He advised that if parents were smart, they would immunize their children against the dangerous virus of bobby sox culture and seek to elevate their taste toward the finer things of life.[8] Hohman may have been the first, but certainly not the last, of parents who would like to immunize their children against what they consider to be the excesses of teenage culture.

NOTES

1. Joseph F. Kett, *Rites of Passage: Adolescence in America, 1790 to the Present* (New York: Basic Books, 1977), 169.

2. Grace Palladino, *Teen-agers: An American History* (New York: Basic Books, 1996), 37.

3. U.S. Bureau of the Census, *Historical Statistics of the United States, Colonial Times to 1970, Bi-Centennial Edition, Part I* (Washington, D.C.: Government Printing Office, 1975), 380, 379.

4. Palladino, *Teen-agers*, 45–46.

5. James Lincoln Collier, *Benny Goodman and the Swing Era* (New York: Oxford Univ. Press, 1989), 190–91.

6. The Oxford English Dictionary credits *Popular Science* (April 1941) with the first use of the term "teenager."

7. "Sub-Debs —They Live in a Jolly World of Gangs, Games, Gadding, Movies, Malteds, and Music," *Life*, 27 January 1941, 75.

8. Leslie Hohman, "As the Twig is Bent," *Ladies Home Journal*, October 1939, 67.

appendix two

A FAMILY FORUM
IN ACTION

Holding a family forum to establish rules is a great strategy for setting boundaries and teaching responsible behavior to your teenager. Chapter 12 offers guidelines for setting rules; but how do you conduct a family forum, and what do you say?

Sometime before your child turns thirteen, call for a family forum with just the teen and his parents. Find an evening when no one has time restraints or is under undue stress. This is how one parent initiated such a family forum.

"Mom and I have called this family forum because we are aware that next week we will have a teenager in this house. We have never had one before but we are looking forward to it with great anticipation." Then turning to his son he said, "Tony, Mom and I have been talking. Over the past twelve years, we have tried to be good parents. I know that we have not been perfect and sometimes we have made mistakes. When we did, we tried to acknowledge them. We have enjoyed these twelve years with you. You have brought much joy into our lives. We are happy about your many accomplishments.

"We know that over the next eight years you are going to experience many changes," Dad continued. "Your world is going to greatly expand. There will be many changes: changes in your body, in your mind, in the world around you. You will make new friends and explore new interests. We are excited for you. We want to continue to be good parents.

"Two things are especially important to us. First, we know that over the next few years, you will become more and more independent. You will want to do your own thinking and make your own decisions. We are glad about that because when you are an adult, you will need to make all of your decisions. We want you to learn how to make good decisions while you are a teenager. Secondly, we know that you want not only more independence but you will want more responsibility. As an adult, you will be responsible for your own family and your own children. We believe that much can be learned about responsibility while you are a teenager. We want to encourage both your independence and your responsibility. Therefore, Mom and I felt we should call a family conference where we could examine together our family rules and decide which ones we should keep and which ones may need to be changed."

Mom, who had been nodding her head during this beautiful speech, felt compelled to say: "This doesn't mean that we are going to throw away our rules and start over. What we want to do is examine them and see what changes need to be made. We wanted your input because we know that it is your life and we want to consider what you think and how you feel. Of course, we are your parents and we will have the final word. But we think we can do a better job of being parents if we know your thoughts and feelings."

I can assure you that Tony's parents have his full attention. He was ready for this conversation, maybe even a little frightened at the prospect of becoming a teenager. But certainly, he was eager for the journey.

Your opening speech at a family forum, of course, may be different. It could be shorter, you may mention things you've noticed that show your teen is ready to participate, showing the beginning signs of wise decision making but also the tendency to make decisions independent of the family. Encourage your teen that this is his opportunity to be heard, and that these rules will benefit him primarily, and the family secondarily. Once you have done this, it's time to enter a dialogue and, with your teenager, to set some rules. Return to chapter 12 to learn how to set up those rules.

Beauty. Message. Ministry.

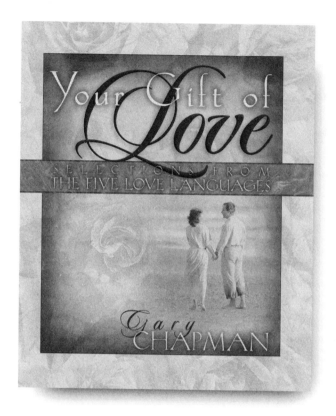

Your Gift of Love
Selections From The Five Love Languages

What better gift to give a couple, new or seasoned, than an attractive book with excellent selections from one of the preeminent books on marriage? *Your Gift of Love* is a beautifully designed gift book containing key passages from Chapman's million-copy best seller *The Five Love Languages.*

Cloth 1-881273-32-6

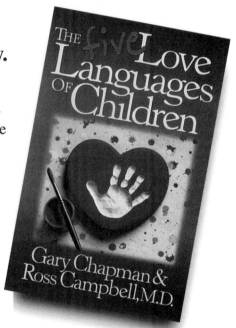

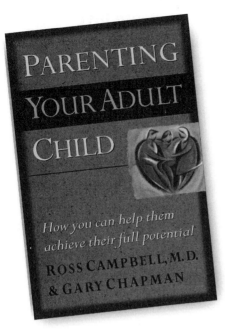
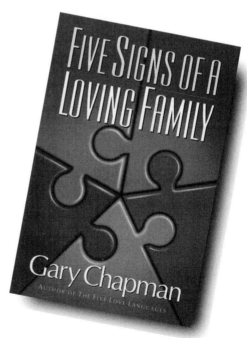

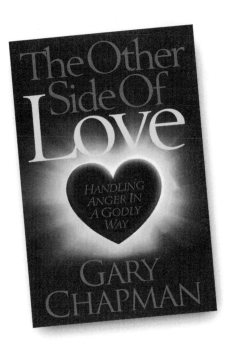

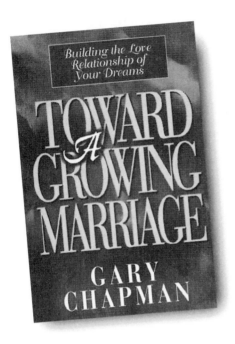
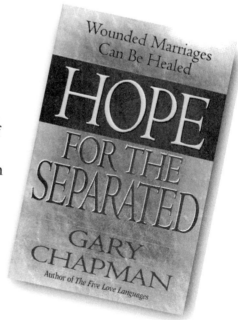

If you are interested in information
about other books written from a
biblical perspective, please write
to the following address:

Northfield Publishing
215 West Locust Street
Chicago, IL 60610